Chris Fogg is a creative producer, writer and dramaturg, who has written and directed for the theatre for several years, as well as more recently collaborating artistically with choreographers and contemporary dance companies.

**Northern Songs**
is his second collection of poems, stories and essays.

His first collection, Special Relationships, is also available from Mudlark Press.

## Plays written by Chris Fogg

The Tall Tree*
To See The Six Points*
**with music by Chris Dumigan*
The Silent Princess
Changeling
Peterloo: The Greatest Show on Earth
Snapshot *co-written with Andrew Pastor & Chris Phillips*
Safe Haven
Firestarter
Trying To Get Back Home
Heroes
It's Not Just The Jewels…
Bogus
You Are Harry Kipper & I Claim My Five Pounds!
One of Us**
How To Build A Rocket**
***writing assistant to Gavin Stride*

**Adaptations:**
Return of the Native
In The Land Of Zorn
The Stone Book Quartet
1984
The Birdman

**For young people and community companies:**
The Ballad of Billy The Kid
Small Blue Thing
Market Forces
Inside
The Sleeping Clock
Titanic
The Posy Tree
Scheherazade
Persons Reported

**Musicals:**
Stag***
Marilyn***
****co-written with Chris Dumigan*

## Responses to Northern Songs

*Chris Fogg is a troubadour – and a true one at that. He's also a song-and-dance man of the imagination. And he's a sharp-eyed chronicler not only of his own life, but of our times. He's a balladeer, a loving memoirist, and an insatiable story-teller. 'Northern Songs' is his Bumper Annual, his Commodious Compendium, where Mr. Punch yarns with Sgt. Pepper out on the Long & Winding Road leading us away from, and always back to, home. It's a book of Wonders in which he honours the advice given to one of his characters: 'Be not forgetful to entertain strangers'. That's the way to do it!*

**Chris Waters** Winner of Plough and Bridport Poetry Prizes,
author of Arisaig and Through a Glass Lately

*If it's possible to be exuberant, compassionate, politically and socially aware, wise, reflective and funny all at once, then Chris Fogg has achieved it here. His Northern Songs is a prose and verse medley that plays with time, telling us in an intimate voice not only his own but others' stories. Writing from the middle of a life fully lived and rich with detail that will trigger memories even in those of us whose experiences have been different, he has given us a wonderful and deeply absorbing read. Don't start this book unless you're willing to miss tea breaks, meals and even some sleep. You may also want to look up from the page, as I did, and read a few of the perfect scenes aloud to anyone within earshot.*

**Irene Willis** Winner of Violet Haas Award and Pushcart Prize Nominee

*One of Chris Fogg's stories is called 'The Memory Box'. To me this collection is like opening just such a memory box. The memories aren't mine but they are written with such a lived clarity that they affect me like my own. As Keats said, all good poetry should strike you as 'almost a remembrance'. My experience of Chris Fogg's writing is exactly that: I am transported by it and moved, for it holds a quiet strength.*

**Ben Duke** Artistic Director: Lost Dog, Winner of The Place Prize 2011

*Evokes fundamental questions of now, who we are and where we are inside ourselves…*

**Mark Bruce** Winner of Sky Arts/South Bank Award 2013,
National Dance Awards Best Independent Company 2015

*The outlines of things I think I know are beautifully re-drawn in Chris Fogg's Northern Songs. Shifting between poetic and prose form, moments that shape a life are beautifully and unexpectedly etched through the series of characters we encounter. In Privet, a young child savours his*

*investigation of the individual leaves of an apparently unremarkable, ubiquitous hedge – finding hidden joy within each one. Waiting nearby in the cold, the poem's narrator knows that his son experiences something that his own senses have become inured to. And so it is that Northern Songs by turns urges us and beguiles us to wipe the dust from our looking and see the brilliant clarity of the world around us in all its vivid, individuality. An individuality that is nevertheless connected both inside and out. Tom Waits once said this about song writing: "You can't wrestle with them or you'll only scare them off. Trying to capture them is trying to trap birds." The 'songs' in Northern Songs, neither wrestled with nor trapped, seem only too happy to offer themselves up for our tender consideration.*

**Lucy Cash** Artist-in-Residence Whitechapel Gallery 2012-13

*He is one of those irritatingly talented people who has an ability to take a simple idea and turn it into something profound. I can't stand it. He is a master at seeing the extraordinary in the everyday bits and pieces of modern life. I have an inextinguishable admiration for his gentle politic, for his ability to weave an apparently simple idea into a thoughtful reflection on what we should value most. I never would have believed it. He has in 'Property Ladder' produced a page turner of a poem. Quietly urgent poetry.*

**Gavin Stride** Director, Farnham Maltings and caravan

*I come to Fogg's words as a poetry novice, still reeling from the memory of a deeply uninspiring English teacher and her still-felt damage on my creativity; words are not my thing, I deduced. How wonderful then to be truly invited in, to have a deeply personal world so well illuminated that I can find myself in those cold mornings, that night sky or rummaging in the back of a wardrobe for heirlooms. His attention to rhythm and imagery lead my curiosity and he lovingly encourages me to look and to look again at my own life, which, of course, is full of rich details, but only if I stop to notice.*

**Theo Clinkard** Associate Artist Dance 4

*The writing in Northern Songs is gripping and poignant. I found myself reading at 'a pace' at times eagerly turning the pages as the narratives unfolded.*

**Kate Wood** Artistic Director, Activate Performance Company

*...poems of acute observation infused with a concern to explore ideas deeply and thoroughly... I hesitate to call the poems gentle because, though that might seem to be the case on a first reading, they are urgently political in their commentary, and the seductive, sometimes almost pastoral veneer can fool the reader so that we're tripped up, bought up short by the currency of the writing - by which I mean the*

*subjects being of now: libraries becoming solicitor's offices; women finding themselves war wives and girlfriends; the press ridiculing public art – which powerfully draws us in.*

**Theresa Beattie** Dance programming, producing and projects

*Chris Fogg's writing is not only powerful, provocative and often playful, it makes your soul sing.*

**Subathra Subramaniam** *Director: Sadhana,*
*former Co-Director of Education: Cape Farewell*

*"Chris Fogg looks at life's moving parts through a watchmaker's loupe. He sees how the tiniest elements can affect the whole mechanism, meshing apparently disparate details, making them not just tick but unexpectedly chime.*

**Quentin Cooper** Broadcaster and Journalist; former presenter of
The Material World for BBC Radio 4

*When reading Fogg's poetry, I hear his voice – it resonates as deep as déjà vu. An evocative, compelling, sometimes humorous, tour of the senses, which makes his poetry so vivid and enjoyable to read.*

***Beth Cinamon*** *Creative Producer*

*Stop a little. Placate that insatiable instinct to hurry on because, like his ten-month old son, Chris Fogg has things to show us. He lovingly reveals worlds spied through the fractures of cracked china, through black spotted mirrors and beyond the words inscribed on timeworn letters. With an adroit capacity as a wordsmith, he tethers a web of ancestral anecdote with personal testimony, boundlessly uniting the formative sensations of childhood with the imaginings and consciousness of adulthood. This is a literary voyage amongst the influence and memory of relatives and friends. Fogg's wistful and humorous encounters draw relatable pictures of amity, love, doubt, loss and the spectacle of life's rich bounty. John Ruskin commandeered a practice of 'word painting' as a constructive means to achieve a deep appreciation of the loveliness of life. I believe wholeheartedly that Chris Fogg is such a word painter. His descriptions of the details of life are unashamedly infused with sentiment but never dawdle into sentimentality. In this arcane and ever complicated world in which we live that increasingly makes attempts to crush the soul, Northern Songs reminds us that we have one. Astounding writing.*

**Ben Wright** Associate Director, Skånes Dansteater, Malmö,
and Jerwood Prize winner

# northern songs

poems, stories, essays
by Chris Fogg

mudlark

First published by Mudlark Press 2015
in a limited edition of 200


ISBN 978-0-9565162-6-8

Published and distributed by
Mudlark Press, 5 Hempstone Park Barns,
Littlehempston, Devon

Cover and Design by Sally Chapman-Walker

Printed by Imprint Digital, Upton Pyne,
Exeter, Devon

With the exception of *The Chairs, Posting to Iraq* and *Property Ladder,* which are works of fiction, and in which any resemblance to actual persons, living or dead, is purely coincidental, this book is a memoir, drawing on the author's own personal reminiscences. For artistic purposes some details of events have been altered and the names of some individuals have been changed.

*No More Heroes* first appeared in Special Relationships, but has found a more appropriate home here. *After the Rain* was written during a period of research and development with Ben Wright and bgroup for a future production of Spectrum and appears here with the company's permission and thanks to the dancers who inspired it.

The front cover image is River Irwell, Manchester 1966 by photographer Shirley Baker and is used by kind permission of the Mary Evans Picture Library, with particular thanks to Mark Vivian and Luci Gosling.

For Amanda, Tim, Kama and Seren

# Contents

**Northern Songs** was a subsidiary company of EMI which published The Beatles' music.

*Looking through the backyard of my life, time to sweep the fallen leaves away...* Paul McCartney

*There were big gaps in all the streets where houses used to be. We used to play over them.* Ringo Starr

*You know, you have all the old records there if you want to reminisce...* John Lennon

*It's only a northern song...* George Harrison

*

*A message to yourself from the past when you believed in different things.*
Neon sign advertising the Mirror City exhibition at the Hayward Gallery on London's Southbank 2014.

*We must all bear witness for when we are in the future. I am in that future now... bearing witness to the past* Kate Atkinson

*The future always looks good in the golden land, because no one remembers the past.... We tell ourselves stories in order to live.* Joan Didion

*Memory is the substitute for the tail we lost in the process of evolution. It directs all our movements... if only because such a process is never linear.* Joseph Brodsky

*Memory contains details, not the whole picture... highlights, not the entire show...* Vladimir Nabokov

*Footfalls echo in the memory*
*Down the passage which we did not take*
*Towards the door we never opened...* T.S. Eliot

*... such a compass of years will shew new examples of olde things, parallelisms of occurrences through the whole course of time, and nothing be monstrous unto him, who may in that time understand not only the varieties of man, but the varieties of himself, and how many men he hath been in that extent of time...* Thomas Browne

*We are so accustomed to disguise ourselves to others that, in the end, we become disguised to ourselves.* François de la Rochefoucauld

*Can I have become a different being while I still remain myself?*
Simone de Beauvoir

*

*We were riding through frozen fields in a wagon at dawn*
*A red wing rose in the darkness.*

*And suddenly a hare ran across the road.*
*One of us pointed to it,*

*That was long ago. Today, neither of them is alive,*
*Not the hare, nor the man who made the gesture.*

*Oh my love, where are they, where are they going:*
*The flash of the hand, streak of movement, rustle of pebbles?*

*I ask not out of sorrow but in wonder...*

Czeslaw Milosz: *Encounter*

# get back

## to where you once belonged

## Dinky Toys

Driving south out of the city
in my old post office van
(green with yellow wheels) slowly
towards the River Bollin

I have to pause for a red light –
traffic in an endless stream –
when just before I make a right,
as if from some number nine dream,

a second green van approaches –
mirror image, the same
yellow wheels, two dinky toys,
magnets drawn towards home –

and pulls up alongside to
watch and wait for a space
to open up and let us through.
I try in vain to see his face

obscured by his windscreen which
reflects buildings, cars, sky
if only to acknowledge
with a gesture or catch his eye –

look, we're driving the same car –
maybe even toot my horn,
when suddenly two gaps appear,
we're each forced to make our turn,

and it's only then I see him;
he turns towards me, smiles –
the shock hits me like a drum,
it's me at both sets of controls –

same face, same hair, same beard,
collisioning parallel lives,
only a different coloured shirt
divides us – two astonished waves,

we head off in separate
directions… They say we all
have a lost twin lying in wait,
a doppelganger, a double –

I'd like to rise up, pull back
to space's outer reaches
slowly, google-earth, and track
their lone, respective journeys…

## What If?

What of all the ifs and buts and maybes,
the roads not taken, the choices not made?

I used to think of them as harpies
jeering at me from the stands

but now I regard them quite differently,
they seem more like guardian angels,

these ghosts of all my yesterdays,
walking parallel pathways

with a wave and smile of encouragement –
what's the view like from where you are,

they ask, you seem to be making a fist of it,
we almost crossed back there, didn't we,

maybe we'll meet up again later?
Maybe all roads lead to the same journey's end…

## Alter Egos

You could always depend on Tonto,
the trusty right hand,
the ever present friend,
faithful Indian companion, who

heard the far off warning sound
of no-good ornery outlaws
or the thundering iron horse
just by laying his ear to the ground,

always kept to the straight and narrow,
reliably saved the worst of days
with a wise, well chosen phrase
and a carefully aimed arrow:

*even good man must wear mask*
*some time, kemo sabe,*
*white man natural state not happy* –
we rode disguised into the dusk…

*

When Gary Sobers strolled to the crease,
bat swinging casually,
collar turned up nonchalantly,
acknowledging the applause,

you knew the sun was sure to shine,
crowds dancing in the stands,
calypso cricket, steel bands,
an endless flow of rum and wine.

I was more in the Barrington mould –
the safety-first art
of implacable dead bat,
extra sweater to keep out the cold.

How I longed to be like Gary,
cast caution to the wind,
throw back my head and sing
even as skies turned gloomy,

so when those storm clouds finally massed
I heard that golden rising song
in cadenced Caribbean twang:
*summer's like Sobers, too good to last...*

*

Punch was a most unusual ally –
holy fool,
lord of misrule,
wicked gleam in his eye –

he wormed his way to my darkest dream
on a pier in North Wales
thrilling me with lurid tales
of revolution, murder, mayhem,

cast off cosy domesticity,
cheated the hangman, tricked the police,
hoodwinked the devil to gain his release,
always courting my complicity

which I gave him, threw in my lot
with him for a while,
adopted his stick, his swazzle, his smile,
thought: that's the way to do it...

*

Unlike many other kids I knew
I didn't have imaginary friends
who'd take the blame or make amends
or be there simply to talk to

until uninvited Camille stepped out
of the dansette in the sitting room
(exotic sounding *nom de plume*
through whom I'd place each daily bet)

straight from Lehar's light opera,
my father's high tenor voice
transporting me to a place
gilded with glamour…

*

But with none of these travel companions
was I able to stay the course.
I watched each one saddle his horse,
leave me behind with my diffidence.

Camille stayed longer than most –
perhaps because he wasn't real
he was someone I could feel
closer to than the rest

but he too left eventually
so it came as quite a shock
when out of the blue he came back –
I thought I'd forgotten him completely –

in Graham Nash's northern tones
*oh Camille, tell me how do you feel*
*now your heart tells you this can't be real*
bringing with him all those former friends

who whisper in my ear slyly,
who hit me for six,
beat me with their sticks –
*time to tell truth now, kemo sabe…*

## Parallel Lines

winter
night

a hard frost glinting
stars arching clear and sharp

black ink sky
breath freezing in statues

a narrow back lane
cuts between backs of houses

cheese-slicing the dark
a fixed point on the horizon

I walk towards –
footsteps pecking the stone

a beat too late – not alone
the cold blurs my eyes

image shifts, double vision
replicates in a tear of ice

focus pulled out and in
slipped frame mirroring

time-warped worm hole
cross-over from the meeting point

horizon shape-shifter
walks to meet me

catches at my frozen breath
sucked back within

*

ship's horn sounds in the fog
grey mass heavy as regret
hanging…

out on the ice
the creature cries
rattling

chains no hand grasps
scraping the deck
splintering

hull stuck fast in frozen sea
edge of the known world
howling

seeking its lost twin –
lashed to the masthead
plunging

butchered bird around my neck
I stare at the fog to lift
listening

voice in my skull
dredged from ocean floor
accusing

the shattering ice cracks
we stand on opposite sides
not seeing

sensing, arriving, retreating
hands raised in recognition
till next time…

*

clearing out the flat
I pack away the years
into cardboard boxes
dispensing a life

back of the wardrobe
an old dusty mirror
black spots behind the silver
wrapped in green baize

hanging it weeks later
above the brick fireplace
air crackles, match sparks
clock skips a second

caught in an altered room
slight shift of furniture
closed curtain rustles –
my reflection turning back winks…

*

parallel lines

fused

## Starting Over

*You can step in the same river, but the water will not be the same.* Heraclitus

Camille and his wife were sitting companionably reading one evening after dinner. Camille looked up from his paper and said, "Listen to this. 'Scientists claim that the brain remembers everything. Every single thought, word or deed remains stored somewhere on its hard drive'. The problem is we haven't yet found a way to access it all."

"Or even some of it," laughed his wife. "Some days I can't remember who I am."

"Who are you anyway?"

"Actually, I think I remember reading that article already, or something similar," she said. "The way that when one part of our brain forgets something, or can't retrieve it, another part is able to create an alternative version of what happened, and how the part of the brain that is searching for the original memory can be persuaded of the truth of the fiction."

"It's probably just as well," said Camille, "for if we ever did find a way to retrieve every single incident in our lives and then recount them, it would take as long to relive it, if not longer, as it did to experience it first time around."

"What a dreadful thought," said his wife. "It would stop you from ever encountering anything new."

Camille, though, thought he would like to try nevertheless. The trouble was that all the millions of memories he could recall, which fizzed around the circuitry of his brain so fast, like racing cars in a grand prix, simply made his head hurt. No sooner had he registered the tiniest fraction of them, than the rest had vanished, seemingly for ever, like sand through his fingers. A few grains remained, tantalisingly glinting in the sunlight, but making little sense. The only course of action left open to him, he thought, was to be selective: pick out random moments he *could* recall and see where they led him; and try later, if he could, to discern any pattern or connecting thread that might link them, that might take him from this, as far back as he could remember, to some sort of beginning.

"Scientists also say," he went on, "that we are not in fact the same person we were when we started out. We shed atoms at the rate of something like fifty billion per second. Our skin cells decay and drop off so frequently that we are literally not who we once were."

He stopped. What he'd also read, but didn't say, was that by the time we reach sixty, as Camille just had, our entire skin will have changed some seven or eight times. So even if he did manage to make it back through all the recounted moments he could muster, who would he find? Not himself, it would seem. A series of different incarnations perhaps, pursuing vaguely parallel lives. Despite the impossibility of his brain grasping all of this, he decided he would set out anyway to try and find where they might meet, and wondered, idly, what that particular infinity might look like…

*

The next night they were watching a film. Its premise was that the central character had the ability to turn back time. He could replay the same day, the same hour, the same minute, a second, a third, or even a fourth time, to try and right a wrong, avert an accident, enable things to turn out better. What would that be like, Camille wondered out loud?

"I wouldn't want to," said his wife. "Oh – there are many particular moments, whole days even, that I'd love to relive, golden times, but I wouldn't want to change them. Once you start doing that, who knows what kind of chain reaction you might set off."

"The butterfly effect," agreed Camille.

"Exactly," she said. "We wouldn't be the people we are now, sitting having this conversation, to be able to go back and alter something in the first place. I'm not talking about skin cells, but something less easy to define. Every intervention you might make would open up so many possibilities, create so many imponderables, that the odds of navigating yourself back to *that* precise moment which led to *this* action, to *that* consequence, so that you could actually change just the one thing, without altering anything else, are incalculable."

"The Enigma Code."

"Precisely."

"But they cracked that."

"They got lucky."

"Besides," he said, "it could be like what Woody Allen says in *Hannah and her Sisters.* 'If I could live my whole life over, would I come back as an aardvark or a moose? I might have to watch *The Ice-Capades* again and again'."

"Cause and effect," she laughed. "What makes a great novel is when the writer presents you with a set of specific circumstances and a group of characters who face them. The choices they make are governed by a combination of so many factors that when one of them carries out a particular action, you don't know how it's going to turn out, what the exact effect is going to be. You can speculate – you have the cause – but the outcome is uncertain."

"I suppose so."

"The whole point is in not knowing, and the fun part is trying to work it out."

"Perhaps that explains why you forget what you've read or seen so often."

"Perhaps," she laughed.

"At least you have the consolation of being surprised all over again when you re-read it."

"Even if I do remember, I still like to consider other possible endings and enjoy the ride," she said and went through to the kitchen.

Enjoy the ride, thought Camille.

His mind went back to the Robert Frost poem they'd all had to learn at school:

*"Two roads diverged in a yellow wood,*
*And sorry I could not travel both*
*And be one traveller, long I stood*
*And looked down one as far as I could*
*To where it bent in the undergrowth…"*

How did it go? He'd forgotten.

*"I shall be telling this with a sigh*
*Somewhere ages and ages hence:*
*Two roads diverged in a wood, and I…"*

Yes, that was it.

*"I took the one less travelled by,*
*And that has made all the difference…"*

"Dinner's ready," his wife called out from the kitchen. "Do you want to put some music on?"

He went to the record player, where still on the turntable from the last time was John Lennon. Why not play it again, he thought?

*Starting Over.*

# this boy

## The Story of the Moon

sick green pumpkin –
gouged pock-hole eyes
cratered nose
gaping toothless grin –

stared down on me
with murderous malice
between rows of bombed-out houses
walking home from grandma

she's hunting me, I'd
whisper, hand clutched tight
in my father's, unlit street
held no place to hide

her searchlight beam
razor-sharp would pierce
slate-less roof, broken glass
the long night walk home

shut your eyes, don't look
my dad would say but
even squeezed tight shut
she'd needle a crack

I'd hear the rustle
of her crow-black skirt
pursuing me, her deep throat
laughter's cackle

## Friday Nights...

... I'd creep downstairs drawn by laughter and music –
my parents back home from dancing
or the pictures, enjoying a drink with friends –
and perch on a stair I knew didn't creak
to peep between the banisters
first towards the kitchen, the men sitting
round the table playing poker,
the overhead light a fug of cigarette smoke,
and then towards the women standing apart
drinking babychams, easing off stilettos,
dancing in the hallway on stockinged feet
to Lonnie Donegan on the blue dansette...

I studied my father's poker face
recognising the slow blink of his eyes,
the barely perceptible cat-like smile
when he had a good hand, and after
he'd pooled all the pennies on the table
my mum would drape her arms around him
cajoling him for one last dance...

It was then he'd usually spot me, or someone would,
a chair would scrape back on the kitchen linoleum
and I'd be beckoned to join them,
my mum would put the kettle on
for a last mug of Maxwell House
and I'd be passed around like a puppy,
cheeks pinched, hair tousled,
remarks made I wouldn't understand
till fast asleep I'd be carried upstairs again
dreaming of when it would be my turn
to enter that magic circle, to join in
instead of merely watching from the stairs...

## Saturday Mornings

*Tic-tac is a traditional method of signs used by bookmakers to communicate the odds of certain horses. Tic-tac men would wear white gloves to allow their hand movements to be easily seen over wide distances across the racecourse.* Wikipedia

1

Saturday mornings meant
running bets for my dad
to the local bookie's round the corner
when betting was barely legal
so you had to use a pseudonym –

my father, Eric, chose Enrico
(after Caruso) which made somehow
the gambling seem more glamorous
a far cry from grandma's dire warnings
delivered daily like a sermon

*... first it's a shilling, then it's a pound,*
*then it's the whole house...*

her hands rising to her face in horror
a gesture a Geisha might make
delicate, rehearsed, designed to deter
but I was in thrall to the litany
of betting slips clutched in hot hands

*they're under starter's orders...*
*... and they're off*

yankee each way treble accumulator
in letters spilling unconfined
beyond pre-drawn lines on Basildon Bond
blue carbon paper placed beneath
for copies he always kept

*

(every week would see the same routine)

- *you're too young*
- *it's not for me, it's my dad*
- *it says Enrico, how do I know that isn't you?*
- *I'd be Camille*
- *our secret then…*

(like father, like son)

2

(like father, like son)
I studied the form
*The Sporting Life* and *Chronicle*

compiling vital statistics
picking winners for the week ahead
recorded in red exercise books

with the old weights and measures
imperial dry, avoirdupois, long or lineal
listed on the back –

*two links one chain*
*ten chains one furlong*
*eight furlongs one mile*

furlongs the measurement of racing
that could all come down to half a length
a neck, short head, dead heat

bushels and pecks, fathoms and leagues
rods, poles and perches
(I never did learn what they were for)

*

each day en route for school
crossing the Ship Canal
I'd stop to swap tips with the Irish Navvies

my grandma needn't have worried
it was never the money for me
more the pleasure in picking winners

working out odds signalled in code
tic-tac men like Masons
black bowler hats, white kid gloves

silent scriptures in the sky
I longed to learn their language
like my granddad's semaphore

fifteen to eight, a hundred to thirty
even money the favourite
twenty to one - bar…

I raced to the bookie's
the following Saturday
to try out my new-learned skill

to my delight he signalled me back –
I still need your father's slip, he called
Enrico… Camille… each way…

3

but soon gambling was commonplace
nom de plumes discarded
we got a telephone – 2587 party line –
and my dad rang in his bets
(though he'd always begin "*Enrico here…*")

and I stopped reading *The Sporting Life*
switched my interest from horses to girls
whose vital statistics I sought out in inches
while weights and measures went metric
(twenty grains equal one scruple)

## Sunday Afternoons

…began straight after breakfast
when my grandmother would scrub
the back of my neck with a pumice stone

hair was brushed and brylcreemed
shoes polished to a mirror
and to cap it all
I had to wear a tie

… but worse than all of this
was having always to be quiet –
never speak unless spoken to
was an unbreakable rule

forced to sit still and listen
to the boring talk of adults
I wasn't allowed to read a book
or colour in, or even play Patience

my swinging legs suspended
by the merest of stern glances
the faintest fidget frozen
by a single raised finger

… I could imagine no worse fate
than to grow up
willingly choosing to endure
the strain of Sunday silences

## Aunts & Uncles

At the start of *Annie Hall* Woody Allen repeats the old Groucho Marx joke that he would never want to join a club which had him as a member. But your family is a club you are born into, and as the saying goes, you can choose your friends, but not your family.

My own family falls into that much-loved cliché of soccer commentators – a game of two halves – for while my mother was an only child, her mother (my grandmother) was one of ten children and my grandfather one of five, so there were always different aunts, uncles and cousins to call on, Wrights and Eves, Heaths and Blundells, each with their own particular foibles, and I quickly got to know them all…

*

First there was fat Uncle Cyril, who sat me on his knee and who pinched and squeezed me too hard. Auntie Alice, his wife, who played the piano for Saturday sing-alongs at the Legion but only hymns on Sundays, both sung with same wheezy smoker's hack.

Then there was fierce Uncle Harry, a foreman at the print works run by my grandfather, who lived in the house where my mum had been born, who rubbed my cheeks with the stubble on his chin, who called me a closet seat, a big girl's blouse, but who would melt like butter for Auntie May, his wife, who polished the chapel brasses.

Cousin Dorothy, their daughter, who caused a scandal by marrying a Catholic and moving to Cheshire, whose daughter Julie I had a crush on, whose best friend was another cousin, Janice, who cut my hair and rode horses on the farm at Barton Moss with her mum Marjorie, who'd once been a showgirl, a dancer in the music hall, but who now mucked out the stables.

Red-faced Uncle Jack, who tied my mum to a tree in the orchard in the neighbouring farm at Rixton, where pigs rooted for wind falls, where thirty wild cats ran about the yard ruled by a fierce tabby with three legs and one eye, where Jack kept a succession of rolling-eyed guard dogs, and where Uncle Hughie, his dad, died in his sleep after milking the cows.

Dorothy's big sister Margaret, who worked in the Soap Works with Auntie Ruby, who married Uncle Stan, who couldn't read or write, but who bred budgies in their back yard. Margaret's husband Bill, who drove a steam engine from the Tar Pit to the Steel Works by the canal, whose oil-slick, polluted surface spontaneously combusted one hot afternoon at Bob's Lane Ferry.

Uncle Frank, who lived in a converted upturned boat on a beach in North Wales, where we played cricket with an oar for a bat, where I got stung by a jelly fish, and where Cousin Derek, RAF pilot and Don Juan, gave my mum the complete works of Byron.

Uncle Tom, who lost his leg on the Somme, who worked for Tootal's in Manchester and who gave me a tie each Christmas. Aunt Mathilda, "our Tilly", who was the first girl in the family to work in an office (instead of in service) and who changed her name to "Laurie" because it sounded posher.

Uncle Gordon who made me eat black bananas every time I saw him, who did magic tricks with match boxes, but who we always had to be quiet around because he was an invalid. I have photos of him sitting on the decks of cruise ships with a blanket on his knees.

Auntie Ethel, who sailed away to Canada, where she bleached her hair and married a jockey. Cousin Alan who grew tomatoes in Jersey, Cousin George who flicked my ear lobes, Cousin Bill who bit my bum and Auntie Barbara who cuffed their ears…

*

My father on the other hand, the youngest of seven children, held no truck with families and was always tight-lipped on the subject. A guilty, lapsed Catholic, these were two clubs he'd abandoned – the church and his family – and we never saw anything of either.

My dad's father, John Fogg, died when my dad was just a boy. I grew up under the illusion he'd been a sign writer, who'd immigrated to a Salford slum from Ireland and proceeded to make his way in the world. I liked this notion that my never-seen grandfather might have left me messages in the signs he'd written, hanging over shops and factories across the city but this, like so much else with my dad's family, proved false.

John was in fact born in Salford, as was his father and his father before that, all of them called John. He worked as a labourer in a lumber yard by the Bridgwater Canal near Patricroft, where the waters of the Bridgwater are carried by the world's first swing bridge aqueduct out across the Ship Canal, which links Liverpool to Manchester, making a wide loop around Eccles and Peel Green, where my dad was cremated, and where his mother would move when she remarried, a fact I only learned recently, for I never knew her.

Tiny and fierce (I'm told) she brought up all seven children single-handed in a narrow, brick-built terraced house in Urmston till, one by one, they all left her, save my dad, the youngest, who finished school early at 14 to start work and help out, nightly trudging the streets of Salford selling insurance, by day a steeple-jack climbing factory chimneys on Trafford Park, till National Service took him away for two wasted years.

From various hints dropped by my mother, I think my father never forgave his brothers and sisters for the way they all left home to pursue their own lives, leaving him, still only a boy, to look after their ailing mother who, when he returned from the army, had begun to lose her sight as well.

This was why, I was told, I never saw this grandmother as a child – she was fearful I'd fall in the canal at the back of her house – but perhaps it was more my father felt betrayed by her remarrying after all he felt he'd sacrificed… Who knows? As far as I'm aware he rarely saw her after that, although she did attend his wedding – a double wedding at which as well as my dad marrying my mum, his best friend Bob married his childhood sweetheart Gladys – for years later, when cleaning out my mum's flat after she died, I came across their wedding album and concluded, by a process of elimination and the evident likeness she bore to my father, that this tiny, indomitable woman staring out at the camera, must be the grandmother I never knew.

I only knew there were never any photographs of my father's family at home, and when, once, I asked him why, he only said, "Not all families are like your mother's," and he never mentioned any of them again.

Auntie Alice Rose, the eldest, who I never knew existed till I researched the Family Tree.

Auntie Florence, named after her mother, but whom I never saw, likewise Uncle Henry and Auntie Joan, yet they all lived close by. I later learned that I had walked past Uncle Henry's house, in a long row called Shaw View by the Candle Factory, every week on my way to Sunday School.

Then there was Uncle Johnny, for some reason my godfather, though I only saw him twice. The first time was when he came to our house on the afternoon of our wedding, the second a chance collision on the corner of the street where my dad had been born and from which all these aunts and uncles had departed, until now, when Johnny had returned to live there with his wife Vera and daughter Susan. I liked him, though I never saw him again.

And finally there was Uncle Jim, who, rumour had it, ran away to sea, made a drunken pass at my mother on her wedding day to my father, and got into fist fights at the Legion…

But now I doubt the truth of any of this. In the absence of hard facts we make up stories to help us make sense of who we are, and now I wish I'd done more to track them down, these relatives, the missing aunts and uncles on my father's side, who I still picture trudging those Salford streets, or climbing those factory chimneys as a young man, and I'm reminded of what Thoreau wrote: *"Most men lead quiet lives of desperation."*

My dad's escape was through singing. Each night he'd come in from work and sing a snatch of Puccini to reclaim some part of who he was.

*

If Sunday afternoons meant visiting relations from my mother's wide extended family, Saturday nights meant sitting in draughty church halls, listening to my mum and dad singing in the Concert Party they'd formed with Bob and Gladys, the couple who'd shared their wedding day. Afterwards I'd go back to my grandparents' house on my mother's side, where I would spend the night, so that I could be up bright and early to get ready for those Sunday family excursions.

My dad never joined in these visits. It was as if he, like Woody Allen in *Annie Hall*, although warmly welcomed by my mother's family, couldn't bring himself to join any club which invited him to be a member.

At the end of each concert, he and my mother would sing that old Nelson Eddy/Jeannette Macdonald favourite, *"Ah, Sweet Mystery of Life, at last I've found thee..."*

"Your father's a man of mystery and no mistake," my grandmother would say, and she didn't mean it as a compliment. "You never know where he is..."

I'm beginning to think I might.

## Carousel

*And the seasons they go round and round*
*The painted ponies go up and down*
*We're captive on a carousel of time...* Joni Mitchell

autumn was conkers
first you collected them
the shiny chestnuts gathering
in drifts by the roadside

then the preparation
the soaking in vinegar
the placing in rows on baking trays
to be cooked and hardened in ovens

next came the tricky bit
the piercing with a skewer
where if you weren't careful
(or even if you were)

it could split
an early lesson in life's unfairness
and finally the threading
with knotted string or baler twine

then you were ready
to do battle in the playground
a contest where for once size
or age didn't matter

if your nerve held and your aim was true
if you could withstand the rapped knuckles and near misses
if you had patience to wait
till just the right moment

you'd be rewarded with the accolade
king for a day
before your conker would crack
give up the ghost

consigned to playground tarmac
trodden underfoot
till nothing was left
but mashed pulp

you'd simply go home
select the next contender
start again
re-enter the fray…

*

winter was always soccer
pumping up the bladder inside the ball
like repairing the inner tube of a bicycle tyre

spit on your fingers
rub along the surface
lower in water in an old washing up bowl

waiting to spot the tell-tale
bubble of air escaping
drying then patching the culprit

before stuffing it back in its outer case
lacing the leather
hard and heavy as brick

then coat after coat of dubbin
to soften last season's shed-abandoned boots
mud baked like concrete

finally
ball tucked under arm
boots laced and looped around neck

you crossed the forbidden main road
climbed the fence to prohibited park
savoured the delicious sound of goal

ball rolling down rope of net
imprint of lace on your forehead
after you headed it home…

*

spring was marbles
all through winter you hoarded them
first in small string bags
later, as your collection grew, in large round tins

from time to time in the long dark nights
you took them secretly like a miser
held them one by one to the light
the glass-eyes, the alleys, the dobbers

laid them out and sorted them
arranged by size and colour
saved for the contests to come
as soon as the clocks went forward

you'd practise for weeks
on the hall carpet or kitchen linoleum
follow the leader, target, donkey drops
perfecting the weight and line

then, when the long slow thaw began
you'd blow on your fingers to keep them warm
kneeling in gravel till tiny stones
embedded themselves in your shins

*

summer, when you were older, was cricket
rooting out bats from the back of the wardrobe

carefully sanding willow blades
liberally applying linseed oil

till they shone like golden syrup
sprinkling talcum on the handles

unrolling slowly the new grips snug and tight
(like you learned to do later with condoms…)

glowing cherry red in your mind's eye
you take the ball from its box in the drawer

your fingers close round raised stitched seam
eyes shut perfecting each grip

off spin, cutter, in-swing
leg-break, googly, chinaman

(since last season you've made do with *owzat*
exquisite tiny metal rollers

annotating each imaginary innings
with neat HB pencil in crimson hardback scorebook

between sky blue lines on pale cream paper
gridded calligraphy of schoolboy dreams)

you whiten pads and boots, screw in studs
bend and stretch rubber-spiked green gloves

air your box, pack and repack your bag
then set off on that long lonely walk

from changing room to nets
pavilion to middle

right arm over, one to come –
rain stops play…

## Water Features

*Rhos Point '62*
a wave somersaults above
my grandfather's car

lifts us in the air
drops us several yards ahead –
that was fun, he says

*

*Clapton '88*
we wade thigh deep through run-off
from rain-sodden fields

our son announces
adventures are fine in books –
I carry him home

*

*'77*
*Lindisfarne* – water lapping
the narrow causeway

vanished in seconds
I put my foot on the gas
it's now or never

*

*Greenham '99*
the century's swept away
water levels rise

flash flood roaring through
tears down bridges, rips up roots
we stand on the edge

*

*Peel '74*
circling the ruined castle
the eye of the storm

we howl to the waves
here we all are, do your worst
young, invincible

## Flash Floods

Flixton '63
coldest winter on record
ice inside windows

frozen pipes bursting
torrents of water cascade
through swollen front door

misery for months
so cold the fire just can't catch
permanent power

cuts, birds stiff on wires
my mother can't stop crying
my dad hardly speaks

I retreat upstairs
huddled under overcoats
waiting for the thaw

doll in a suitcase
fixed stare piercing the darkness
scratches at the lid

*

later that summer
marooned by sudden flash floods
Chassen Road Station

rescued by firemen
who carry us one by one
like Angel Clare's Tess

to dry land safety
of Salvation Army hut
biscuits and Bovril

I miss induction
at the local grammar school
turn up in autumn

confused a day late
*sans cap, sans tie, sans blazer*
catching the wrong bus

with exercise books
not backed in plain brown paper
plimsolls not whitened

satchel like a girl's
grey babyish short trousers
belted gabardine

head dunked in toilet
taking turns to hold me down
repeat flushings

no fireman rescue
this time, no break in the clouds
just more of the same

the weather forecast
prophesies more long winters
a cold front coming

*

lie low, my dad says
keep mum – what would Tonto do
or the Lone Ranger?

*yes kemo sabe*
*white man speak with forkèd tongue*
*where is that masked man*

I'm easy pickings
too easy, soon they grow bored
seek out different prey

I'm asked to take part
(if you can't beat them join them)
follow the arrow

obscure codes in chalk
mirror-writing on smeared glass
invisible ink

arcane rules, secret signs
complex hand-shakes and high fives
initiations

I pass the fire test
hand held over naked flame
thumb-pricked mingled blood

fingers crossed I play
the role of double agent
*si kemo sabe*

to each new victim
I leave a silver bullet
hidden in their desk

and keep making trails
of dead leaves and bird-feathers
a silent shadow

sweeping footprints
no longer needing flash floods
to cover my tracks

*

fifty years later
the floods return carrying
the detritus spoil

of lost memories
washed up along the shoreline
the rains receding

head of a child's doll
ravens pecking at the eyes
stares out accusing

a severed hand thrusts
splayed fingers through mud pointing
back where it came from

vainly reaching out
a battered suitcase bobs by
spilling its contents

guilty reminders
an assortment of odd shoes
and abandoned dreams

## Age of Discovery

When I was 12 years old, on the last day of term before breaking up for the long summer holidays, I volunteered to do an extra summer history project. Sad, isn't it? I didn't have to, and nobody was even asking for anyone to. I simply approached Mr Vaughan, my History teacher, and asked if I could. Somewhat nonplussed he agreed and then asked me what I might be interested in. This hadn't occurred to me. I think I expected to be told what it would be, as we were the rest of the time. There was an awkward pause, and I realised he was waiting for me to suggest something. On the wall behind him was an early map of the world with illustrations of sailing ships and Latin inscriptions proclaiming *Terra Incognita* and *Here Be Dragons*. That looked interesting, I thought, and since I'd be spending all of the summer holidays in Wales with my grandparents, where I knew my granddad had lots of atlases, I randomly came up with: "Age of Discovery, sir."

"Excellent choice," he said. "Here's a new exercise book. See how much of it you can fill up." Quantity, as opposed to quality, always seemed to be the benchmark of my school days. "But don't spend all the summer cooped up indoors. *Mens sana in corpore sano,* what?" And he was off down the corridor making his own end-of-term getaway.

*

My first day in Penrhyn Bay turned out to be rainy, and so my grandmother, who did not want me under her feet all day, packed me off to the library in Llandudno. This was one of those marvellous 1920's municipal affairs, with a large dome, imposing stone steps flanked by lions, marble pillars and an oak panelled reference room accessed by a spiral staircase – absolutely the proper place to be carrying out important, serious research, I told myself. Fortunately there was a very good History section and before long I was rolling the names of those early explorers around my unfamiliar tongue like a litany: Amerigo Vespucci, Vasco da Gama, Hernando de Soto, Nunez de Balboa. I imagined myself discovering the North-West Passage, charting the coast of America, canoeing down rivers, hacking my way through jungles with daring portages through Panama, warding off marauding Indians, boarding the ships of scurvy sea dogs and hoisting the Jolly Roger. Much more drama than history. (Why let the truth get in the way of a good story, as a friend of mine often says still?)

But the more I read, the more drawn in I became to the blind faith of all those who sailed aboard such tiny vessels, who literally did not know where, or if, they might sight land again. Spending half the year as I did in those days by the sea, it was easy to imagine that the world was flat, like a dinner plate, and that if you sailed to the far horizon, you might simply drop off the edge. The facsimile of the early map of the world that hung on my History teacher's wall showed a round, flat earth being carried on the back of an elephant, which in turn was supported by a giant turtle. I was also very much taken by Christopher Columbus's notion that by sailing west, across the Atlantic, he would eventually arrive right around the other side of the world at the Spice Islands, not realising that the little matter of the continent of America lay in between.

That idea of travelling in a perpetual circle, eventually arriving back at exactly the same spot you started from, continues to intrigue.

*

For the rest of that summer in Penhryn Bay the sun shone and I spent all of my time playing cricket, and so when the time came for me to go back home to Manchester in readiness for the start of the new school year, I hadn't even begun, let alone completed, my voluntary project on the Age of Discovery. Hastily the night before, I copied various bits and pieces from my grandfather's encyclopaedia and handed it in to Mr Vaughan on the first day of term. Clearly he had forgotten all about it and did not look too thrilled at the prospect of having to read through something extra he hadn't bargained for.

Weeks passed and, when half term approached, I plucked up the courage to ask him if he had had chance yet to read through my project and what he thought about it. Once again it was quite apparent that he had not given it a moment's thought. "Ah yes, indeed, most interesting. Don't happen to have it to hand just now, but first thing after half term – promise."

When the Christmas holidays loomed and still it had not materialised, I began to suspect that he had in all probability mislaid it, or worse, thrown it away, and I said so. "Lost at sea, is it, sir? Like Marco Polo?"

"Are you trying to be clever?"

"My project, sir. The Age of Discovery."

"Well, see if you can discover where the school playing fields lie and give me twenty laps."

Rendered speechless by such injustice, I found myself lapping the football pitch at the back of the school, dragging my feet through the thick crust of mud which covered it. Round and round I ran, going nowhere, my legs as slow and heavy as that turtle's must have been, supporting both the elephant and the world on his shoulders. Round and round, back to where I started from. I tried to imagine myself as Amerigo Vespucci once more, charting every inlet and headland from the Hudson Bay to Tierra del Fuego, or Ferdinand Magellan circumnavigating the globe, but I couldn't. All I could think of was putting one foot in front of the other, trudging through the mud, as the icy rain stabbed my face like needles.

(Ten years later I remember a student friend describing a journey he had just completed across America. He was delivering a car from New York to California, a cheap way of seeing the country. For one whole day he drove through a corn field in Kansas, as vast and limitless as an ocean with no other features except the sky and the corn. One whole day. The corn really was as high as an elephant's eye, so he could see nothing but the straight empty road stretching for ever in front of him. "I thought that in the end I'd simply drive off over the edge," he said. "Or go crazy. Like the Ancient Mariner.")

Round and round I continued to run, finding a rhythm, feet getting surer. I began to realise that I had lost count – had I done twenty laps or not? – but also that it didn't matter. Nobody was watching me. I could stop whenever I liked, but I didn't. I kept running, round and round, on and on. I didn't know where I was heading, but it would be somewhere, and I would know when I'd got there.

It was my own age of discovery.

## Cross Country Running

Every Friday morning, whatever the weather, we were sent out cross-country running. We were given a route – a lap of the school playing fields, then out along Bradfield Road towards the Humphrey Park Estate, across Urmston Lane down into the meadows (always flooded) by the banks of the Mersey, then back across the main Stretford Road to the school playing fields – which we were meant to complete three times. The PE teacher – the sadistic Mr Rapson – issued his instructions then breezily sent us on our way, while he stayed behind in his office by the gymnasium for a cigarette and the chance to pose in front of the naked pin-ups he had on the inside of his locker door, which he didn't know we knew about, and which we once caught him preening himself in front of.

He particularly liked to do this after he had taken the slipper to all of our bare behinds on some jumped-up pretext or other. Once, when we were mere first years, he left us alone in the gym one time and naturally we started fooling around, till the noise levels grew quite high. We weren't organised enough then to have someone on look-out, so his sudden reappearance caught us unawares. To punish us all for the noise we'd been making, he ordered us to form a queue so that he could slipper us one by one. A very quiet, nervous boy – Michael Stone – clearly terrified, begged Rapson to spare him because he himself had not been talking. This was true; Michael wouldn't say 'boo' to a goose. Rapson curled his upper lip in what for him resembled a smile and quietly informed Michael that in that case he would receive six strokes of the slipper to everyone else's three. Unthinkable in these modern, health-and-safety conscious days we live in now, but nobody thought to complain about either his bullying, or the lack of supervision for our weekly cross country run, and away we all went.

Except that for me, Ian Cloudsdale and Pete Jackson, we had ourselves our own private little wheeze. Pete lived on

Bradfield Road (less than a hundred yards away) and both his parents were out at work all day, so once we had lapped the playing field, while the rest of the class trundled out through the school gates, we ducked under a hedge by the adjoining allotments and scooted on down towards the gate at the back of Pete's house, where his mum would always hide the spare key. Then we would ensconce ourselves in their kitchen, brew ourselves a pot of tea and watch the rest of the class as they struggled past. Forty minutes or so later, when they passed by on their final lap, we'd slip out of the front door and join the pack somewhere in the middle, having first ensured that we had splashed a few bits of mud up and down the backs of our legs to make it look as though we had been running down by the Mersey meadows.

To finish the race 'somewhere in the middle' was important, as we successively made our way past Mr Rapson's baleful stare, avoiding the random clips round the ear he casually administered to those within easy reach. Too near the front might have risked us being selected for the cross country team (which would have meant spending Saturday mornings with Rapson in the back of a minibus) and too near the rear would have brought further bouts of sarcasm, derision and, probably, the slipper – so the anonymity of the middle was the safest place to strive for – a goal that suited our whole school's philosophy rather well. Its motto was "Manners Makyth Man", and it was always impressed upon us that it wasn't really polite to win or excel in any way. Not that we needed any encouraging – what was the point, we felt, in running round and round the same piece of ground, over and over, week after week, round and round and round...? Done that. Got the T-shirt.

To be sure, on the annual Speech Nights, prizes were awarded, but as much for "progress" as for coming top, and so that way most of us usually received something – a book token, always – although Rapson eschewed the whole notion of progress and only doled out prizes to what Americans would term "jocks", or his bum-boys, as the rest of us called them back then, I recall now somewhat shamefacedly.

Of much more interest was the anticipated length of the

headmaster's annual address, which was always interminable, made only moderately manageable by the book I used to run on how long his speech would be. We all placed sixpence on the time we thought it would last, and if no-one guessed correctly, I would clean up. He was called Mr. Babb, Mr W.H. Babb (we none of us ever knew what the initials stood for, so he was affectionately dubbed "Wilf", and he had the shortest neck I can ever remember, giving the impression that he had a coat-hanger in the shoulders of his black, hooded, academic gown which he always wore and that he had just been hung up by it).

Afterwards we'd serve parents cups of tea. I remember one of the dinner ladies saying to me, Ian and Pete, whose turn it was to do this one year, what good tea-makers we were. "Well," said Pete, "we get plenty of practice. Every Friday morning."

## Amo, amas, amat

In addition to Mr Rapson, my school had its fair share of bullies among its teachers, as well as one or two who were truly inspiring, but it's the bullies you tend to remember the most, isn't it? Like Mr Johnson, the Art teacher, a bluff Geordie with a rasping tongue. He didn't mince his words and what few he chose to utter were by and large scathing. Once, I recall, while we were struggling over a still life he'd set up for us to draw, he walked around the class throwing out withering, caustic jibes and comments as he passed each one of us. On reaching me, he dismissed my admittedly weak effort with barely a glance, adding, "Hey, laddie – why not use a poker next time?"

I stopped drawing instantly and have never been able to take it up again, although I love to look at art: visiting galleries and exhibitions I count among my keenest pleasures.

When Tim, our son, was just three years old, he was sitting on my knee one evening and I was trying to draw a car for him. With disarming, artless candour, he remarked helpfully, "You're not very good at drawing, are you, Daddy?" He himself has proved to be an excellent artist, a talent clearly inherited from his mother, and is currently working on a graphic novel with his partner.

But he, too, suffered from early discouragement. Like all children he loved singing, and would often be heard unselfconsciously singing to himself, sometimes songs he had heard, but mostly songs he simply made up. But when he reached primary school, his first teacher informed him once that he must be tone deaf, for his singing was dreadful and it would be better for everyone if he stopped. Which is what he did, of course, despite all of our encouragement to the contrary, and still, to this day, you will not hear him singing. How differently things might turn out if teachers weighed their words more carefully. Parallel lines…

*

At secondary school, there were three teachers the memory of whose sadistic bullying has for ever stayed with me. First there was Mr Martin, the music teacher. He was a round, plumpish man with a chin beard, which misleadingly made you think he was quite jolly. He made lots of jokes and he would dash off improvisations at his piano to underscore whatever mood he was in or whatever opinion he was delivering at the time. But he also had a darker side cloaked within that gnome-like demeanour. Once, during an interminable hour in which he had us drawing page after page of treble clefs on a particularly hot summer's afternoon, I was sitting by the window where, outside on the playing field, a cricket match was taking place. At that age – 13 years – cricket was my absolute passion, and so naturally I found my gaze being drawn to events on the cricket pitch away from the treble clefs more and more, until, inevitably, Mr Martin spotted me.

"And what is out there, boy," he asked in his lilting Welsh accent, "that can possibly be more interesting than the task in hand?"

"Cricket, sir."

"Oh cricket, is it? What the fascination is in watching adolescent boys rubbing a red leather ball up against their crotch has always eluded me."

"Yes, sir. I mean, no, sir."

"So why were you staring so avidly?"

"It's the House Final, sir. I was just curious as to who was winning."

"So you're a curious boy, are you? I should say so – a very curious boy indeed."

By now everyone else had stopped working, scenting blood.

"Curiosity killed the cat, and besides, I don't think it's curiosity at all. I prefer to call it nosey. Are you a nosey boy?"

"I'd like to think not, sir."

"You'd like to think not, sir, would you, sir? Well, boy, I have a cure for nosiness. Step up here."

Sensing everybody's eyes upon me, I walked slowly towards the front of the class.

"Face the blackboard." It was one of those blackboards on a roller that you could pull up and down with the aid of a metal strip which ran along the bottom edge.

"Do you see this?" Mr Martin went on, and he drew a small circle in chalk on the board just above my head. "This is what we do to nosey boys. Place your own curious little nose into that circle." I rose up on tiptoe and tried to do as he asked. "Now put your hands behind your back and make sure you keep that nose of yours inside the circle." He then proceeded, agonisingly slowly, to raise the board inch by inch while I tried in vain to keep my nose within the circle. "You're not trying, boy. I think you need a little extra motivation…" Whereupon he suddenly, without warning, thrust the metal strip at the bottom of the board upwards at lightning speed, so that it nearly emasculated my nose as it sped on up and past. The rest of class giggled nervously at my discomfort.

"I'm bored now," declared Mr Martin. "Into the cupboard with you," and he bustled me towards the stock cupboard behind his desk, threw me inside, then closed and locked the door behind me, where I lay on the floor in total darkness, surrounded by piles of musty, yellowing music manuscript paper. He often threatened us with locking us in there; he kept a tiger in there, he said, who liked little boys, especially first and second years, for afternoon tea, and though none of us believed him, this was the first time he had actually put any of us inside, and the thought that maybe, somewhere, in a far corner, a tiger was lying in wait did cross my mind as I waited for the lesson to end.

After what seemed an eternity, I finally heard the bell go for the end of the school day, followed by the mass scraping of chairs as my classmates stood up to be dismissed. Gradually I heard everyone leave and waited for Mr Martin to open up the stock room door and let me go too. Except that he didn't. I waited and waited and waited… In a panic I started banging on the door asking, please, to be let out. Eventually, the door opened and there stood one of the cleaners, plainly put out.

"Goodness, you gave me a scare with all that banging. Mr Martin mentioned something about a boy being in the cupboard, but I didn't believe him – he's always saying such things – you made me jump out of my skin. Whatever did you do to get yourself locked in there, you silly boy?"

"Mr Martin locked me in, miss."

"Did he now? Well then, I expect you deserved it. Off you go."

Not a shred of sympathy. It was like – years later – when I was 19 years old, I was in Newcastle visiting my then girl friend who was at university there. We had just spent the evening at a folk club and after seeing her back to her Hall of Residence, I was walking through the city centre towards a house where she had arranged for me to sleep on the floor of some friends she had. It was just after midnight and the streets were quietening down, when round the corner came a bunch of skinheads. At that stage in my life, I had very long hair and looked, no doubt, a bit of a hippy to them, and I could see at once that look in their eyes – not dissimilar to Mr Martin's – which said, "Let's have a bit of fun." Instantly they set upon me, knocked me to the ground, and began kicking me with their not inconsiderable "bovver boots", only to be interrupted by an elderly woman coming out of her front door to wonder what all the noise was about. To my great relief, the skinheads ran off down the street and the old lady walked towards me. Looking down at me, lying beaten in the gutter, she matter-of-factly remarked, "Well let that be a lesson to you," after which she merely turned on her heels and walked back inside, leaving me all alone to lick my wounds.

All those years earlier, liberated from the Music Room stock cupboard, I legged it to the bus stop, only to arrive there just as my bus was pulling away. Our school on Bradfield Road was directly opposite St Paul's, a Roman Catholic secondary modern, and such was the rivalry between the two schools that start and finish times for the beginning and end of the respective school days were carefully orchestrated so that we wouldn't all be arriving or leaving at the same time. By missing my bus, I would, I now realised, have to walk the gauntlet of all the St Paul's crowd, who would be arriving at the bus stop within the next few minutes, which they assuredly did. I tried to keep apart, hanging back from them, and this seemed to be working, until just as the bus arrived, a group of lads and girls suddenly barged into me, knocking off my cap, pinching my satchel and emptying its contents out onto the pavement, so that by the time I had gathered everything back together, the bus pulled away, leaving me with no option but to walk home.

When I eventually got there, I was more than an hour later than usual, but this caused no comment, other than a "What kept you?" from my mum, busy fixing the tea – it was a Tuesday, so that meant tripe and onions – to which I merely replied, "I just got caught up watching the cricket and lost track of the time."

On another occasion, once again bored in a music lesson, I was caught by Mr Martin as I was rocking to and fro on the back legs of my chair. "Oh," he sneered, with a growing glint in his eye, "so you like to balance, do you? See me after school in the car park."

When I turned up, he led me by the ear to a large stone pedestal that looked a bit like a giant mushroom, or a font, which had a manhole cover on the top leading down no doubt to some labyrinth of pipes and sewers. "Up you get," he said, and I slowly clambered on to the top, where I stood feeling very foolish and exposed. "Now," he said, his Welsh accent relishing the vowels, "you know the Statue of Eros in Piccadilly Circus, don't you?"

"I've never been to London, sir."

"Don't you be clever with me, boy! You've seen pictures, haven't you?"

"Yes, sir."

"Well then, off you go."

"Sir?"

"Adopt the same pose. Pretend to be firing a bow and arrow and stand on one leg."

By this time quite a crowd had gathered. The giant stone mushroom on which I was standing was situated right next to the bike sheds. About 500 boys attended Urmston Grammar School at that time and at least half of them travelled there each day by bike.

"This boy," proclaimed Mr Martin to the assembled throng, "likes to balance. So now he's going to demonstrate his prowess to one and all. I give you: the Urmston Statue of Eros! Let's give him a round of applause, shall we?"

Everyone started clapping, mixed with cat-calls and whistles, while I attempted to stand on one leg and hold an imaginary bow and arrow.

"Right, boy, you stay here till I come back," and off he strode.

The next 15 minutes, as I stood there while more than 200 bicycles paraded around and past me, were among the longest I've ever known. Needless to say, Mr Martin did not return any time soon. Eventually, the school caretaker, taking pity on me, said, "I'd go home if I were you, son. I'll tell Mr Martin that I gave you permission. And next time," he added as I climbed back down, "don't get caught."

More disturbing than Mr Martin, however, who was mostly irrelevant to us back then, was Mr Rhoden, the French teacher – or "Rodin", as he sometimes asked us to refer to him, for reasons that will become unpleasantly clear.

Most of the time Mr Rhoden was great: he was quiet, calm, well organised, an excellent, methodical teacher with an obvious love of both France and the French, and he made us all want to go there, and once there, speak the language fluently. He tapped into my own near-photographic memory, setting us lists of nouns to learn with all the masculine words on the left hand column and the feminine words on the right. As I tried to remember them, all I had to do was conjure up which side of the page I had first seen them written down on, and they would float back into my memory, and, because I experience synaesthesia, I still picture all the 'le' words as navy blue, with all the 'la' words being a bright, vivid yellow.

But Mr Rhoden had a dark side, and he would reveal this suddenly, unexpectedly, as if at the flick of a switch. "Maintenant, mes amis," he would say, and we would come to recognise this sudden shift into French as a warning sign, "amis" flashing up in neon red for danger. "Alors," he would continue, "Marat is coming round to see you. Je suis "Rodin" and I am bringing mon compagnon, Marat, to inspect your work."

Marat turned out to be a long, three-sided cane, with each of the triangular bevelled sides sharpened to a pointed edge. He would brandish this before him, rather like a magician's wand, as he walked up and down, pausing by each desk to check our work. Whenever he saw an error, he would remark, "A-ha, Marat is most displeased," and he would ping the wand on the top of our heads, which would truly hurt because of its sharpened edges. We all of us dreaded the appearance of Marat. "And when Marat is displeased, mes amis, we know what he must do next, do we not? He must bring out his friend Madame La Guillotine," and down would come Marat again onto one of our cowering, undeserving crowns.

Sometimes, Marat in hand, he would pause by some hapless individual (thankfully I never suffered this particular fate) and, having admonished him with Madame La Guillotine, he would then insert his hand inside the boy's shirt and proceed to squeeze his nipple hard.

Thankfully he was replaced after just a year by the effervescent Mr McKenna, an ebullient cockney, who acted out his lessons with outrageous mimes, and when our laughter grew too uproarious, he would put his finger to his lips and whisper, "Doucement," and proceed to walk in an outrageous fashion on tiptoe, which we would all copy, whispering back, "Doucement, doucement," in a hushed, northern unison.

And finally there was Mr Lever, the Latin teacher – or Jasper, as he was universally known. His actual name was Johnny, but everyone knew him as Jasper, even other teachers, I suspect, for he was something of a legend. I don't know how old he was – at 11 every adult looks old – but he had been my mother's Latin teacher when she was at school, so that tells you something, and he wore glasses with lenses so thick that they magnified his eyes to such a huge extent that he resembled some kind of ancient, giant bullfrog. His reputation preceded him, and we all knew about Jasper and what to expect long before we actually had our first lesson with him, which was as second years.

He had a ferocious, terrifying temper and frequently cuffed boys around the ears for no apparent reason, roaring like a bull till his face would turn purple with rage. On one occasion we rendered him momentarily speechless because we couldn't come up with the one word in the English language that has four consecutive consonants in the middle of it. "Come on," he bellowed, "what's the matter with you? Don't they teach you anything these days at primary school?" When he finally realised that no answer would be forthcoming, he yelled back at us with incredulity, "Pulchritude, you imbeciles!" (We were, you will recall, just 12 years old, but it's a fact that has stayed with me ever since, such was the force of his presence in the classroom). "I don't know," he lamented, "education today, it's nothing more than a three-ringed crackpot circus. Why, for two pins I'd walk out right now." At which point, Derek Marshall, the class clown, would always hold up two fingers offering Jasper these imaginary two pins, until one afternoon, when he was noticed by Jasper, who normally saw very little that was in front of him, and who interpreted Derek's actions as an altogether different two-fingered gesture.

"Are you saucing me, lad?"

"Who? Me, sir?"

"Yes, you, sir."

"No, sir. Not I, sir?"

"You're doing it again. You're saucing me. How dare you? I'll give you something to sauce about in a minute," whereupon he launched into a sudden and terrifying assault.

We were well used to Jasper's bouts of violence, which occurred on at least a weekly basis, but none of was prepared for the ferocity of this particular attack. He proceeded to knock Derek right around the classroom, up and down the aisles between the desks, until he finally cornered him near the door, where he repeatedly rammed his head against the light switches. The suppressed laughter that had greeted Derek's initial remarks had now given way to a frightened silence; it was as if the term 'shock and awe' had been especially coined for this one moment. Although we were quite accustomed to regular beatings by teachers, with a ruler, a slipper, the cane, or, more usually, the casual back of a hand, the scale of this attack was unprecedented.

This was in the days when in the classroom the teacher's word was law, was never challenged, and we would never have considered complaining about such treatment to our parents, but something must have happened after this occasion, for we never saw Jasper again. He had retired, we were told, (which was quite possibly true, for to our eyes he was at least a hundred years old), and he was replaced by the young, good looking and dynamic Mike Ryder, an ex- fighter pilot, who was also a brilliant sportsman, and suddenly Latin was no longer a dead language taught by some old fossil, but cool and hip, and I ended up carrying on with it right through to 'A' level, where I developed a life-long love of Virgil, Ovid, Catullus and Pliny (both the younger and the elder!)

I remember Mr Ryder walking into his first lesson with us carrying under his arm a copy of *In His Own Write* by John Lennon. "Turn to page 46," he said, and there we read:

*"Amo, amas, a minibus*
*A marmyladie cat..."*

And suddenly Latin was fun. It was John Lennon. It was the new zeitgeist. It was where it was at, and the three-ringed crackpot circus had found itself a new ringmaster. We had moved away from *"magister discipulum vacuum verberat"* (the schoolmaster beats the lazy pupil) to Mr Ryder's RAF motto *"per ardua ad astra"* (through adversity to the stars).

## Criss Cross Quiz

Criss Cross Quiz was a TV general knowledge game based on noughts and crosses. It was first aired on Granada in the 1950's, and in 1963 a children's version was launched, hosted by Danny Blanchflower, former captain of Tottenham Hotspur and Northern Ireland.

when Elvis starts to sing
in German *Wooden Heart*
I know at once but tongue-
tied on live TV blurt

Harry Belafonté
instead (it's so uncool)
and I know there's no way
I'll live this down nor feel

each time I see the sign
'Granada Studios'
I blew the chance to win
on Junior Criss Cross Quiz

**(then we will remember)**

# things we said today

## Wedding Dresses

My grandmother, who looms so large in my dreams, was, it seems, tiny, a mere slip of a girl.

Two years ago, when clearing out my mother's flat, we came across her wedding dress, white, neatly folded, in a dust-covered blue box, tied up with string, stuffed in the back of a tallboy.

My mother, who was not in the least sentimental, who never once, as far as I knew, looked backward over her shoulder, preferring instead to inhabit the present, for some reason kept it down the years, like some family museum. She inherited my grandmother's catchphrase of "waste not, want not", with occasional grand spring cleans and clear outs, sporadic bouts of sorting through her cupboards, though she was never that methodical, and somehow her own mother's wedding dress escaped these culls, so that there we found it, together with her own, also white, moth-balled and forgotten, neither having seen the light of day since their single airing.

My wife, Amanda, when we got married, did not know of either of these dresses at the time. Nor did she opt for a white one for herself. Instead her Auntie Nellie made her by hand a beautiful long blue skirt with matching wrap-around blue top, so that she might, if she chose, wear it again on future occasions. But this did not happen, as far as I can remember, so it, too, remains on a hanger, covered to protect it. When she rescued my mother's and grandmother's wedding dresses, she tried them both on. My mother's was a perfect fit, but she could not even fit her arm into the sleeve of my grandmother's, it was so tiny.

"She must have been like a sparrow," she exclaims, though the one photograph we have of her actually wearing it does not suggest this, but then, I remember now, my grandfather, whose arm she is linking, standing next to him coming out of the chapel, was himself quite small, dapper, so that, together, side by side, they make the perfect couple. She looks quite *à la mode*, with newly bobbed hair, a jaunty hat instead of a veil, while the dress is calf length, revealing graceful, white-stockinged ankles and dainty court shoes.

They say women look for their fathers in their husbands, while men marry their mothers. Well, I've come to think that I married my grandmother, and Amanda and I often joke about this – the same feisty northernness, the fierce appraising look, the raised warning forefinger (always in jest) – but she was also, I later learned, a woman who, like Amanda (and like her daughter, Stella, my mother), enjoyed dancing, listening to the big bands on the wireless, Henry Hall and Geraldo, and who stares out of the photograph, bird-framed in that wedding dress, about to take flight.

Now the dress has been hand washed in Lux Soap Flakes, gently rinsed in cold water, lightly pressed then neatly folded, wrapped in special tissue paper, and put back into its now dusted blue box, tied up with new string. It's up in our attic, back in the dark, (along with her daughter's), while we decide what's to be done with them. A museum? A collector? A second hand retro vintage shop? A charity? I suspect we may simply keep them.

Why, I wonder? What are we clinging on to? Are we hoping that something of these no-nonsense women's determination to make the most of their lives, to live in the moment, to plump for the new over the old (as they both unfailingly did), to look forward instead of back, will somehow rub off on us? Is this the reason why they, too, held on to these dresses so surprisingly, so uncharacteristically, so that we might one day look in the mirror and see them standing behind us, smiling and pointing forwards, urging us on?

## Wibbersley Park

My grandmother was the third of ten children, eight of whom survived. She was born the daughter of a miner in Ellen Brook, close to Chat Moss, but when she was still just a girl, the family moved across the other side of the Moss to Irlam in a three bedroom terraced house on Astley Road, and her father became a labourer at the local tar works. She was christened Esther Hannah after each grandmother, whom they visited on alternate Sundays. This necessitated her parents having to remember to call her by the appropriate grandmother's name, depending upon which one they happened to be with, and this proved too much for her exasperated father. "From now on, we're calling her Annie, and let that be an end of it," he'd said, so from that day on she was known to all as Annie, later as Auntie Annie to the literally dozens of nieces and nephews (plus other less connected children) who came her way.

So when her elder sister Ethel decided she wanted to emigrate to Canada, it was to Annie she turned for advice as to how she might best appease her father. When "our Tilly", as Mathilda, the youngest girl in the family, was universally known, suddenly announced that she was considering adopting her middle name Laurie as what she would prefer to be known by, it was to Annie she confided first, and it was Annie who made sure that none of the others attempted to tease her. She was a tigress, too, when it came to protecting Stanley. Stanley was a little slow; he never went to school and he never learned to read or write. But woe betide any other street kid who dared to make fun of him. It was she who encouraged him in his love of animals and, especially, in the rare gift he proved to possess with birds: he nursed them, ringed them, later bred them. Stanley was the middle of three brothers who survived infancy (with David and George, the twins, dying when they were just a few days old). Jim was the eldest, named after his father, and Annie hero-worshipped him, as did her closest sister, Edith; while Harry, the youngest, was hot-headed with a fiery temper. Many was the time when Annie would intervene to save Harry from himself.

She seemed earmarked for the role of carer from early on, helping her mother with all these children who came after her, and generally looking after the household, from feeding and wringing the necks of the chickens they kept in the back yard, (before plucking the feathers and removing the innards, and then helping her mother to roast them), to cooking, cleaning, polishing and mending. While all her other siblings would leave the house one by one to work – in the Soap Works, Margarine Works, council offices, on the railways, at the printer's, on a farm – Annie stayed at home. Except for once. When she was 13 she was asked to go and work up at the Big House in Worsley as a maid. She stayed just a month. Returning for her first day off, she was greeted by her family as if she had been lost at sea, and she simply didn't return. "She's needed here," her father said, and the matter was never spoken of again.

It was no surprise therefore that when the First World War broke out, when Annie was 17, she would volunteer as a V.A.D at nearby Wibbersley Park, a gracious house built by a Mr & Mrs Stott in the 1870's standing in its own modest grounds, which had been seconded for the duration to serve as a Military Hospital. Wibbersley Park was a few miles away in Flixton. This meant that she had to borrow her brother Jim's bike and cycle all the way to the Ship Canal, cross the lock gates, then down to the ferry, a row boat which took people, bicycles and animals across to Flixton for a penny. Then it was a further mile's cycle up Irlam Road till she reached Wibbersley Park. Not being a trained nurse, she was initially used as a ward maid, cleaning up after the doctors and nurses had changed wound dressings, but it soon became clear that she was a natural carer and a quick learner, and before long she was being allowed to do more nursing duties, at which she quietly, unfussily, excelled.

The day after war was declared, her brother Jim enlisted. He joined the Royal Scots Fusiliers because, he said, he wanted to wear a kilt, and he went up to Edinburgh for initial training and was then piped aboard the troop train, marching the length of Princes Street to thousands of cheering crowds. On his brief leave home before being posted to France, he had his photograph taken standing in full regalia behind Annie and Edith, modestly seated below in white blouses with enamelled brooches at their throats. (I have this photograph above my desk as I am writing this). In the spring of 1915 he was due a second leave. Annie was at home in Astley Road having just cycled back from her shift at Wibbersley Park and was resting on the settee in the parlour, the rarely used front room, when she heard the door open and in walked Jim. He put down his kit bag and perched on the arm of the settee.

"I hope you're taking good care of that bike of mine, our Annie," he said. "I shall want it back after this show's over."

My grandmother told me this story about Jim when I was 10 years old. "I can't remember what it was I said back to him," she said, "but I usually gave as good as I got."

"Well," Jim went on, "I just want you to know that you needn't worry about it." She went suddenly quiet.

"What is it, Nanna?"

"I think I must have nodded off – I was always tired in the war – but the next thing I know there's a knocking at the front door. I got up to answer it, and there's this postman with a telegram. I knew straight away what it was. Jim had just come on ahead, to prepare me…"

The telegram baldly stated that Private James Eve of the Royal Scots Fusiliers had been killed in action on the first day of the 2nd Battle of Ypres, 21st April 1915.

His name is listed in the book of honour always kept open in Edinburgh Castle, and Annie and Edith travelled up to read it there after the war was over.

"Was that your brother's ghost?" I remember asking in wide-eyed wonder.

"I don't like the word 'ghost'," she replied. "That sounds frightening, and this wasn't frightening in the least. It was…" she paused, "like being tucked up with a blanket when you're not feeling well."

“I wish I could see a ghost,” I said. “Then I could tell everyone at school all about it.”

“You’ll see the back of my hand,” she said, “if you don’t get out from under my feet. Now off you go into the fresh air. Unless you want me to give you some chores instead. There’s always the brasses to polish.” And away I would run…

After the war ended, the Stott family never returned to Wibbersley Park, and the house lay empty for years, falling into neglect until it was pulled down in 1925, and a dozen small semis were built on the land, plus a community hall, which for a time was a youth club. The Stotts retired to another gracious house, on Church Road, with a wild, overgrown orchard behind, the back of which was next door but one to where I lived after our family crossed over the water of the Ship Canal from Irlam. I used to climb the railings to play there with the other kids living nearby. Later, when I was a teenager, we all used to take a short cut through it up to the youth club at Wibbersley Park, not realising till my grandmother came to live with us after my granddad died, that this was the place where she had been a V.A.D.

*

Fast forward fifty years to May 1968. I’m a couple of months shy of 16 and it’s a Saturday night. My grandmother still lives with us in a different house in Flixton. Near the station. About a mile and a half from Wibbersley. My friend Dave, who lives just round the corner, across the iron bridge, calls round one Saturday afternoon while I’m listening to the football results on the radio.

“Why don’t you come round after tea?” he says. “Pat’s bringing the new Beatles single.” Pat was Dave’s girlfriend and the new Beatles single was *Lady Madonna.* Dave knows I won’t be able to resist that, and so, just after 7 o’clock, I cut through the cobbled back alley that runs from the iron bridge down the side of his house, slip over the wall and walk through his back door into their kitchen.

Mrs Randall is there, Dave's mum, standing by the kettle. "Hi, Chris. Just go straight into the front room. Dave said you might be coming round. They've got a surprise for you, I believe."

"Thanks, Mrs Randall. Dave said..."

"Did he now?" She turns away slightly, suppressing an amused smile. "Well, just make yourself at home. I'll bring in the tea in a minute."

From the front room I can already hear the strains of *Lady Madonna*, Paul's honky tonk piano thumping through the closed door. "*... listen to the music playing in your head...*" I bound in, about to say something about how great it sounds, when I see what Dave's mum means about the surprise, and I'm frozen to the spot.

"Hi, Chris," says Dave. "This is Sue."

And there, sitting on the sofa by the window, is this beautiful girl with shoulder-length dark hair, like a Madonna herself, but wearing a short black mini skirt and matching boots.

"Hello," I think I manage to stammer.

"Pleased to meet you," she replies instantly. She sounds confident and assured.

"Sue's a friend from school," says Pat helpfully. Pat lives in Irlam, across the canal, so that must mean Sue does too. I don't know any girls really, for the school I go to is all boys.

*Lady Madonna* has finished, and the hiss of the needle on the vinyl as the record keeps spinning round fills the sudden silence. "What do you think?" says Dave. I turn to him in panic. "The record, I mean. I'll play it again, shall I?"

At that moment Dave's mum breezes in with a tray. "The tea's brewing, and there's chocolate digestives. Are you alright, Chris? Why don't you sit down? There's plenty of room on the sofa."

"Thanks, Mrs Randall. I'm fine." Sue, I notice, has moved her handbag from the sofa, so that I can sit down beside her.

"Well, I'll just be in the back if you need anything. It's nearly time for *The Avengers*." And off she goes. Right now, I am wishing I could be there with her, watching Steed and

Emma Peel, instead of here, and then it strikes me that Sue bears more than a passing resemblance to Diana Rigg. Does she do karate, I find myself wondering, as I sit on the sofa beside her? Just relax, I tell myself, it'll be fine.

Dave puts the record on again, while Pat pours the tea. "Sugar, Sue?"

"No thanks."

"Sweet enough," I say, before I can stop myself. Even though Dave has his back towards me, I can feel him rolling his eyes, but Sue just smiles, sweetly.

"*Tuesday afternoon is never ending...*" sings Paul.

"Which one are you?" asks Sue.

"Eh?"

"Which child?"

I must still look perplexed.

"What day were you born on?" she adds patiently.

"Oh, I see. Monday, I think."

" 'Monday's Child is fair of face'," she says, smiling.

"Chris is the exception that proves the rule," remarks Dave. I shoot him a look.

"What about you?" I ask.

"Saturday," she says, then starts to laugh. " 'Saturday's Child works hard for a living'!"

"Tell me about it," says Pat. They've both worked all day in their local Woolworth's, yet somehow have managed to arrive here this evening fresh, clean and shining. Whereas I, who don't have a job, look like I've been dragged through a hedge backwards.

"And we'll both be starting full time in a couple of months when we leave school," adds Sue.

I feel awkward, for Dave and I will be staying on.

Perhaps Dave feels the same, for he gets up to put on a different record – *Rain* – the 'B' side to *Paperback Writer*, while Pat gets up to pour the tea.

Outside it is raining quite hard. "Appropriate song," I say, trying to steer the conversation to a more neutral topic, gesturing to the window.

"I don't know why this wasn't the 'A' side," says Dave. "It's much the better track." He's right, and we all nod sagely.

He flops back onto the armchair, and when she has finished pouring the tea, Pat sits down on his knee, and immediately they set to with some serious snogging. Sue and I look at each other, then look down. "*When the rain comes, they run and hide their heads…*"

We've been set up. Sue, I think, must have had some inkling, for she's really made an effort and dressed up, while I, in blissful ignorance, have turned up in dirty jeans and an old jumper with holes in. Sue has washed her hair, which shines lustrously, while mine hangs lank and streaky. She smells alluringly of shampoo and soap and perfume, while I… I don't like to think what I might smell like. But she seems unperturbed and gamely tries to talk above the music.

"You like The Beatles then?" she offers helpfully.

"Yes, I… do," I peter out.

"I prefer The Stones."

"Oh, I like them too."

"Do you want to dance?"

Alarmed, I clutch at the only straw I can think of. "I'd prefer to go for a walk."

"It's raining," she says.

"Yeah, but still… We could always take your umbrella," I say, noticing it bright and red by her handbag.

"OK," she shrugs. "I'll just get my coat."

"Right. Er – Dave, Pat? We're just going out."

They don't even come up for air. Dave merely signals a thumbs-up with his free hand, which Pat then wraps back around her.

Once outside, Sue puts up her umbrella and we start walking along the road. "Where are we going?" she asks, reasonably enough. "This is your neck of the woods, not mine."

"Oh," I say. I haven't thought this far. Then inspiration hits. "The youth club."

If she feels disappointment, she doesn't show it, and it occurs to me that I unexpectedly have the chance to be really smooth and cool. "Here," I say, "let me carry that." And I take the umbrella in one hand, while in the same movement seamlessly put my other arm around her shoulder.

Immediately, and quite thrillingly, Sue places her arm around my waist. I know that I'm instantly blushing. But suddenly it all becomes easier. Conversation begins to flow, she even laughs at one of my jokes, and as the warm spring rain falls softly on our hands and faces, the nervousness drops away.

We approach the pub where it is rumoured they serve anyone – not that I know first hand – but we pass it by. It's not worth the risk of a humiliating refusal in pursuit of the dubious kudos of a pint of shandy and a Cherry B, and as we arrive at Wibbersley Park, at the youth club, I know it's going to be fine. It's a Saturday and so it's only the older teenagers who are there, and because, mercifully, there is no disco on that night, it is fairly quiet. We find a secluded corner to sit, we drink *Cidrax*, a non-alcoholic cider, and we chat – about school, what we hope to do after 'O' levels (in less than a month's time), TV programmes, where we live, our families. It turns out that Sue lives in Astley Road, at number 24, just a couple of doors away from where my grandmother lived when *she* was 16, and here we are, in Wibbersley Park, where she had worked as a nurse during World War 1. I don't share this coincidence with Sue, I keep it to myself, a warm, quiet secret – like being tucked up in a blanket when you're not feeling well. Except that I feel great.

But all too soon the evening comes to a close. At half past nine Sue indicates that we should be heading back. "Mrs Randall will drive me and Pat back to the ferry, and my dad will be there to meet us on the other side. If I'm later than half past ten, there'll be hell to pay."

We walk the mile and a half back to Dave's, where he and Pat seem to be locked together in the same clinch as when we left them, and Mrs Randall duly drives us all down Irlam Road to the ferry, retracing the route my grandmother would have taken on her brother's bicycle half a century before. The rain has stopped but a mist is rising from the waters of the canal. As the ferry is rowed across towards where we wait, Dave and Pat are still kissing, while Sue and I have fallen silent. At the last moment she turns and says, "Thanks, Chris. I've had a lovely evening." Then she closes her eyes and lifts up her face towards me. I know I'm expected to kiss her, but suddenly I'm struck down with nervousness once more. I've never kissed anyone before and I'm acutely aware that I'm not really sure what to do. I bend my face towards hers, clumsily, our noses get in each other's way, and my lips brush hers for barely a millisecond, when Mrs Randall calls out, "The ferry's here." Before either of us can say anything else, Sue is standing aboard with Pat and disappearing into the mist and the darkness. Like Eurydice.

But I am no Orpheus, and as the days and then weeks slip by, and I get caught up in exams, all of a sudden the summer is over and I haven't tried to get in touch with her. I hear from Dave that she has left school and got a good job in an office in Manchester, while I am indeed staying on in the 6th form. She won't want to go out with a schoolboy, I glumly think, and so I never contact her again. Years later I learn that she has become engaged to another boy I was at school with, Carl, who himself lives next door to the girl I will eventually marry, but on that dark and misty Saturday night I don't even know of her existence. Carl and Sue emigrate to Australia, where, for all I know, they still are. But all of that is years ahead. After the ferry has finally slipped completely out of sight, I turn to Dave and Mrs Randall and say, "If you don't mind, I think I'll walk home. It's not far."

And that is what I do. I walk the mile and a half back to Flixton, thinking of Sue heading back to the same road my grandmother had grown up in, who, when I finally reach home, is just making a hot water bottle to take up to bed. My mum and dad are out, probably to the pictures and afterwards a drink.

"Goodnight, Nanna. I hope you didn't wait up for me."

"Oh no. I've had a proper telly night – *Dixon of Dock Green, Morecambe & Wise, Opportunity Knocks*."

"That's alright then. Who won?"

"A lovely Welsh lass – Mary something-or-other… *Those Were The Days.*"

"So you've had a nice evening?"

"Yes, love. I have. But not as nice as someone I could mention."

"What do you mean?"

"You look like the cat who's got the cream. What's her name?" My grandmother never misses a trick. "But you've not been out like that, have you? Fancy," she continues, looking disapprovingly at my dirty jeans, "going on a date in your overalls!"

"She lives on Astley Road."

"Does she now? That speaks well of her. And where did you take her?"

"The youth club. Wibbersley Park."

"You certainly know how to sweep a girl off her feet, don't you?"

And she tells me again about how Wibbersley Park had been turned into a military hospital during the first World War, and how she had cycled there as a girl, all the way from Irlam, across the lock gates, over the ferry, and volunteered as a nurse, except this time I properly take it in.

"The things I saw there," she says. "Terrible things. I'd never have imagined that it would see happy times again. I wasn't surprised the Stotts never went back, nor was I sorry when the house was pulled down." She walks towards me and pats me on the shoulder. "Those were the days… Goodnight, Christopher. I'm so pleased." She climbs the stairs, humming Mary Hopkin to herself, thinking of her lost brother.

Later, in bed, I replay the whole evening again and again, like each time I buy a new Beatles record, over and over till I've got it by heart.

*Monday's Child has learned to tie his bootlace…*

*See how they run…*

## May 1968

May 1968. The world was turning. On the streets of Paris students and workers stormed the barricades and nearly brought down the De Gaulle government; in Grosvenor Square thousands protested outside the US Embassy against the Vietnam War; in America first Martin Luther King, then Robert Kennedy were assassinated – and I had my first kiss. But more momentous than any of these events, May 1968 also saw Manchester United win the European Cup, the first English side to do so, and, with it, my second kiss…

The story begins five years earlier.

*

1963

Every Friday night, when my mum and dad went out – for a drink, to the pictures, dancing – I had a series of baby sitters. Mostly these were young men from where my dad worked who came round with their girl friends, and who no doubt wanted me packed off to bed as soon as possible so they could get down to some serious canoodling. I remember not being able to sleep one time – I must have been about 8 – and coming downstairs to find the most regular of these sitters – Wes – and his girl friend of the time who was sitting on his knee for a kiss and a cuddle, and the look of disappointment on their faces. Sometimes Wes's brother, Baz, would come too (if Wes didn't have a girl friend that night) and occasionally Baz would bring his friend, Phil, along.

Phil was Phil Chisnall. Now – you have probably never heard of Phil Chisnall, but he played for Manchester United. At that time he played mostly in the youth team (he was probably about 18) and sometimes in the reserves. This was the early 1960's when United were still recovering from after the Munich air disaster of 1958. That team was known as the "Busby Babes", they were so young, including a teenage

Bobby Charlton (who survived the crash) and the legendary Duncan Edwards (another teenager, who did not). Those were the days of small teams, not large squads like today, and United lost 8 players that February evening, from a squad of about 14. So in 1961, when I first met Phil, United were rebuilding, but still with a focus on bringing through local Manchester boys – like Phil Chisnall.

Phil was from Urmston (my home town, which is about 4 miles from Old Trafford) and he used to cycle there for training sessions. Can you believe that? Cycle! Over the next couple of years he began to make his breakthrough. In 1963 he made his first team debut, and from 1963 to 1965 he played quite frequently but was always on the fringes, never, quite, a regular.

1963 marked the first time that United had been to Wembley since 1958 when, amazingly, with a scratch team of local young lads and older players brought out of retirement, plus one or two survivors from the Munich crash – Charlton, Bill Foulkes, Harry Gregg (the goalkeeper) – carried along on a tide of national fervour, somehow made the final against Bolton Wanderers after a series of emotion-packed ties and replays, only to lose to two controversial Nat Lofthouse goals, (though to be fair, Bolton were the better side and United were by that time simply exhausted). So five years later, having narrowly escaped relegation, there they were at Wembley again, very much the underdogs – can you imagine that: United as underdogs? – for Leicester had finished the league in the top four or five. (I don't know who won the League that year, though I do believe Manchester City were relegated – not that we're gloating).

1963 had also seen Matt Busby buy the first ever £100,000 player* – Denis Law, whom he brought in from Torino. Against the odds, United won that cup final 3-1 with goals by Law, Charlton and Herd (an old fashioned "up-and-at-'em" centre forward).

* As a footnote to this, when Jimmy Greaves was transferred to Spurs, also from an Italian side, Roma, the previous year, the asking price was £100,000, but the then Spurs manager, Bill Nicholson, refused to pay this on principle, and so Greaves was accordingly signed for £99,999. 19s 11d in old money!

Denis Law was, it was rumoured, the first non-Catholic player to play for United. Originally, larger cities formed two football sides – one for Catholics and one for non-Conformists and Anglicans. Hard to credit these days when clubs feature players from all over the world. So, City were the Protestant team and United the Catholic side. (Similarly, Liverpool were Protestant and Everton Catholic. Just as – still, in terms of their respective fan bases – in Glasgow, Rangers are Protestant and Celtic are Catholic; while in Edinburgh, Hearts are Protestant and Hibs are Catholic). When Busby signed Law it was a definite signal that his ambitions were in fact well beyond the FA Cup. His sights were firmly set on Europe and the European Cup, which of course you could only enter by *winning* the League Title back then.

This European trophy became something of a holy grail for Busby. United had, in fact, been the first British side to play in Europe, entering the European Cup in the 1956-57 season, much against the wishes of the FA, who were, if such a thing is possible, even more stuffy and out of touch than they are today. This, remember, was only 6 years after England had entered the World Cup for the very first time, disastrously in 1950, when a team including Stanley Matthews and Tom Finney had lost 1-0 to an amateur side from the USA. Yet this caused barely a ripple, for it was not even reported on by the BBC, so insignificant a competition was it then considered. England at that time still assumed they were, by some kind of divine right having invented the game in the first place, simply above all that kind of thing and naturally the best team. Further warning signs appeared in 1953, when England were thrashed 6-3 at Wembley by the then best team in the world, Hungary, the first foreign team ever to win at Wembley, and then 7-2 over in Budapest the following year.

The major figure in that groundbreaking Hungarian side was Ferenc Puskas, and it was he, together with Alfredo Di Stefano, who formed the heart of the great Real Madrid side who dominated the early years of the European Cup, winning it every year from 1955 to 1960. United played in two consecutive European Cups – in 1956-57 and 57-58 – and on each occasion they lost in the semi-finals to Real Madrid. In

1958, of course, this match took place after the Munich air disaster, and the feeling had been that the Busby Babes might have overcome Madrid on that occasion, had fate not intervened.

But as a consequence of those years, and particularly because the Munich air crash took place after a famous victory by United in the quarter finals of the European Cup (over Red Star Belgrade), Busby and United became obsessed, both with winning the trophy and with beating Real Madrid, with whom a very special and lasting bond of friendship was formed.

It's impossible today to fully recapture the glamour and exoticism that Real Madrid possessed at that time. People did not travel much in those days; football was not televised; we didn't have access to overseas players; we had simply never seen anything like Real Madrid, who, so tanned and handsome beside the pasty English, seemed like gods.

So – while United were rebuilding in the aftermath of Munich, as a mark of friendship and respect, each year United played a friendly against Real Madrid, usually in the middle of the season, alternating between the Bernebau and Old Trafford for the venue, and this was regarded unequivocally as the highlight of the year, a reminder of former glories and a promise of future possibilities.

After the FA Cup victory of 1963, two high profile stars of the team – Johnny Giles and Albert Quixall – requested significant pay rises. Busby refused and they were each placed on the transfer list. Their subsequent departures opened the door to a certain scrawny-looking Belfast boy called George Best…

And this is where Phil Chisnall re-enters the story.

*

One cold, foggy November night, aged 11 years old, I went with my dad to my first ever United match. (Football grounds were very different in those days: they were largely uncovered, almost all standing, and not very child-friendly, so 11 was about the youngest you could safely go). It was to see the friendly between United and Real Madrid, always a sell-out. Phil Chisnall had got us the tickets and he was playing.

There's something about the atmosphere of a night match that is incredibly special: the cold night air, the freezing breath of all the spectators, the floodlights, the rain caught in their beams; the noise seems louder, the players closer, more sharply etched somehow; the outcome uncertain, a one-off, like a cup-tie or replay. Although it was a friendly, both teams had put out their best available sides and the roar that greeted the referee's whistle to start the game was electric, spine-tingling, especially to a small boy, whose first match this was…

So here I am – walking along the Warwick Road (later to be renamed Sir Matt Busby Way) towards the Scoreboard End (now the Sir Alex Ferguson Stand) past the Munich Memorial Clock (with the fateful date of 6th Feb 1958 engraved upon it, still there today) and round towards the Stretford End, where we are to stand behind the goal. I'm holding my dad's hand and wearing a red and white scarf that my mum has knitted specially, which is so long that, if I don't wrap it round my neck several times, it will drag along the floor. ("Well," says my mum, "you'll be able to grow into it." And she is right, for this scarf will see me right through all of the years I will go to watch the Reds at Old Trafford). We take up our places quite near the front, so that I can sit on the fence right at the edge of the ground itself, along with other boys, their dads standing a few rows behind to keep an eye on us, with no tall people in front of us.

The game starts in a blur. We catch Madrid cold and Denis Law scores twice inside the first ten minutes. We have never beaten Real Madrid – could this be the night? – but, like the true champions they are, they begin to play their way back into the game, and pretty soon they are stroking the ball gracefully between them and we can't get a kick. On the stroke of thirty minutes they pull a goal back and half time can't come quickly enough. Inevitably, though, within ten minutes of the restart they equalise. But we pick up our game and suddenly it's end to end, a really thrilling contest that could go either way. Then, with just ten minutes to go, Phil Chisnall picks the ball up on the right wing, cuts inside and unleashes an unstoppable shot from 30 yards out that screams into the top corner of the net right in front of where we're standing. The crowd goes wild and Phil celebrates right in front of us, sees me and gives me a wink and a smile. I cannot believe it. Real Madrid then bombard our goal with attack after attack but somehow we hold out; the ref blows for full time and Chisnall is carried shoulder high from the field by his delirious team mates.

My dad picks me up and hoists me on his shoulders, just like Phil, as we make our way out of the crowded Stretford End – it is the only safe way to leave, for as the crowd moves like a human tidal wave, I would be swept along without my feet touching the ground. We reach the bus stop, but it is far too crowded, we know we don't stand a chance of getting on, so we walk to the next stop, then to the next, and then to the next, till in the end we decide to walk the whole four miles home, not reaching our house till after 11 o'clock. My mum is waiting for us and we tell her all about the game, then we put slices of bread on a toasting fork in front of the coal fire, with mugs of *"hot chocolate, drinking chocolate"*, before climbing the stairs to bed, where the inside of my bedroom window is already frozen up with icicles on the panes.

"Do I have to go to school tomorrow?" I ask my dad.

"Well, I have to go to work," he says, "so I don't see why you shouldn't go to school!"

And secretly I am pleased, for the next day I will tell all my friends about how Phil Chisnall, my baby sitter, scored the best goal ever to help United beat Real Madrid for the very first time…

Winning the FA Cup in 1963, followed by this symbolic victory over Real Madrid, paved the way for a period of greatness for United. But Phil Chisnall could not establish himself as a regular. He made a number of appearances but never had another moment like that night when he scored against Real Madrid. He didn't train hard enough, it was said, he drank too much, and although he gained an England

Under 23's cap, he was eventually transferred to Liverpool, in 1965 I think, by which time I was too old for babysitters and we lost touch. Phil didn't establish himself at Liverpool either and gradually drifted down the leagues.

The last I heard of him was when I was at University and my friend Kevin (who is an avid United fan) played against him in a non-league team. He was in his thirties by then, overweight, but still with prodigious ability. He completely controlled the game, Kevin said, so much so that Kevin's team were played off the park. Afterwards he learned who he was and was in absolute awe of his profligate, sadly unfulfilled talent.

But I will never forget the magic of that foggy November night, when the United player who scored the goal that beat Real Madrid was the same guy I knew as Phil, Wes's brother Baz's best mate, who used to come round to our house and kick a football with me against a wall in our street!

*

1966

In February 1966 I went to my first European Cup tie, a quarter final match between United and Benfica, the then holders of the trophy, led by the wondrous Eusebio, the Black Pearl.

It was a bitterly cold, rainswept night, and as exciting as only European Cup nights can be. The air bristled with the electricity of anticipation. Confounding our worst fears, right from the kick-off Eusebio broke through our defence and laid on the simplest of tap-in goals for their centre forward, Torres. But United gradually played their way back into the game and after an hour were 2-1 ahead. Benfica pressed for an equaliser, but with about 5 minutes remaining, United scored a third goal on a breakaway attack, and the tie seemed safe. But unfortunately, United seemed to think so too, relaxed, momentarily switched off and Eusebio once more broke through to set up a second goal for Torres, and the match ended 3-2. The return match, at the original Stadium of Light, the *Estadio da Luz* in Lisbon, appeared a daunting prospect, for Benfica had not only never lost a home European tie; they had been unbeaten at home in any competition for the whole of that decade – more than six years since their last home defeat – and United, then as now, were not renowned for their defending.

Two weeks later the 2nd leg was played on a balmy Portuguese spring evening. This was 1966 – the height of Beatlemania – and George Best had begun to establish his reputation as a celebrity, the first such in British football, but he had not by then cemented his footballing credentials internationally. (He was still only 19).

Half an hour before kick-off he was nowhere to be found. Things were more lax back then and the team, staying in a nearby hotel, had walked to the ground! (Can you imagine that today?) And somehow Best had gone missing – it would not be the last time that this happened…

At the last minute he turned up, as nonchalant as you like, and while the team waited nervously in the dressing room just before kick off, he proceeded to indulge in a solo game of "keepy-uppy", only to lose control of the ball and smash the dressing room mirror. His team mates, already edgy about a match they were widely tipped to lose, were not best pleased as you can imagine, but before they could express how they felt they were called out for the start of the match. Busby, it was reported later, said to them as they made their way on to the pitch: "Just sit tight for the first ten minutes, then begin to press."

Well, the rest, as they say, is history. You probably know this story, but in case you don't, Best scored an extraordinary hat trick all inside the first ten minutes, two of the goals being solo specialities. United ran out 5-1 winners, away from home, the first time Benfica had ever lost a home European tie, and the Portuguese press hailed Best "El Beatle", United were in the semi-finals for the first time since the night of the Munich air crash, and Best's reputation was established.

In the semi-final United drew Partizan Belgrade – and

we were all delighted we had avoided Real Madrid – and felt that, having defeated Benfica, surely we could overcome Partizan. But of course football doesn't work like that, does it? There was added piquancy about the tie, for it had been against Belgrade's other team, Red Star, whom United had played the night before Munich, and in the weeks preceding the tie, United were hit by a spate of injuries. They travelled to Belgrade without Best or Law. It was a freezing night and the game was played in a snowstorm. Yugoslavia were, back then, one of the stronger European footballing nations, still under Soviet rule, and Partizan were not the push-overs they would be today, and they ran out 2-0 winners. Still, we were confident that we could overturn this deficit in the return leg at Old Trafford, which I duly attended.

United, still without Best (who had to have a cartilage operation) and Law, who suffered throughout his career with knee injuries, lay siege to the Partizan goal for the full 90 minutes, but the Yugoslavs were highly organised, put all eleven men behind the ball and tried to soak up the pressure. With less than ten minutes to go, United pulled one back; then, in the final minute, they scored an equaliser – that is, everyone in the ground saw the ball cross the line, as did all the press photographers, with images in all the papers the following day to prove the fact, but unfortunately neither the referee nor the linesman did, and so we went out 2-1 on aggregate. The cries for goal line technology are not new…

Real Madrid duly won their semi-final, and so the dream final, which had been so close, was denied us. Real too found Partizan a tough nut to crack but eventually won 2-1 and regained the European Cup for the first time since 1960. United, meanwhile, just three days after losing to Partizan, lost 1-0 to Everton in the semi-final of the FA Cup – Everton went on to win a thrilling final, coming back from 2-0 down to beat Sheffield Wednesday 3-2 – while United also finished runners-up in the League, which, in those days, meant no European Cup the following season: only the champions qualified back then.

United would have to wait at least two years for another crack at Busby's Holy Grail, but they did not begin the 1967 campaign at all promisingly. By Christmas they had yet to win a single away game and had actually lost 6 matches by the halfway point in the season. But after Christmas they won 18 games on the trot and travelled to West Ham for the penultimate game of the season, knowing that an away win would bring them the title, pipping Nottingham Forest, while West Ham were lying third. (This was the West Ham side that contained the World Cup trio of Bobby Moore, Geoff Hurst and Martin Peters). Amazingly, given the pressure of the situation, United went 4-0 up in the first 20 minutes, featuring another George Best hat trick, and two second half goals from Denis Law saw them run out 6-1 winners and 1967 Champions. They could compete in the 1968 European Cup.

(But they could no longer strive to be Britain's first winners of the trophy, for in an unforgettable match Glasgow Celtic came from behind to defeat Inter Milan (conquerors of Benfica in the semi final, who had themselves knocked out Real Madrid in the quarters) 2-1 in the final with a side that contained eleven players not only all from Scotland, but all from Glasgow – arguably the greatest single achievement by any team ever: real Roy of the Rovers stuff. That would be quite impossible today...)

*

1968

United's progress to the semi-finals in 1968 was relatively smooth – I can't now remember whom they beat on their way, (apart from their demolition of Anderlecht of Belgium 10-1 at Old Trafford in the 1st Round, with Denis Law scoring five, I think). But in the semi-finals we drew Real Madrid. This was the first time we had played them competitively since 1958, some ten years before. The friendlies of the early 60's (when Phil Chisnall scored that unforgettable winning goal) had now lapsed. The first leg was at Old Trafford and, in a really tight contest, George Best scored the only goal of the game with about 15 minutes to go. Despite further pressure United couldn't manage a second, and the general mood among the fans was that one goal would probably be not enough, particularly as Law was again to be sidelined with a recurrence of his knee trouble.

The 1968 season also saw a titanic battle for the League Title between United and City. Rather like the 2012 season, City came from behind in the last few games to pip United for the title in the last match, as Busby rested key players for the 2nd leg of the European Cup semi-final. The Bernebau Stadium was then, as it is now, something of a cauldron, and more than 130,000 people crammed in to see the return leg. Real Madrid took an early league, but with five minutes to go before half time, United's right back, Shay Brennan, scored his one and only goal for the club to equalise, but then Real hit back with two more goals, and we went in at the interval reeling at 3-1 down.

These games were not of course televised back then, and there was only an arrangement for radio commentary for the second half, so when I switched on the radio at the appointed time, I was instantly downcast by the score, especially as the commentator expressed his view that United were fortunate they weren't 6-1 down, and that the situation looked hopeless. In those days, they did not apply the 'away goals' rule, and so I remember thinking that if we could just pull one goal back, that would mean a 3-3 aggregate draw and a replay on a neutral ground. (Replays! Do you remember them? Those were the days).

The second half began much as the first half had ended with Real Madrid completely in the ascendancy and all over us, as I sat in the kitchen nervously listening to the radio while wearing my United scarf! Somehow they contrived not to convert any of their myriad chances and gradually United began to claw their way back into the game. Against the run of play, David Sadler, the stand-in for Law, though more of a defensive midfielder, cheekily back-heeled a goal, so now it was 3-2, the aggregate scores were level, and Real Madrid poured forward once again in wave after wave of attacks in search of the goal that would take them through. In the final few minutes, George Best took the ball on a mazy run towards the corner flag trying to keep possession and waste a few more precious seconds, but then he cut in towards the goal and side-footed a pass back towards the edge of the penalty area, where, unbelievably, the United centre half, Bill Foulkes, was standing….

(We have to pause here while I tell you about Bill Foulkes. He was one of the great unsung heroes of the club. With Bobby Charlton he was by 1968 the only survivor from Munich still playing for the team. He was by then something of a veteran, around 35 at least, who, when he first started playing for United, still had another job – as an apprentice plumber, I think – and he would catch the bus to home games after working in the morning! He was one of those rare breeds – a one club player; and after Ryan Giggs and Charlton he has played more games for the club than anyone else. He was not the most skilled or graceful of players. He was big, strong, could win most balls in the air, would simply kick the ball into touch if it reached him on the ground, and he never, ever, ventured beyond the half way line…)

… Except there, on that sultry night in the Bernebau, he did. Best squared the ball back to him and, calm as you like, he side-footed the ball into the corner of the goal, more of a pass than a shot, and suddenly it was 3-3, which meant United were winning 4-3 on aggregate. The stadium fell eerily silent and Foulkes simply trotted towards the goal, picked up the ball, tucked it under his arm and ran with it to the centre spot, where he neatly placed it. Then he shook Best's hand, as if thanking him for the pass…

So – United were in their first ever European Cup final, and we can now return to the story of my second kiss.

*

May

Cut to two weeks before the final, which is to be at Wembley. Tickets go on sale at 8am on a Sunday morning at Old Trafford. I have arranged to meet up with friends at the Jubilee Tree, (a tree at a cross roads near where we live in Flixton, planted to mark the diamond jubilee of Queen

Victoria), before dawn from where we will walk the four miles to the ground to make sure we are early enough to get a ticket.

It must be about 5.30am by the time we get there and already there's a huge crowd milling around excitedly, forming a series of queues at each of the turnstiles, where the tickets will go on sale. To qualify for a ticket, you have to produce a sheet of paper (provided in the programme for the first game of the season) onto which you have to stick tokens that are printed in every subsequent home match programme, both for the first team and the reserves. There are 42 spaces and, if you are to have any chance of securing a ticket, not only do you have to be early to get your place in the queue, you have to have a full token sheet. I have 41 tokens. I missed one of the reserve games – number 28, I can remember it still – and I am sure I'll have no chance, but we have a cunning plan. Another friend – Bri – is not able to go to the final. (We are all of us only 15, except Bri, who is younger, and Bri's mum will just not let him go, no way). Now Bri doesn't have a number 28 token either, but he has a number 18, and we reckon we can risk putting his spare number 18 in the place where the number 28 should go, and alter the '1' to a '2'. We reckon that there'll be so many people that the ticket sellers won't check too closely; they'll just want to see a full token sheet. The week before, when we'd hatched this scheme, it felt like an ace plan, but now we're there, approaching the ground in the early morning light, it feels stupid: we're bound to get found out. My other mates, Alan and Bernard, have got full token sheets, so to be honest they don't really care that much.

We reach the ground and the scene is almost biblical – a series of make-shift stalls have sprouted outside the ground: they're selling bacon butties; mugs of tea, or Oxo, or Bovril; some enterprising chaps have set up a table selling individual tokens at exorbitant prices (more than a shilling each!!), while others are even selling glue to stick the tokens in – "a penny a dab…" The hell-fire preacher, who attends every game, week after week, year after year, wearing a bowler hat and a sandwich board with religious tracts painted on it, is there too, of course. He stands on an old vegetable crate and harangues us cheerfully: "Where will YOU spend eternity?" he cries. "In the Stretford End," we chime back, at which he laughs hugely, before embarking on another sermon.

We leave this bazaar behind us and make our way towards the queues, hearts in our mouths. We check we have the right money: the tickets cost ten shillings (that's only 50p in today's money but it's four weeks pocket money back then), and I've had to borrow half of it from my dad. The sun rises, the turnstiles open, and the tickets go on sale. We seem to be miles away, as the queues snake around the ground. An hour passes; then two; we edge agonisingly slowly towards the front.

Then, suddenly, one by one, the turnstiles start closing as each sells its allocation, until there are just two queues left. I creep closer; then the other gate shuts. I'm in the last queue; there are 7 people in front of me; 6,5,4,3,2 – then it's me. I squeeze through the turnstile, sheepishly present my token sheet, certain I'm going to be rumbled – it's going to be so humiliating – but the man selling the tickets is completely knackered and he barely gives it a second glance. I pay my ten shillings, he hands over my ticket; then, after just one more person, he closes his gate. I've got the last-but-one ticket for the European Cup Final and I rush back out onto the forecourt to rejoin Alan, Bernard and Bri. Immediately someone offers to buy my ten shilling ticket for ten pounds! But there's no way I'd sell this ticket for anything. We walk the four miles back home and I place the ticket on the mantelpiece next to the ship in the bottle that is my dad's pride and joy…

The next two weeks drag by. I even cross each day off on a calendar in the kitchen. My mum gives the red and white scarf she knitted for me for when I went to watch Phil Chisnall score his wonder goal some five years previously its one and only wash ready for the Final. The Saturday evening before the game (which is scheduled for a Wednesday) is when my mate Dave fixes me up on the blind date with Susan Molloy. All I can really talk about is the game – I must be boring her to death – but when she lets me kiss her goodnight she sweetly says as she boards the ferry, "Enjoy yourself at Wembley. I hope you win."

The day of the match dawns, a Wednesday, and it's a glorious one – really warm, brilliant blue skies – it must be a good omen. I have taken the day off school (of course) along with practically everyone in Manchester. For once old rivalries between United and City fans are laid to one side. This is history – the first time an English team has reached the European Cup Final, and the realisation of a dream for Matt Busby just ten years after that dreadful night in Munich, when nearly an entire team was wiped out. I think the whole country was on United's side that day. As I walk to the bus stop that will take me to the station in Manchester, where they are running a series of 'specials' directly to Wembley, I am wearing my newly washed red and white scarf and complete strangers come up to me and wish me luck, or shake my hand, or call out from across the street, "Give them a cheer from me," or "For the Busby Babes…"

I meet Alan at the bus stop (Bernard has gone separately the day before to stay with a cousin near London) and it feels as though everyone there is going to the game. Alan had polio as a child and he has an iron calliper on one of his legs, not that that stops him from doing anything: he plays in goal for the school team, and he's the fastest cyclist I know, even peddling with just one leg, but walking isn't easy for him, and our aim is to get to the ground as early as we can, to get a good place, and where we can sit on the steps of the terraces while it fills up. Which we duly do. The train pulls into Wembley and we walk down Wembley Way towards the Two Towers that were still there then, past all the souvenir sellers, and find our place, which is behind the goal near where the tunnel used to be.

It is while we are waiting that we meet the two American girls. What they are doing there, I've no idea, nor how they got to get tickets, but there they are – beautiful, blonde, tanned – like creatures from another planet, certainly a different planet from the one spotty northern teenage boys inhabit anyway. They decide to stick around with us as the ground fills up, and we're not complaining, especially as they keep squealing with delight every time we say anything, declaring our accents to be "just so cute!"

The atmosphere builds and builds, and the excitement is getting practically unbearable, when the two teams walk out below us to huge cheers. There are 30,000 United fans, 30,000 Benfica fans, and 40,000 so-called "neutrals", but it feels like United have the biggest support, or maybe it just feels like that because we are standing among all the United fans. Both teams traditionally play in red, but for this game, for some reason, neither side is wearing red: Benfica are all in white and United are wearing an all blue strip unlike anything they have ever worn before, plus black socks. (United have worn black socks ever since Munich). Then before you know it the match has started.

I want to try and savour every second for I know I will probably never experience anything like this again, but of course, once the game starts, all you can do is to get caught up in the ebb and flow of it as it unfolds. You probably know about this game, so I won't dwell on it too much. After a canny, tight, very even first half, it is goal-less. The revelation has been John Aston on United's left wing. Generally regarded as the team's weakest player, and frequently the butt of the crowd's displeasure, in part because he is the son of one of the coaching staff, tonight he has a stormer, easily the best game he will ever play for United, and afterwards he will deservedly win the man-of-the-match award.

But it is at this point that I need to bring in another, hitherto not mentioned United legend – Nobby Stiles. How can you not love Nobby? With his two front teeth missing, he will be for ever remembered for his jaunty, joyful dance along the touch line clutching the Jules Rimmet trophy after England had won the World Cup just two years previously (famously immortalised in the Lightning Seeds' *Three Lions* song). Back then every team had a Nobby, someone who snapped at other players' ankles, who would lay down his life for his team, who would have adopted, had they known it, Gandalf's immortal line from *The Lord of the Rings*, "You shall not pass!" City had Mike Doyle; Chelsea had the original Ron "Chopper" Harris; while Leeds had Norman "bites-yer-legs" Hunter. Well, United had Nobby, and he was Eusebio's nemesis. Never once, in all the games between Benfica and

United, or England against Portugal in those years, did Eusebio score if Stiles was marking him. But he went mighty close, though, as we shall see...

At the start of the second half, Benfica feel that Nobby is paying Eusebio rather too much close attention, and they surround him. For a few moments it threatens to get ugly, but Bobby Charlton does his usual peacemaker bit, and the referee halts the game for a brief spell to calm things down. The two American girls, confused by the turn of events, ask, "What's going on? Is it a time-out?" This memory comes back to me now all these years later – time out indeed: time out of mind out of time out of mind...

Gradually United begin to get on top and after a sustained period of pressure, score the opening goal – a rare, collector's item: a Bobby Charlton header! Then it's all United. Almost immediately, George Best scores a second, only to be (wrongly) ruled out for offside, but we feel more goals will come, for Benfica just can't cope with our pace. But they don't. Somehow Benfica keep scrambling the ball clear, and as the final whistle begins to draw tantalisingly near, United start to play for time and allow Benfica back into the game, until the inevitable happens. With just eight minutes left that man Torres again leaps higher than the United defence and heads in the equaliser.

Suddenly the tide of the game has turned completely. Now it's Benfica who are in the ascendancy; they pin United back in our own penalty area. Inside I start to feel sick; I can only see one result: that Benfica will snatch it. It is then that the game's defining moment happens. Eusebio, for once, escapes the shackles of Nobby Stiles and races clear. He is one-on-one with Stepney, the United goalkeeper. As Foulkes tries to close him down Eusebio unleashes a ferocious, unstoppable-looking shot heading straight for the top corner, but somehow, Stepney not only manages to save it, he actually clings onto it, so that there is no opportunity for Eusebio to follow up. Then, unforgettably, the greatest act of sportsmanship I have ever witnessed on a football field takes place. While Stepney begins to pick himself up from the ground, still clutching the ball tightly to his chest, Eusebio moves towards him, helps him to his feet, and shakes his hand to congratulate him on his save. This is not ironic; it is entirely genuine.

The referee blows for full time: Eusebio had almost won the game for Benfica; Stepney had saved it for United. But as the teams get ready for extra time, we are all of us sure that United have run themselves into the ground – several of the players are lying on the ground clearly suffering from cramp (the curse of the old Wembley) – while Benfica seem as fresh as daisies. Only Matt Busby seems calm, as he walks round all of the players with a quiet word for each of them. He was just eight minutes away from fulfilling his long-held dream, but he seems unperturbed.

Extra time gets underway and immediately Benfica are back on the offensive, but a long up-field clearance from Stepney sees George Best suddenly pounce on a moment's indecision by one of their defenders; he dispossesses him and races past another couple, rounds the goalkeeper, then, cool as a cucumber, strokes it slowly, agonisingly, into the empty net. We are back in front, and this time there is no sitting back. Best, at just 21 years old, has been named European Footballer of the Year (the youngest ever and completing an extraordinary hat-trick for United, with Charlton receiving this honour in 1966 and Denis Law in 1967, but Law is missing this final – he is in a Manchester hospital where he has had to have another knee operation watching the game on TV: reportedly he nearly injured himself again celebrating Best's goal in extra time). And now Best starts to torment the opposition, running rings round the defenders, going back and beating them a second time just for the fun of it; he crosses the ball to young Brian Kidd (in for the injured Law, playing just his 5th game) who heads the ball onto the crossbar, then heads in the rebound, and now it is 3-1. It's his 18th birthday – what a way to mark it! Then a couple of minutes later, a one-two between Charlton and Best sees Charlton clip in his second and United's fourth, and now we know it's all over.

There's no way back from there for Benfica. United have scored three goals in just five minutes. We are all of us delirious, and suddenly the two American girls seem to get what football – or "soccer", as they insist on calling it – is really all about. One of them, Carly, throws her arms around me as United's fourth goal goes in, and gives me the most glorious kiss, my second, and somewhat more extended than Susan Molloy's chaste peck. I'm afraid I don't recall much of the second half of extra time. There were more kisses, but no more goals…

The game ended; United received the trophy – there are marvellous photographs of the occasion with Matt Busby embracing the two Munich survivors, Bobby Charlton and Billy Foulkes – but it was the beginning of the end for this second great United team. Having won the European Cup, Busby retired at the end of the following season. Law never really recovered his fitness. Charlton, Foulkes and Stiles were all coming to the end of their careers. Best began to go walkabout. There were occasional great moments: a run to the semi-final of the European Cup in 1969; George Best scoring 6 goals in a single cup tie against Northampton in 1970; Best's wonder goal against Sheffield United in 1971 (still shown on TV); but he started to go missing more and more. Denis Law left the club when Tommy Docherty became the third manager in three years after Busby retired and rejoined Manchester City. On the final game of the 1974 season United played City at Old Trafford, knowing that they had to win to have any chance of avoiding relegation. With just seconds remaining, with the score still 0-0, Law scored for City; the crowd was stunned into silence; Law, usually the most gladiatorial of goal celebrators, put his head in his hands and walked off the pitch; the referee blew for full time, and United, just six years after being European champions, were, unthinkably, relegated. Although they would bounce back up immediately the following year, it would be another twenty years before United would again win the League title…

But no one who was there that balmy, hot May night in 1968 will ever forget the rapture and joy of United becoming the first English team to win the European Cup and see Matt Busby's long-cherished dream fulfilled. And to win it in such style too – 4-1 against the great Benfica after what had been in normal time such a close end-to-end contest.

Alan and I parted ways with the two American girls to catch the night train back to Manchester, the Milk Train, as it was called then, arriving back north with the dawn. Alan was met by an uncle off the train, who was taking him further north towards Preston for the weekend, and so, because the buses had not yet started to run, I decided to walk the six miles back to Flixton as the sun rose. Once again, as had been the case less than 24 hours previously, people stopped and chatted: "Were you there? Did you see the goals? Wasn't it great? Aren't you lucky?" And I was, and I did, and it was, and I was – so lucky. And for that golden morning all the world seemed to be as one, all caught in the sun's rays, celebrating United's success, which, because of Munich, transcended football and "united" the whole country, it felt, in a shared joy.

When I reached home, after a second dawn walk in that momentous May of 1968 when the world turned, my mum and dad were just about to leave for work, while I just fell into bed. But I didn't sleep. I grinned blissfully from ear to ear remembering celebrating golden goals and kissing golden American girls.

*

Epilogue: 1963

We are back in 1963, back on the street where I was born. It is a weekday afternoon – I think it's a Friday – and for some reason I am not in school. Maybe I am sick, or maybe it's a half day holiday, I don't remember. But Wes's brother Baz is there, keeping an eye on me till my dad gets back from work. We are outside kicking a football against the wall in front of our house, when around the corner comes Phil Chisnall on his bike. "On me 'ead, Chris!" he calls, and for the next half hour or so we play a game – me and Baz against Phil and of course he wins: we simply can't get the ball off him. Then I see my dad walking briskly towards us…

A note here now about my dad. When he was 17 he was signed up by City. It's true! He was a tricky winger but very slight of build. Then, as now, players tended to be big, and he was told by City he would need to build himself up more if he wasn't going to be knocked off the ball too easily. (In those days, although the game was much slower than it is now, it was rougher, in the sense that more physical contact was an accepted part of the way the game was played). My dad was then a United supporter and also a Catholic, but by the late 1940's (when this was happening) City no longer adopted a Protestants Only policy (unlike United, who were then still only fielding Catholics). Naturally he was thrilled to have been spotted by one of their club scouts while playing for a park team on a Sunday afternoon, but football was not then the gateway to riches for young men that it is today. Even as late as the 1950's there was a statutory top salary for footballers of just £30 per week! I don't know what happened in the early 60's that brought about a change in the law, but somehow that £30 ceiling was eventually broken, and 1962 saw the first ever £100 a week salary, causing the same kind of outrage that the £100,000 per week salaries cause today, though even allowing for inflation the two figures are in no way comparable. (And do you know who the first player to receive £100 per week was? Useful pub quiz fact coming up – it was… Johnny Haynes of Fulham. Who, I hear you ask? One of the Brylcreem Boys on ITV, along with Denis Compton). So back in 1947, when my dad was signed up, being a footballer was pretty low down on the wages scale.

However, before he could play his first game, he was called up for National Service, which there was no getting out of. So, just a few weeks after starting training with City, my dad was packed off to an army base in Catterick in North Yorkshire, where he would be based for the start of the next two years, before being transferred to Copthorne in Shropshire.

"Wasted years," my dad would always recall bitterly. I don't know much about his army experiences – he never talked about them. In fact I know precious little about my dad's childhood or youth at all, except that his own dad died when he was just eight years old, that he was the youngest of seven children (only one of whom I ever met), and that he left school at 14 in order to get a job and help his mum out. The only things I know about his National Service experience were that he became an excellent marksman (in later years he would always win on the fairground shooting booths), that he set up a kind of concert party in which he sang songs from the shows, that he missed going to Korea by just a few weeks (his National Service ending just before we went to war there), and that he continued to play football: for Shrewsbury Town.

But this was not such a big deal as it sounds either, for back then Shrewsbury were in what was known as Third Division North, and such teams were largely amateur, often struggled to field eleven players and came to rely on local army camps based nearby (for whole swathes of the male population were taken out of circulation by National Service) to boost their teams. But it still shows what a good player he was. When he turned out for Shrewsbury, they used to play in what was the old gloriously-named Gay Meadow ground, which was situated right next to the River Severn. Frequently the ball would be kicked into the river, so frequently, in fact, that they used to employ an old man in a coracle (a round wicker boat a bit like a Moses basket) to fish the ball out and throw it back! It was while my dad was playing for Shrewsbury one afternoon that he incurred a bad knee injury, and when he returned to Manchester after his National Service had finished, City felt he was too much of a risk and so did not take up the option on his contract. But though obviously disappointing, it was not the blow that this would be to a young man today in such circumstances. Back then most footballers, even those who played for First Division teams, often had to have other jobs as well (like Bill Foulkes). So my dad did a series of different jobs for a while – collecting insurance in Salford, climbing tall factory chimneys to re-point them in the Lancashire coalfields, and finally in an asbestos factory on Trafford Park – but he continued to play football twice a week for local league teams.

So – that Friday afternoon when he came round the corner into our street on his way home from work and saw me, Baz and Phil Chisnall playing football, he was still a young man, perhaps 34 years old at most. I remember him taking off his coat, folding it and placing it on the pavement, then calling to Phil to pass him the ball. "Come and get it," said Phil, "if you can." My dad caught my eye and grinned. He then proceeded to dispossess Phil and dribble the ball past him again and again.

We set up coats and jumpers as goal posts in the street (there were hardly any cars then to worry about) and me and my dad played Phil and Baz till the sky grew dark and the street lights came on and the air filled with the smell of scores of smoking chimneys from the coal fires burning in the grates of every house. We played for what felt like hours as Phil and Baz tried to get the ball off my dad, who would pass it to me when he felt it was impossible for me not to score, right until my mum came home from work, when she sent me off to the chippy for a fish and chip supper all round – the perfect end to a perfect afternoon…

## No More Heroes (part 1)

My friend said shagging was quite alright –
he liked to do it on Friday night –
depending upon the bird,
but not like watching George Best score.
Now *he* had goals and girls galore –
I wonder which he preferred?

I nearly saw The Beatles twice –
each time I couldn't afford the price.
My friend went, though: his favourite bit
was when John sang, "She Loves You – Shit!"
Of all the four I liked John best –
I wasn't fussed about the rest –
he sang of pain and class and sex,
and wore those National Health-type specs.
When I wore them in primary school,
the other kids said I looked a fool.

In '67, the Summer of Peace,
I really got into Chief Cochise –
all that stuff on ecologies…
I thought: "Far out, this'll do me,"
and went to live in a Welsh tepee;
tuned in, dropped out – went home for tea….

(to be continued…)

Sometimes, on those skives from cross country, Pete, Ian and I would be joined by Bernard and Jamie. Bernard lived just around the corner from me, over the iron bridge which crossed the railway line that ran from Manchester to Liverpool, while Jamie lived in Glazebrook, a small village on the Moss a couple of stations further along. As we progressed through each successive year at school, Bernard became my best friend, while Jamie emerged as the cleverest boy in the class. He and Bernard (together with Ian) would later all go to Cambridge together. When he was 11 or 12, Bernard was a quiet, reserved, timid sort of a boy, but as he got older he came into his own. He grew his hair – longer and longer, until it went way down his back past his shoulders – and developed a biting, dry, ironic wit. He worked in the summer holidays as a hospital porter and spent all his money on the latest music technology – state of the art reel-to-reel tape recorders in those days – and listened to more avant garde music than even John Peel would play. "It's worth it," he'd say, "after the shit I have to put up with at the hospital."

His tales from working at Park Hospital, Davyhulme were the stuff of legend. He'd regale us with descriptions of the underground passages and corridors, not used by the public, by which he would transport human waste, blood, fingers, thumbs, hands and other body parts to the incinerator, as well as patients who had died en route to the morgue. At night, he said, these passages were carpeted with cockroaches, which would scuttle and crack beneath his shoes. Once, when it was very late, he was trundling a recently deceased male to the morgue. The corridor was dimly lit and, as usual, festooned with cockroaches. He entered the morgue, wheeled his gurney to the designated metal, refrigerated drawer, only to discover – too late – that he'd been mistakenly given the wrong number, for this drawer was already occupied, and as Bernard pulled it open, the body that lay inside suddenly sat bolt upright. (Apparently this transient breaking of rigor mortis is not uncommon). In the fastness of the night, Bernard, normally the most unflappable of characters, shrieked and fled. But as he was trying to make his escape, the loop of the belt in his porter's overalls got tangled up in the door handle. "He's got me," he yelled in a blind panic.

But this next story is from the autumn of 1968, when Bernard still listened to mainstream music, before he discovered Captain Beefheart, his Magic Band and *Trout Mask Replica,* and before he had begun his holiday job in the hospital.

I remember vividly one Saturday morning in November Bernard and I taking the train to meet up with Jamie, something we had been looking forward to with increasing relish all of the preceding week, for it was on that particular Saturday morning that The Beatles' White Album was being released; Jamie had saved enough to buy it, and Bernard and I were travelling down to spend the day listening to it. Glazebrook is a small village situated on one of the many mosses that are strung along the edge of the East Lancs Road which runs between Manchester and Liverpool. There is Barton Moss, Chat Moss (to which we'll return later), Irlam Moss, Cadishead Moss (where my mother grew up as a child), Rixton Moss (where some of my family still live) and finally Glazebrook Moss. Back in those days the 11+ exam was still in operation, and the only Grammar School for miles around was at Urmston which, for those families living on these outlying mosses, meant a long train ride through the Steel Works at Cadishead, past the Tar, Soap and Margarine Works in Irlam, over the Manchester Ship Canal, across the iron bridge, then alongside the Mersey flood plain and meadows, and finally into Urmston Station, from where it was a further 25 minute walk to the school.

Bernard and I caught the train that Saturday morning at Flixton, and Glazebrook was two stations along. When we got out, we followed the instructions Jamie had given us to walk through a nettle-strewn back lane, then out across a kind of levee that crossed the boggy fields of the moss towards the village where he lived. This makes it sound quite rural, which I suppose it was, but it was/is not pretty. It is flat, open, exposed land, where swedes are grown for cattle, and the rain drives hard and horizontal, forcing you to keep your eyes fixed on the marshy, muddy ground. If you did lift your head for a moment, what greeted your eyes was the steel works back at Cadishead, or the petro-chemical works of Shell over at Partington. Both of these massive factory complexes belched smoke and fumes twenty-four hours a day, and at night, mighty plumes of red fire roared into the sky. From the safe distance of Flixton, on the other side of the Ship Canal, this scene at night resembled Mordor from *The Lord of the Rings.*

On that November Saturday morning, however, it wasn't raining. Instead a damp fog hung just a few feet above the moss, and we made our way with growing excitement as we anticipated listening to the almost mythical White Album that Jamie would by now have purchased. Just as we were nearing the final turning to his house, he suddenly appeared, waving. "Bad news," he said, as we arrived within earshot. "I didn't get it." Our faces fell. He shrugged apologetically, then said. "It's just across here. Come inside and we'll have a brew."

Bernard and I said nothing and simply followed. The disappointment was as palpable as the dank layers of mist that clung to our clothes and hair.

The Beatles' White Album had assumed almost iconic proportions before it had even been released. Back then, The Beatles still retained that aura of somehow managing to be both anti-establishment and part of the mainstream at the same time. They didn't merely react to the mood of the times, they shaped it. They had grown up on streets just like ours, less than twenty miles away from where we were walking, and since they had stopped touring and playing live (less than two years previously) their influence and mystique had, if anything, grown even more. If 1967 had been the year of love and peace and psychadelia, 1968 was when it started to turn angry.

The riots on the streets of Paris, followed by the protests outside the US Embassy in Grosvenor Square, had raised our political consciousness. Bernard and I had spoken in a debate at school attacking the American involvement in Vietnam. Earlier that summer I had gone to London for the very first time and, en route coincidentally to see The Beatles' film of *Yellow Submarine* in Leicester Square, had been stopped on Piccadilly Circus next to the Statue of Eros by a barefoot hippy girl with flowers in her hair selling copies of *The International Times*, who told me all about the Russian tanks crushing the green shoots of the Prague Spring, while The Beatles had been in India studying transcendental meditation with the Maharishi, and rumours were circulating that the new album would mark a shift back to more simple, direct recordings.

After the drug-fuelled experiments of *Sgt Pepper, Strawberry Fields, Magical Mystery Tour* and *I am the Walrus,* there had been virtual silence. Then in the summer, in yet another new approach, they had launched their own label – Apple – with a beautiful, if naïve, manifesto about putting the artists in charge of the decision making, and their first recordings, Apple 001 and 002, were the achingly beautiful *Hey Jude* juxtaposed with the ambiguous politics of *Revolution* – *"But if you talk about destruction/Don't you know that you can count me out – in..."* Out – in: what did that mean? We had debated that endlessly at school, and each of us wondered which side of that particular fence we were on.

(Meanwhile, in a parallel universe, Amanda, who in just eight years from that November Saturday would be my wife, but whom I hadn't even met yet, even though she lived in the same town, would be spending that evening at the after-show party for Eccles Operatic Society's production of *Robert & Elizabeth,* in which she had danced the Spirit of Autumn, sitting on the knee of a boy called Keith Wiggins kissing her way through the entire eight minutes of *Hey Jude,* though her only abiding memory of that experience would be of suffering a stiff neck!)

And now The White Album was being released, The Beatles' first LP since *Sgt Pepper,* and not only that, but a double album to boot. Nobody had put out one of those before. And while Pepper's cover had been a riot of colour in Peter Blake's amazing design, the new cover was completely unadorned – plain white, with "The Beatles" stamped on in further embossed white. We all knew that this was clearly the influence of Yoko Ono and we were thrilled by its daring.

In those days, when there was no internet, no illegal downloads, the only source for hearing any previews was via Radio 1, and in the week before its release, Kenny Everett had been playing selected tracks each night on his early evening show. The first track he played was the still little-known *Sexy Sadie,* which I'd loved for its clever lyrics, witty backing vocals and glorious guitar work. (I didn't know then that Sexy Sadie was a private nickname John had coined for the Maharishi, and that already they had begun to see through him). In his typically irreverent way, Kenny Everett had tantalised and teased us with snippets of other songs here and there, so that by the time that Saturday morning came and the album was available in the shops, it was still by and large unknown and unheard. No singles were released beforehand to promote it; The Beatles didn't need that kind of publicity. In fact, it was the mystery surrounding almost every aspect of it that was a large part of its appeal. You can imagine therefore just how intense was the disappointment Bernard and I felt when Jamie announced that he had not been able to get it after all.

We arrived at his house just as his mother was coming out of the front door on her way to visit a family member living nearby. "Hello, boys," she said. "The kettle's already on, and there's a packet of Jaffa cakes on the kitchen table. Enjoy yourselves listening to your new record." And she scooted her bike away down the lane.

"But…" we stuttered.

"It's true. *I* didn't get it. *She* did. She had to go into Warrington first thing this morning and so she picked it up for us."

"Why you little….!"

And we tumbled into the back kitchen where, lying on the table next to the biscuits, was The Beatles' White Album.

"Come on," said Jamie. "Let's have a brew and some bacon butties."

We then proceeded to listen to all four sides of the double album straight through three times, taking it in turns to pore over the lyrics and the photo-collage that came with it. Back in those far-off days of vinyl, each side was carefully constructed with a strong opening and closing track to hook you in and then make you want to turn the disc over to hear the other side. The White Album's four sides each have their own particular style and aesthetic: side 1 is largely 'pop'; side 2 more acoustic; side 3 rock; side 4 more eclectic and experimental. The range of material is simply astounding and those three consecutive plays couldn't do it justice, and so when I went home afterwards I dropped big hints to my parents that, if they were stuck for what to get me for Christmas, The Beatles' White Album had just been released, and so sure enough I unwrapped my own mono copy on Christmas morning, and have it still, nearly half a century later, having been played almost to the point of nonexistence.

Over the years different tracks have emerged as my personal favourite, but it is the concept of it as a whole that still lingers. On that first hearing of it in Glazebrook, Jamie really liked the sly, wicked humour of tracks like *Bungalow Bill* and *Glass Onion;* Bernard unsurprisingly responded to the avant-garde *Revolution 9* with its seemingly random edits of radio stations, fragments of music, overheard conversations, resembling nothing less than you were tuning into the end, or beginning, of the world, while I was haunted by the simple melodies of tracks like *Julia* and *Blackbird*, and all of us thrilled to the raw power and energy of *Yer Blues* and *Helter Skelter.*

*"It's coming down fast…"*

*"We were only waiting for this moment to arise…"*

Those lyrics really spoke to us. Such a happy, innocent day. None of us knew then that half way across the world, in a California desert, Charles Manson and his crazed followers were also hearing those lyrics but reading into them unintended messages telling them to embark upon their orgies of killing in San Francisco's Laurel Canyon. The Beatles always channelled the mood of the times, but this was an outcome that could never have been predicted, and for a time it made it hard for me to listen to The White Album in that same state of original innocence.

Less than a year later The Beatles would break up. There would be two further albums – *Let It Be* and *Abbey Road* – but The White Album, for me, will always remain their apotheosis. In it they did indeed 'get back to where they once belonged', which made the break-up, so painfully captured in Michael Lindsey-Hogg's sprawling documentary of the making of the *Let It Be* album, all the more poignant. In it there is one particularly telling scene. Paul is trying to enthuse John with an idea he has to 'get back' on the road, to turn up to small venues unannounced and just play, without any of the hype and paraphernalia of a huge stadium tour. They could reinvent themselves, he argues. John sits throughout in complete silence. Watching that moment up there on screen, one knows at once that the game is up.

But that idea stayed with Paul. A couple of years later, when he was launching Wings, he knew that there would be far too much expectation and pressure on any new post-Beatles band, and so he would simply turn up at university student unions, just as he had imagined it in that conversation with John, and ask to play. When I was a student myself at Manchester University, I vividly recall one particular Friday evening. That, too, was in November, and the foyer of the student union was unusually empty. It was around 6.30 in the evening, before the bars would start to fill up, and there were only a few people milling around. I had just finished making a call from a pay phone to my then girl friend who was a student in Newcastle, when in strolled Paul.

Casually and without any fuss he walked up to the porter's desk and said, "Hi, my name's Paul McCartney and I was just wondering if my group might play a small gig here tonight."

The foyer fell suddenly quiet. The porter, unimpressed, looked up. "Tonight?" he said.

"Yeah," said Paul. "If that's OK."

The porter licked the end of his stubby pencil and flicked through a ledger in front of him. "It says here," he said, stabbing the page with the pencil, "that Jazz Club have got the room booked."

"Right. Well – is there another space? Or maybe Jazz

Club might be able to move somewhere else…?

"It says here… What did you say your name was again?"

"Listen. It's cool. Don't worry. We'll try somewhere else." And out he walked.

Those few of us standing there who had witnessed this immediately rounded on the hapless porter. "Do you realise who that was?"

"I can't let just any Tom, Dick or Harry walk in here and think he can just do what he likes…"

"That wasn't any Tom, Dick or Harry. It was Paul!"

"Whatever his name was – it says here…"

"… Jazz Club have got the room booked – we know," we all chimed back.

"It's more than my job's worth…"

Later we learned that Wings played that night a few miles down the road at Salford University.

It was the third time that I nearly saw The Beatles (or some of them). The first time was in the summer of 1963, when they appeared in a tent at Urmston Show, a kind of glorified village fete on Chassen Park. But the tickets cost 12/6 – that's sixty-two and a half pence in decimal – but back then represented five weeks pocket money, so there was no way I could afford that. My next door neighbour, Pete, went though. "What were they like?" I asked him. "Rough," he said, "raw, but really exciting."

The second time I nearly saw them was at the Llandudno Odeon in 1964. My grandparents lived in North Wales at the time, but the date didn't coincide with when I was visiting. My friend there, Richard, went and what he remembered most was the screaming of all the girls. It was the height of Beatlemania by then and it was mass hysteria. He said, "You couldn't actually hear what they were playing. Except for once. Just for a second the screaming died down, as if the girls were all taking a deep, collective breath. In the sudden quiet, ringing out across the aisles where we were standing, you could hear – as plain as day – 'She Loves You Shit, Shit, Shit'…" Years later John would recall that they knew no-one could hear them and that they would sometimes sing anything.

In 2001, when I visited New York for the first time, I walked across Central Park, through the part known now as Strawberry Fields, past the *Imagine* mosaic, out towards the Dakota Building, when Yoko Ono suddenly stepped out of a side door and into a black, chauffeured limousine. I remember being struck by how tiny she seemed. And I share the same birthday as Ringo – 7th July – who in an interview for *The Beatles Anthology* so movingly recalls how the very last words recorded by the band, which appear at the close of *Abbey Road,* fittingly called *The End,* capture exactly what he felt their work was all about:

*"And in the end the love you take*
*Is equal to the love you make..."*

I was never in later years one of those who yearned for some kind of reunion. "That was then," as John said. "If you want to reminisce, you can always listen to the records." And it's true: you can. No, I prefer to remember that final concert on the rooftop of their Abbey Road studios when somehow, after all the wrangling and the rows that punctuated that painful period of breaking up, they had the crazy, spontaneous idea to do what Paul had been suggesting to John all along – just turn up unannounced and play. That rooftop concert is now iconic and has even been satirised in *The Simpsons,* but it is still thrilling to revisit it, to see the looks and expressions on the faces of people in the streets below as they gradually realise what is going on and who it actually is up there playing for free, and then of course the arrival of the police to break it all up and almost arrest them, with John's final words in an exaggerated scouse accent perfectly capturing the essence not just of that concert, but the whole era of The Beatles.

"On behalf of the group we'd like to thank you very much and we hope we've passed the audition...."

As the evening drew in and the mists rolled once more across Glazebrook Moss, Jamie turned to Bernard and me and said, "I think we've time to listen to it once more before you get the last train home."

## And Our Bird Once Sang

There now appears a short intermission,
like there used to be before the *Early Bird*
(launched by The Beatles for *One World*)
when there was no longer a need
for the potter's wheel or test card,
but now this unwanted omission
where, instead of this, you should have read
a Lennon and McCartney collage,
(not forgetting Harrison,
as we so often did, the "quiet one")
fragments of lyrics, an *homage*
to their lasting legacy,
their influence over both you and me:
it shouts at us like a black hole

beyond our deep space exploration
(95% of which is unknowable
anti-matter awaiting discovery);
a billion dollar corporation,
self-appointed guardian
of what is deemed allowed for use,
denies us access, information
in the guise of dubious protection –
so thank you, Multi-National Company,
and all the rest in the Upper Circle:
why don't you, in the words of one whose
others now you keep from us
crowding below in the cheaper seats,
"swing your beads and rattle your jewellery"?

*Truth is Beauty, Beauty Truth* – that's all you need to know,
except to say she leapt out through the bathroom window…

## Gwenda Takes Me In Hand

*Each day has its always*
*A look down life's hallways* The Moody Blues

"The trouble is you look like a school boy."

"I *am* a schoolboy."

"Not for much longer. You'll be at university in a few weeks. You don't want to turn up looking like this, do you?"

Personally I couldn't see much wrong with how I looked, but then again I'd never given it much thought either, just grabbed whatever was at hand. This evening I was still in what passed for my school uniform. So was Gwenda. Though I had to admit she looked a lot better in hers than I did in mine. I leant across to kiss her.

"Later," she said. "Homework first. English. I've got a Hamlet essay. You?"

"T.S. Eliot."

*"We are the hollow men,"* she chanted, *"we are the stuffed men,"* dancing round the living room with comical, stiff scarecrow arms, her father's white shirt (which she'd commandeered and customised for school) dangling low over her wrists. She was a complete one-off, with a real flair for design, inherited perhaps from her older sister, a fashion student, who lived wickedly with her boyfriend in a flat in glamorous, bohemian Didsbury.

"We'll take you to Manchester on Saturday and see what we can find for you. You can use your birthday money." (I had just turned 18).

"We?"

"I'll see if Kathryn can come too."

Gwenda's shoulder-length raven hair fell across her pale Vivien Leigh-like face as she bent over her book. I smiled.

"What?"

*"O what a rogue and peasant slave am I…"*

"In that case I'd better start cracking my whip," she said. "Work."

We settled in companionable silence to read, make notes, begin our respective essays. After an hour, she stood up and stretched, her long white sleeves slipping below her elbows.

"Cup of tea?" she said.

"Please."

When she came back in from the kitchen, she placed the mugs on the floor and sat down next to me on the sofa. She took hold of my hand and said, "Are you looking forward to it?"

"Being a Drama student?" I said.

She nodded.

"I can't wait."

"Have you decided where you are going yet?"

"I'd like to go to Exeter, but my dad thinks I should stay here, go to Manchester."

"It's not his decision though, is it?"

"He has to sign the acceptance form, don't forget."

"But that's ridiculous. They're lowering the age of consent to 18, aren't they?"

"Not till next year. So you'll be OK. Technically, I'll not be an adult till I'm 21."

"It wouldn't apply to me in any case. My parents would support me wherever I chose."

I shrugged.

"It'll work out," she said. "He'll come round. Let *me* talk to him. I'll charm him."

"Right," I said, smiling. "My mum and dad don't really approve of you."

("You've changed since you met that Gwenda," they'd said.

"Good," I'd replied).

"Well *I* don't approve of *them*."

*

The next Saturday we took the number 5 bus to Manchester where we met Kathryn at *The Kardomah*, already sipping an espresso and smoking a sobranie. (I'd only just experienced my first Maxwell House).

"Well," she said, "we can start on New Brown Street if you like. *Stolen from Ivor* have just opened their first out of London store there – what do you say to a Ben Sherman shirt, Chris? – but personally I'd head for the second hand market stalls in The Corn Exchange and the textile warehouses on Ancoats Street. What do you think, Chris?"

The two sisters looked at me expectantly.

"Do I have a choice?" I said.

"Honestly," said Gwenda, "he's hopeless." And off they went, arms linked, with me trailing in their wake.

"Right," said Kathryn, as we reached the first shop. "Ready for the fray?"

"As ready as I'll ever be," I said.

"You don't really need me, do you, Gwenda? I promised to meet up with Barry at eleven. We'll see you in Tommy Duck's in a couple of hours, and we'll take stock, shall we? Have fun, Chris," and with a wink she was gone.

"Come on," said Gwenda, looking at my less than enthusiastic expression. "It's not like going to the dentist's." Just at that moment, going to the dentist's seemed a much more preferable option.

She took my hand and for the next couple of hours or so we traipsed from shop to shop, with me trying on item after item that she picked out for me.

"I've only got £15," I said.

"It'll be enough. Trust me."

And so it proved. Come the end of the day, I discovered I was the surprised owner of a pair of bottle green cord flares, a button-down paisley shirt, an orange skinny-rib jumper, a pair of brown shoes with a gold buckle instead of laces, with still enough change for a string of turquoise beads Gwenda insisted were needed to complete the outfit. I was dubious about the beads but Kathryn turned up at that point with Barry, her boyfriend, who gave me the once-over and an encouraging thumbs-up.

"All we need now," said Gwenda, "is to do something with his hair."

Barry, seeing the look on my face, laughed. "Just go with it, mate. Come back to our place and we'll have a beer. It'll help to lessen the pain."

For someone who'd only recently been into a pub to order an under-age shandy, this was heady stuff indeed.

*

Catching the bus home in the evening, Gwenda said, "I don't feel like staying in tonight. Let's go for a drink. I'll just stop off and get changed first, alright?"

While I waited for Gwenda to get ready, I was paraded in front of her mum, who immediately expressed her approval. Mrs Hughes (or Denise, as I was daringly encouraged to call her) was always so easy-going. "Cigarette?" she said.

"Thanks," I said nonchalantly, trying not to let it look like this was the first time a grown-up had offered me one.

Gwenda came down a few minutes later wearing her grandmother's white wedding dress with heavy black eye make-up, black lipstick, and ankle-length black stiletto boots. My jaw hit the floor while Denise burst into applause. "Have fun," she said. "Go knock 'em dead, though I'm not sure that Flixton's ready for the two of you!"

As we walked the half mile to the pub Gwenda had picked out for us to make our appearance, cars hooted their horns, cyclists nearly fell off their bikes and passers-by gaped open-mouthed.

"See," she said. "You're causing a stir already."

I laughed. "I don't think it's me they're staring at."

The old *Union Inn*, at the bottom of Bent Lanes by the overgrown stream known locally as the Bent Brook, which dribbled its way very slowly to the Mersey, had recently changed hands, been refurbished and had just re-opened. (How did Gwenda always seem to know these things?) Renamed *The Fox and Hounds*, its décor was all hunting brasses and Toby jugs. It was still reasonably early and the pub was quiet, but (unbelievably since this was not his usual watering hole) standing at the bar was my father.

He was with one of his friends from the local Operatic – Peter, whom I knew by sight, but who didn't know me. As we walked in, Peter put down his pint glass, turned to my father and said in a voice of utter disgust, "My God, look what the wind just blew in."

My father, embarrassed and appalled, pretended not to know me. "Kids today, eh?" he said, turning away.

"They should bring back National Service, that's what I think," said Peter.

"Let's go," I said immediately, completely mortified.

"No way," said Gwenda. "We've as much right to be here as they have." She was enjoying herself hugely. "I'll have a glass of red please."

I went to a different bar to order the drinks, so as not to have to face my father again and cause yet more embarrassment. When I returned to where Gwenda was sitting, I was still seething inside.

"Cheers," she said.

"He'll never sign that acceptance form now."

Gently she placed her hand on my arm. "Give him time to get used to the idea."

I could barely contain myself. "He refused to even acknowledge me."

"He doesn't know who you are."

*

A week later I wore the new clothes for a second time. My hair, in its somewhat alarming Afro, had settled down a bit, and I no longer got a shock each time I caught sight of my reflection.

"I suppose this was that Gwenda's idea," was the only comment my mother could muster. "I expect she thinks it makes you look with it."

And now I was back on the number 5 bus again, heading off to Manchester once more, but alone this time, going to meet up with a couple of mates to see The Moody Blues playing live at The Odeon. Gwenda wasn't coming.

"Why would I?" she'd said when I asked her if she wanted to. "They're rubbish."

I couldn't argue with this. When I'd bought their most recent LP (*To Our Children's Children's Children*), her derision knew no bounds. "I can't believe it," she said, after the opening poem. "Did he really say what I thought he did? '*With the force of 10 billion butterfly sneezes…*'? Pur-lease!"

Despite their penchant for pretentious poems, declaimed against a background of gongs, roaring winds, electronic bleeps, their overblown, half-baked concepts and their appalling album covers, I retained a huge affection for them, ever since I'd heard their first album a few years back, and I'd kind of grown up with them. *Tuesday Afternoon, Nights in White Satin, Visions of Paradise, Melancholy Man,* they had all somehow *"walked along with me to the next bend"*. (I never was at what you might call the cutting edge. No Cream or Captain Beefheart for me sadly). Ah well, as the Moody Blues' song *Another Morning* so profoundly puts it, "yesterday's dreams are tomorrow's sighs…!"

I arrived at The Odeon just as Robin and Jonnie, my long-term fellow fans, did too. As I crossed the road to join them, they could hardly contain their laughter. "What do you look like?" said Robin.

"What d'you mean?"

"Your hair for a start," mocked Jonnie. "You look like you've been dragged through a hedge backwards."

"That's good then, isn't it?" I said.

"And those shoes?" pointed Robin, grimacing. "You look ridiculous. Like a highwayman."

I rather liked the idea of that. "Stand and deliver!" I said. "Have you got the tickets?"

We went in and the concert was much like previous ones I'd attended. Jonnie and Robin were full of it afterwards. "Fantastic," they enthused.

"I never thought they'd play *Legend of a Mind* live," said Jonnie, and he and Robin immediately began to sing. *"He'll take you up, he'll take you down, he'll plant your feet back on the ground…."*

Gwenda's right, I thought. This really is rubbish. I'll be at university in a few weeks, while Jonnie and Robin are still just schoolboys. I could feel myself leaving an old life behind. Jonnie had the new record he'd just bought from the merchandise desk after the concert tucked under his coat to protect it from the rain that was now beginning to fall. "Want to come round tomorrow to listen to it?" he said.

"Absolutely," said Robin. "Chris?"

"I don't think I can, mate. I think Gwenda and I have got something planned."

"Suit yourself," said Jonnie.

Just then the bus came up, driving straight through a deep puddle soaking my new cords and shoes.

"Shit," I yelled, while they just pissed themselves laughing.

"Serves you right," they said.

*

Two months later Gwenda dumped me. The next day I started listening to Leonard Cohen.

# come together

## First Day

This first day, sitting in regimented rows, we wait for people to arrive, for things to begin.

Some have already broken the ice; halting laughter mixes with the scrape of chairs on vinyl as ranks break, then reform into conversation groups. Not me though – I watch from the sidelines feeling suddenly very young.

What am I doing here? How will I fit in with all these mature, confident, cultured accents? The young man next to me reaches across, holds out his hand formally for me to shake, announces his surname and the school he's from.

Moments later the Professor arrives. The room quietens, heads turn towards him expectant. He describes the syllabus (names I haven't heard of) and I'm even more convinced I'm in the wrong room, there must be some mistake, I didn't get a place here after all.

Around noon, dismissed for the day, I find myself walking down Oxford Road – the local boy sharing the sights, the cabbie displaying the knowledge, the trader shouting his wares, desperate to impress.

This is the theatre, there's the cathedral, here's the oldest pub in the city – The Shambles… (Before the IRA bombed the Arndale, before there even was an Arndale).

We stumble through the demolition, the building sites, the cranes, our own unimagined futures forming in the dust and ruins, sprawling scaffold towers blocking out the sun, reinventing phoenix-like the city we climb up out of, the wreckage of past lives shed like an old skin, glimpsing the ghosts of who we might become, waiting there to greet us in hard hats.

Beside me walks a future CEO, heroin addict, politician, playwright, and a girl who'll read the news. The hard hats reach across the rubble smiling, before they haul us back up to the light.

## Skinny-Dipping in the Med

Le Vieux-Nice, 1971

*there are heroes in the seaweed*
*there are children in the morning*   Leonard Cohen: from *Suzanne*

high on cheap wine and cannabis
thirty British students touring France
in a beat-up red London bus
taking the Scottish play across Provence
hang out all night on a beach near Nice

I play many parts – the Doctor
witnessing the sleepwalking scene,
*half* of Birnam Wood, a Murderer,
reporting portents as an Old Man
and, this night, the Drunken Porter

singing, badly, Leonard Cohen
while others frolic and cavort –
I strum along impressing no one,
the girl I fancy's making out
with the guy who's playing Duncan

*and I want to travel with her*
*and I want to travel blind*
while the sound of lust and laughter
surges with the tide across the sand
and the camp fire flames rise higher

*All Right Now* and *I Feel Free*
the party ratchets up a gear
we're on our feet and dancing wildly
it's what we've *come together* for
and *where we're meant to be*

and all as one we race into the sea
howling the moon, tearing off clothes
our new shiny bodies slippery
eels diving through and over waves
and suddenly she's next to me

the water round her rages, boils
she rises like a mermaid from below
we try on this new skin, these scales
her tail's ferocious undertow –
but I can't follow where she calls...

washed up like seals basking in the sand
the sea now just a hush, a whisper
more smokes and joints are passed around
*After the Gold Rush, Helter Skelter*
tomorrow and tomorrow and –

although I won't remember what we said
or did or any of those other things
WE WENT SKINNY-DIPPING IN THE MED (!!)
and what next year, next day, next minute brings
who *gives* a shit – we might be dead

## Circuit Training

my girlfriend's in serious training
for next month's north of England championships
which means early to bed and early to rise
no alcohol, no chocolate, no sex
only endless circuits, round and round

in readiness for the big race
the four hundred metres
one final circuit, a single lap
taken at full speed till completely spent
the final dip before she breasts the tape

high on fumes of embrocation
I didn't make it past the warm up track
consigned to back-straight backwaters
carrying the kit, holding the thermos
behind-hand butt of backseat jokes

but still I persevered, kept the faith
wore the T-shirt, waved the rattle
shouting her name from the back of the stands
snapping her photo on top of the podium
she won my heart, I lost the race

## Snake in the Grass

Sevagram, Maharashtra, Central India

a night snake secretly unseen
slides down towards me from the eaves
to where we sit sipping spiced tea
on the makeshift verandah

silently, inexorably
it seeks me out, its slow moves
patient, stealthy and sure
till, ready, it rears its head to strike –

with barely a backward glance
she plucks it from behind my ear
hurls it in a high wide arc
through the bougainvillea leaves...

this morning, she tells me, she woke
with one coiled close beside her
on the pillow peacefully
winding out and through between

the knotted rope and crack
of fevered truckle dreams
tomorrow it will shed its skin
which she'll nail to a boundary fence –

a warning, don't come near –
a trophy to discarded loves...

later her father takes me back
I ride pillion on his scooter
head thrown high, a rictus grin
racing past abandoned farms

beneath a hunter's moon
we tear through unmarked field graves
where snakes new hatched writhe in wait for me –
they've been waiting ever since...

## Pebble

La Ciotat

words roll round your tongue
unfamiliar and strange
pebble swelling against palate
roof, speech and thought

slurring, each tiny droplet
in fierce Midi heat
you suck evaporates
each dry consonant, grates

no English, she says –
no French, no kisses –
bikini top unhooks
*attise érotique*

slides slow and down
stopping at shoreline
she turns, waves, walks
into the sea, sucks

the sand beneath your feet,
undertow heart beat,
urging you to come
deeper where water's warm

salt speckling skin and lips…
your first few tentative steps
stutter at water's edge
from where, rooted, you watch

her swim away, each stroke
sure and confident takes
her from you further –
you do not try to stop her

no words, just thoughts
half formed stick in your throat
each disgorging reflex
gags, convulses, chokes

expels the pebble whole
smooth and worn with all
those unsaid words, those unlived lives
spits it, skating on the waves

on and on you watch it skim
towards the far horizon's rim
caught by the sun's green ray
*le rayon vert qui s'est fané...*

treading water, the long wait
her hand shoots up to pluck it
from the air, place it deep inside
her skin to catch the next tide

a life imagined, a moment lost...
clouds mass in the east
you pull on your coat, turn
back to more known terrain

## After the Rain

after the rain
each droplet of water
hangs
tremulously
from each
bare
branch
waiting to fall

drip

drop

drip

and within
each
separate
droplet

is an entire world

where
you and I can swim
a lifetime

suspended

hopes and dreams
caught in your fingertips
dripping with memory

you hang here

each droplet of rain
patient to be held
swelling till you burst
to come to rest at last

on the dry
                waiting
                                earth

## Looking Out / Looking In

the title of a 2014 exhibition of paintings and sketches by Andrew Wyeth at the National Gallery of Art, Washington D.C

Andrew,

you'd know this scene
high scudding clouds raking across
cut fields freshly green

pockmarked now by crows
whose ragged mob and swoop
black as liquorice

pecks at Helga's sleep –
you'll paint the space her body's left
beside a rusting tap

ladder to the loft
bed of dried straw
from where you lift

Christina, carry her
to her known world's farthest edge
set her down where

you can rearrange
delicately each twisted limb –
she yearns to reach

beyond horizon's rim –
each grass blade, skin cell you paint
will hold back time

stretch this single moment
beyond the borders of a dream
the bleak truth can't taint

a blank grey room
trapped bird fluttering against glass
exiled in sight of home

coolly you record this
your part-concealed reflection
feathering the canvas

for you focus attention
in the most figurative portrait
on formal abstraction

you paint squares of light
in geometric interplay
white on white on white

the long slow decay
frost-bitten apples on the sill
shutters closed to the day

the house quiet and still
dead leaves on gnarled elm floor
toy soldiers in mock battle

wind-up Victrola
stuck groove replaying scratched silence
dust motes spiral where

your hard cracked peasant's
hands grind crushed roots, mix paint
recording absence

ghostly forms which can't
be seen save in a certain
layered glazed imprint

wind rustling a curtain
lifted by fog rolling up
in flat white cotton

wisps, lines left by scrape
of forks on white table linen
peeling paint-strips on the stoop

the silent unseen women
dried seed pods on makeshift racks
your paintings summon,

bundles of stacked sticks,
haul the hard won harvest home
along ice-cracked cart tracks

to Chadds Ford, roof beams
like bleached bones, a ship's upturned keel,
sheltered from storms

by torn scraps of net, pale
paper hands rest on a worn coat
hung on a bent nail

remnants of lives cut short
(freeze-framed Marie-Celeste)
the moment they stepped out

only a palimpsest
remains, a patina of years,
lingers to the last

the Helgas and Christinas
whose images you fix
to our retinas'

haunted swollen backs
soldered to the brain
in pinprick pencil strokes

so that even when
they're not there, we see them still
looking out, looking in…

Andrew, the son of NC Wyeth, another famous American painter, worked from his father's studio in Chadds Ford, Pennsylvania, and also made annual pilgrimages to Maine, where he took daily walks over a period of more than twenty years around the neighbouring farms, including the Olsen's, where he met Christina, a disabled woman who became the subject of his most famous painting, Christina's World, which depicts the known limits of her existence, the furthest Christina was ever able to take herself, by crawling down into a field to look back up towards her house, a scene he painstakingly recreated, reimagining her younger self.

During the 60's and 70's Andrew embarked upon an obsessive series of 240 drawings and paintings of nudes and portraits, all of a German immigrant and neighbour in Pennsylvania, Helga Testorff, which were kept hidden and secret for many years. Many of these works were not seen until after his death in 2009.

## Skin Memory

eyes closed
fingertips probing
the narrowing space
between us

igniting sparks
sensed
before touched

our
personal antennae
transmitting
imprint of years

brush
stroke
caress

each barely perceptible
tongue
tipped
lick

reconnects us through time

skin memory

## What I Saw / All Things Fall

I saw a cat chase a leaf
I saw a dog chase a cat
I saw a girl chase a dog
I saw a leaf chase a girl

I saw a seed in a trench
I saw a trench grow a tree
I saw a tree bear a fruit
I saw a fruit drop a seed

The blossoms fall in the orchard
The silk threads fall from the fingers
The soldiers fall in the battle
All things fall

I saw a man ride a horse
I saw a horse plough a field
I saw a field grow with corn
I saw the corn clutch a hare

I saw a hare hide in the moon
I saw the moon shine on a dog
I saw a dog hunt for a man
I saw a man scythe down the corn

The moonlight falls on the mountain
The poppies fall in the meadow
The heroes fall in the forest
All things fall

I saw a worm on a hook
I saw a fish eat a worm
I saw a man catch a fish
I saw a worm eat a man

# happiness is a warm gun

## bang bang, shoot shoot

## Trefoil Arch

a little used corner of Central Park, 2014

I glimpse an opening
follow the squirrel-droppinged path
down towards a low arch
beneath a worn stone bridge

inside the shade is cool, the air
surprisingly fragrant, sage and leaf-mould
downloads of memory, clawed
bird tracks scratched on floor and walls

and at the far end a hanging
curtain of ivy, dried paper
feathers, louvred light
one world to another

the ivy rustles as it parts
whispering close-kept secrets

## Loeb's Boathouse

Manhattan 2014

1

sitting in Central Park
beneath peeled plane trees
a lone sail boat tacks
this way then that
across the still Pond –

how long should I stay here
watching? – time to go, I think…
like Godot's tramps I do not move
the boat becalmed and drifting
waits for a breeze

2

it's only later I learn
the boats are radio controlled
operated by old men on benches
crested blazers and cravats
companionably engrossed

a small boy in outsized
yachting cap dances at water's
edge where his father
earnestly absorbed
operates a remote

not noticing his son's
urgent clamour to steer
nor his complaining stomp
back to his mother eager
with camera, cap discarded

3

the minute the sun sets
a young Chinese boy
gathers the beached boats
*stella maris, kittiwake*
with shepherd's crook

hauling each one home
covers the old men's knees
with plaid travel blankets
dozing in the evening light
feeling the wind pick up

fallen leaves carpet the water
the abandoned yachting cap
bobs and floats beyond all reach
we stare into the darkness
rearranging the rugs

## The Hits Keep Coming

T-shirts on Bethesda Terrace, Central Park, NY

*Jesus is my number one*
*the Devil has the best tunes*

a choir is singing –
by an adjacent stone wall
an addict shoots up

*

*this is not Facebook*
*stop checking me out*

leaning forward she
poses Monroe-like, shimmies
while the cameras flash

*

*I used to be a plastic bag*
*(now I'm just a waste of space)*

glasses, puppy fat
scooter disconsolately
trailing behind her

*

gay wedding couple
wearing matching pink T-shirts
under dove grey suits

*I'm Bride* and *I'm Groom*

*

confetti falls like
autumn covering them all
the hits keep coming

## Three Cool Cats

Metro Center Subway Station DC

hustling on the subway platform
singing old soul classics *a capella*

they've still got all the moves
and soon we're all dancing in the streets

taking time out from working on the chain gang
the hits just keep on coming

papa's got a brand new bag
put your money where your mouth is

and the nickels, dimes and dollars
rain down under the boardwalk

papa's still a rolling stone
but he ain't too proud to beg

we keep on waiting in the midnight hour
till we hear it through the grapevine

war – what is it good for?
is it just my imagination

or are we for once in our lives
one nation under a groove

reaching out till we'll be there
boarding the love train

for a rainy night in Georgia
sitting on the dock of the bay

but lawdy Miss Clawdy, the moment passes
they pick up their dollars, bow to the four corners

then drift away down the tracks of my tears
these ghosts of wonder and temptation

standing in the shadow of love
ain't that a shame… Freddy may be dead

and only fools may fall in love
but uptight everything is alright

we know we may be waiting, still anticipating
for all those things we may never possess

but till then we must try a little tenderness
this old heart of mine's gonna keep on truckin'

till we finally bring it on home
oh yes, I'm the great pretender

## The Chairs

Harvard, Cambridge MA 2014

at first there's just one
it appears unexpected
one week day morning

glowing, white, pristine
smooth, sleek lines, functional, clean
washable plastic

announcing itself
boldly as an alien might –
the monolith from

*A Space Odyssey* –
we give it a clear wide berth
as we pass it by

where has it come from,
why has it chosen this spot
to claim for its home?

we take its picture
with our cell phones uploading
it on to Facebook

soon it goes viral
ten thousand hits on you tube
in less than two hours

but that's just the start
the next morning there are two
a cell divided

an exact copy
angled towards the other
obliquely as if

in coded discourse
each waiting for an opening –
you made it? me too…

by week's end eight more
have sprouted on the lower
lawn, within a month

you can no longer
count them in a single sweep
they've arranged themselves

as site-specific
live art, bold conversation
pieces inviting

our interaction
except that we don't, no one
ever sits on them

or rearranges
their mute configurations –
each day there are more

soon they occupy
every corner, every nook,
multi-coloured now

black, brown, yellow, red
every pigment in between
proliferating…

the rumours are rife –
are they breeding, do they have
hidden unseen roots

underground tubers
multiplying tentacles
cracking the concrete

or is some divine
hand at work here whose purpose
is withheld from us?

then one day someone
dares to sit on one of them –
his claim's not believed

till he posts selfies
on all the campus websites,
smiling survivor

it's not long before
copy-cat violations
spread like forest fire

the chairs, some argue,
splitting public opinion,
are a gift from God

to be revered, while
others see them as the new
must-have, measuring

their new-found status
with rituals of observance
springing up, kinship

people start leaving
coins, keepsakes, flowers, photographs
messages of hope

then one semester
students kidnap one, replace
the Chancellor's Chair

with it in Founder's
refusing to hand it back
(this is Year Zero)

against such daily
proliferation, they claim,
what does one matter?

the general public
is outraged demanding that
the chair is returned

in the tense stand-off
which follows the National Guard
places a cordon

around the campus
but soon they are over-run
not by the students

but the surge of chairs
spreading unstoppably, an
ebola virus

so when the missing
chair's returned they can't agree
where it should be placed –

till someone has the
bright idea of siting it
alone on a piece

of empty ground in
the next county to see if
a new colony

will grow... I'm looking
at it right now from inside
our new storm shelter

strong, self-sufficient,
patient, but my daughter thinks
it's looking lonely

she wants to bring it
inside but I am fearful,
it may replicate,

some giant seed pod
biding its time in the dark,
she wants to take out

one of her old dolls
I tell her to wait a while
let's see what happens

but she puts it there
anyway while I'm sleeping –
next day both are gone…

# fixing a hole

## Only in Brighton

Sauron the Dark Lord
playing Frisbee with his pals
on a Brighton beach

launches a high wide
perfect parabola, one
ring to rule them all

## No More Heroes (part 2)

While still at University
Lord Olivier asked me round to tea –
no kidding, how could I refuse? –
but I felt so nervous I got quite pissed,
can't recall what he said, not the slightest gist –
my acting ambitions went straight down the tubes.

Next I plumped for a real old-timer –
Ebeneezer Elliott, the Corn Law Rhymer.
Now he was a really radical geezer:
"Bread not Blood!" Right on, Ebeneezer.
But the more I read, the same old story –
just another closet Tory.

I never went through a rebellious phase,
no Ho Chi Minhs or Maus or Chés,
no, those were my folk revivalist days –
I strode like a figure from Mummers' plays:
Jack-in-the-Green or Mr. Punch,
who deep down, surely, harboured the hunch
that I wasn't cut out for a night with the boys –
so I swallowed my swozzle and sought my own voice.

I don't have heroes now, they fall
too easily from their pedestal,
lie scattered far and near.
Like plaster ducks upon a wall,
whose frozen flight and mocking call
lead you precisely nowhere at all,
they look away, don't give a damn –
they're not who've got me where I am,
so: "where do we go from here…?"

## Guilty Pleasures

I must have spent a thousand hours
in darkened cinemas – such guilty pleasures
especially in the afternoons,

such profligate waste, such indulgence
when you know you should be in the fresh air
doing something useful and you can still hear

your grandmother's voice chastising you
'haven't you anything better to do?'
but when the lights begin to dim

and you hear once more the familiar strain
of MGM or Pearl & Dean
there's really only one answer:

over the rainbow lies buried treasure
and the place you're travelling to is home.

## Cut

NYC – first trip

it's like stepping into a movie
(Woody Allen, Scorsese)
everything feels so familiar –
the Sikh cab driver, the pretty young
girl I share the ride with from JFK
who tells me her life story
who gives me her number
who asks me to come up and see her
some time as we drop her off near
the drug store – *you are now entering*
*Queen's* – then across the East River
*(I could've been a contender)*
I'm on such a high five roll
that even when you don't appear

to meet me as arranged I just call
from the phone booth on the corner
like I've seen a thousand times before
in God knows how many film noir
scenes and when you're not there
to pick up I know just what to do –
take the subway up to Herald Square
ride the elevator right on
up to the top of the Empire
State *(An Affair to Remember)* when
before I've even reached a couple
of blocks I walk smack right into you –
they couldn't script this – best to quit
before some director calls out 'Cut!'

## Vicarious

I seem to live each day by proxy
through music, movies, books,
experiencing the roller coaster
of other people's journeys
more than my own which takes,
it seems, a back seat always,
my default position to tell
stories and incidents from my past,
anecdotes ever so slightly
embroidered to raise a smile
here, elicit a response
there, sometimes I almost
think I've lived even a dull
approximation of that experience

but in art it's all so different,
frequently it stops me in my tracks –
I walk into a gallery of Rothkos
and at once am overwhelmed with tears,
or when Tess's note is pushed beneath
Angel's *rug* as well as his door,
or Miles Davis playing *Blue in Green* –
each of these contains a moment
so intense, so heightened, it unlocks
a door once opened I never want to close
evoking longings, dreams, fears
not embodied in real life

and it's not just art – if anything
cheap sentiment is worse,
an unlikely happy ending,
small acts of self-sacrifice
or, especially, when somebody is *nice*,
the slightest thing unhinges me –
in movies I've learned how to feel,

how to react, how to behave,
things I can't translate to what is real,
which always seems to matter less –
I've heard the mermaids singing
and though they haven't sung for me
I keep on listening just in case
the anaesthetic's wearing off

for even these old songs and films
are from a former bygone day –
I can't relate to *now*, it seems –
Astaire dancing cheek to cheek,
Garland lighting up the screen
lamenting the man who got away,
Chet Baker's funny valentine
who despite having a physique
(like mine) that's somewhat less than Greek
implores me still to stay –
I'm not such a fool,
I never did, never will, possess
Gable's charm, or Kelly's grace,
Flynn's dash, or Bogart's cool

but something keeps pulling me back
(like the bracelet on Barbara Stanwyck's
ankle in *Double Indemnity*)
the promise and allure
of a life fully lived, not
filtered down vicariously
or played safe, but on the edge,
reckless, without fear or shame –
humankind, we're told, cannot bear
very much reality but
the dvd seems permanently
on pause – either I'm
going to walk through that door, or watch
the re-run for the umpteenth time…

## Reading Signs

My wife's friend's younger sister Ruth
views the world as literal truth,
assiduously registers
those cartoon, clip art characters
on road signs, rest rooms, traffic lights –
obediently she imitates:
for green crouch low, get ready, set;
stand tall and primed for red alert.

*

I daily walk past different signs:
bargains, sales, the ends of lines,
closing down, prices slashed,
two for one, while stocks last,
one time offer, don't miss out –
I always do where Ruth would not.

## The Joys & Perils of Cataloguing

*Procrastination is the thief of time.* Edward Young: Night Thoughts

So –

after you have arranged all of your books,
non fiction by subject, fiction by author
alphabetically on shelves around your room

and after you have transcribed all your old video tapes
painstakingly, one by one, onto dvd,
catalogued, indexed, cross-referenced,

systematised your collection of old records, cd's and cassettes,
sorted all the loose photographs
into albums labelled and dated,

rationalised receipts,
shredded all the bills and bank statements,
filed (late) this year's tax return

and then looked around with satisfaction
at what you have accomplished,
what does it all add up to?

Is this, in the end, all that a life
comes down to – a series of lists?
And although there is always pleasure

to be had in ticking each item off
until there is nothing left to be sorted,
how then will you fill that long stretch of hours

that await you down the hall way
and navigate the uncharted road without a map?
These 'night thoughts' of my own

arrest my sleep with troubled dreams
of old and unresolved failings from the past.
How many more distractions to delay

must I find before I start to live the moments
as they chance upon me?
Perhaps this poem's just one more of them…

So –

## Pile of Pennies

you spread out before me
six well-worn brass pennies:
one coin represents *you*,
you say, the rest are friends,
family, other people
in your life; place yourself
first, then arrange the rest
to represent the way
each relates to you and
you to them, notice the
pattern they make and how
*you* fit into it all.

I look down, I'm nowhere,
just a single pile of
pennies with me at the
bottom – some day, I know,
I'll need to knock it down

# tomorrow never knows

## Golden Hill

former local library in Urmston

a low wooden hut
in the middle of the park
a short cut from school

inside a haven
(the playground's raining children)
shelter from the storm

oases of books
escaping to distant lands
keep the world at bay

now leaves pile the door
an empty roundabout turns
rusty swing creaking

## Brook Road

former local library in Flixton

here at the cross roads
a giant granite boulder
dropped by the ice age

stands at the entrance
a direct link with the past –
promise of secrets

to be found inside
its 1930's curved dome
bowed stained glass windows

like a cruise liner
inviting you to set sail
on a long voyage

of discovery –
now it's pulled up its gangplank
and shut its port-holes

a wreck cast adrift
weeds like barnacles crusting
its once leaded roof

looted long years since…
if I could dive beneath its
great barrier reef

for one single book
to bring back to the shoreline
which one would it be…?

## Woodsend

former local library near Davyhulme

on a round about
with no tree, let alone wood
in sight, litter-strewn,

a high bell tower
loomed darkly incongruous
above steep gables,

concrete breeze-block walls,
flag pole, more like a fortress
than a library –

a bell I never heard
ring out as welcome, warning
or distress until

the day it burned down,
whether by arson or chance,
caught in the updraft

of paper licking
flames, splintering glass, struck down
in the *kristallnacht*

of broken pipe dreams,
its motto-bearing banner
fluttering on the breeze –

"books can be dangerous,
the best ones should be labelled,
they could change your life" –

tolling its death knell,
once rung could not be silenced:
*quamvis sum parva*

*tamen audior*
*ampla per arva* – "I may
be small but my voice

nevertheless will
call across far distances…"
I can hear it still.

## Prospect

former local library in Cadishead

at the junction of
Liverpool and Prospect Roads
the edge of the moss

stood the library
two bay windows flanking steps
in white Portland stone

blackened by dark years
of steel-works-belched dirty smoke
hung above the town

sulphurous yellow
staining the stone like droppings
from an extinct bird

fading in the mist
rolling always from the moss
where folk still clung fast

houses built on stilts
patrolled by cut-throat pirates
with wild unchained dogs

or old wizened crones
who flung unwary children
in black cooking pots

hanging their bleached bones
on gnarled and blasted hawthorns
as wordless warnings –

keep out you, go back –
the huddled warmth and blanket
of books lay waiting

light burning behind
those two grimy bowed windows
to welcome us home

free from harm lurking
in fevered imaginings
rescued from danger

but when we were asked
what kind of books we wanted
we'd in a heart beat

clamour at once for
wizards, fairies, leprechauns
pirates, witches, ghosts

mysteries to solve
that thrilling frisson of fear
we secretly craved

to brighten the blank
realities of a life
whose only prospect

was the eight hour shift
the fiery furnace steel mill
Dante's Inferno

books were my ticket
my map for hidden treasure
over the rainbow…

the library's closed now
steel works gone, school boarded up
the Portland stone cleaned

housing a lawyer's –
wills, probate, conveyances –
duller, safer worlds

## Great Aunt Lily's Tea Set

Scheherazade of the Moss

Great Aunt Lily's tea set
sits now at the foot of our stairs,
a family heirloom in a corner
cupboard, fragile blue and white

china, twelve cups, saucers,
each with matching plate,
sugar bowl, cream jug, for those days
you were descended on by whole families

for high tea in stiff starched straight-
-back crinoline, Sunday collars and neck ties –
you can tell that once its use was regular
for some of the pieces let in light

when you hold them up, crazed over
with cracks like Great Aunt Lily's
face, or how I conjure it,
for I've never seen her picture,

only heard stories of her
from my mother, so that now she's
the stuff of legend, and I conflate
her with the tea set, past its prime but

still defiant, as I imagine her
gaze would be if her portrait
lay before me on my lap with the other
family albums, daring trips to the Swiss

lakes and mountains years before
package holidays, no cheap flight
then, only overnight sleepers,
wrestling with labelled suitcases,

railway timetables and souvenirs
of walking stick enamel badges,
apostle spoons, my grandfather's camera
(an early Box Brownie) recording for

posterity with place names he wrote
in meticulous handwriting where
they announce still in immaculate
copper-plate Interlaken, the Brenner Pass

where my grandmother slipped and broke her foot –
the walking stick put to frequent use
on future bracing Cunard cruises
to Madeira, Cape Verde, the Azores

for grandfather's damaged lungs each winter,
then back home, to work, a printer
on the edge of Cadishead Moss
where Great Aunt Lily rented a house

from him, her own money all gone, caught
in the net of some South Sea Bubble or
Wall Street Crash, or the fall of Weimar's
Republic, some such calamity, all of it

lost, even her husband whose
name my mother never knew – he was
simply known as "uncle" – whom Lily met
while in Canada (he was trying to cross

the Yukon on a mule) and somehow their
lives collided on the wide open prairies
of Saskatchewan, (we have a blanket
still from those fabled far-off days –

Canadian Pacific). As well there was
a painting hung above the fireplace
in Great Aunt Lily's meagre house
stuck out there alone on the Moss

like some ancient lone pioneer
in her cabin on the frontier,
her homestead, her own little house
on the prairie, rabbits hung on the door,

shot gun propped up in the corner
ready to fight off Indians or a grizzly bear –
it showed a train, an iron horse
roaring across the plains, plumes of white

smoke belching from its belly as it
tried to outrun marauding Iroquois
and Chippewa whose war-paint faces
framed with coloured braids and feathers

screamed for scalps and justice
while Great Aunt Lily, face like a squaw's,
stoked the embers of the parlour
fire flickering beneath far-off teepees…

How my mother longed for that picture
on the wall, she never did find out
what eventually happened to it
when Great Aunt Lily died, when the house

was sold and all her treasures parcelled out,
but as I would remind her later
she had it still for it would pour
out in the thousand and one stories

she'd tell of Sundays at Great Aunt Lily's
(Scheherazade of the Moss)
where each week the prized tea set
all the way from Canada was brought out –

how it crossed the Rockies, canoed down rivers,
survived the Lusitania
before fetching up here in this nowhere,
this patch of bogs and marshes

still forgotten a century later
(two non-descript brick bungalows
occupy the nettle-strewn hollows
where Great Aunt Lily's rented cottage sat)

where every month she read from Old Moore's
Almanack sucking on mintoes,
savouring each foretold disaster
with such relish and delight

that if ever my mother asked her
some question she couldn't answer
she'd croak, "Let's see what Old Moore's
got to say about it – oh yes,

nothing good can ever come of it,"
throwing back her head with a shout
of pure undiminished pleasure,
and away would go the tea set

until the next time when my mother
would gaze with longing at the picture
of the Indians and the Iron Horse
and spirit herself away there…

Now Great Aunt Lily's tea set
is an heirloom, a treasure
far too fragile and precious
for use, handed down, each plate,

saucer, cup pale and delicate
as an egg, a long dead dodo's
egg that can never hatch again, but:
if I hold a cup against the light

and if I flick the rim of it
I hear in the final fading of that
resounding ring Lily's cracked voice
rasping down the years

further doomed predictions from Old Moore's,
and though she believed every word of it,
she'd rock back in her chair, relight
her pipe, call to Stella, my mother,

a wide-eyed child of eight, to pour
another cup and damn the consequences…
Maybe if we took the tea set out
from its cupboard on the stair's

bend and drank just once from it,
we might imbibe as well that spirit
of derring-do, adventure,
indomitable recklessness,

risk and riot and devil-may-care –
but every time I pass it on the stairs
in what now serves for daily exercise
its low rattle sounds like distant thunder…

## Crofts Bank

I'm sitting in the library where I wrote my first play (more than forty years ago) and it's unrecognisable. Gone are the fixed, polished wooden shelves; gone are the separate rooms for newspapers and periodicals, where the old men would sit each day, gathering like rooks from the sycamores in the park across the way, their wives having tipped them out for the morning to keep them from getting under their feet so they could get on with their chores unencumbered; gone is the reference library on the upper floor, its hushed walls lined with atlases and encyclopaedias; gone, too, is the desk where you queued to have the books you'd chosen stamped and ticketed. Now it's surrounded by a shopping mall; the inside resembles an airport, with all the ducts and pipes of its central heating and air conditioning systems defiantly on show beneath a grey, industrial, metal warehouse roof. People wander in and out carrying cappuccinos in Styrofoam cups; the librarians' desk is more like a supermarket check-out, all bleeps and pings, as bar codes are scanned across computer screens.

A boy in school uniform comes in with his father. I see myself at his age, coming in here half a century ago with my grandfather, when the librarian knew every book she had in stock. "If you've enjoyed that," she'd say, "why not try this…?" Now it's all self-service check-in and check-out, and the school boy is ignored. I watch a pensioner fumble with the mouse of yet another computer terminal, looking around in vain for someone's eye to catch for help. The staff, walled in by a circular battery of terminals, like something out of NASA, do not notice her, their eyes glued to their screens, fingers tapping fervently at keyboards, headphones clamped to their ears, with signs directing "customers" to further remote computer stations. I find a single plastic chair and table, forgotten in a corner, perch precariously and begin to write this down.

*

My grandfather, however, would probably have welcomed many of these changes. He loved anything new and embraced the latest innovations. He died long before digital technology but he would have surfed every wave, I'm certain, and would now be completely at ease with i-pads, mobiles, apps, tablets, Facebook and twitter. He would read e-books on kindle and subscribe to articles on line; he'd write blogs and post entries on YouTube: "How to Make a Garden Pond…"

Earlier today I'd visited the printing works he'd built and run for more than forty years. This autumn it celebrates a hundred years, like the First World War, and, having lain derelict for several years, now hums and buzzes with the sound of children playing, for it has reinvented itself as a pre-school nursery – *Flutterbies* – and the printing presses have given way to toy cars and tricycles, which the children alight upon like multi-coloured butterflies. A small group is busily occupied with potato prints, which Tina, their teacher, is pinning up on a wall in readiness for the Anniversary Party in a month's time. I could imagine my grandfather incorporating these into the design for the invitations. As I leave, Tina claps her hands together and calls, "Gather round, everyone." They all cluster together on what Tina calls the "story mat" to listen, rapt, thumbs in mouths, to her reading *The Gruffalo* to them from one of the many books they appear to have there.

Here, back in the library, I notice a poster above the Children's Section exhorting us to "log on, download, sign up" – not a mention of "read" or "listen" – while one of the librarians, with a local authority name tag around her neck, briskly requests that I vacate my perch, for the table I'm leaning on is needed for a new printer she's carrying…

*

At the top of the stairs leading down to the shopping mall is a small exhibition to commemorate the centenary of World War 1: posters, photocopied photographs, some books. I pick one up. "Please put that back," hisses a different librarian.

"Books in the exhibition are not for reading."

At the exit there's a shop selling lego, birthday cards, fluorescent stickers and "ready-spex reading glasses", but nothing to actually read.

## The Memory Box

I came across it while clearing out my mother's flat after she died, at the bottom of the closet by the front door, in what she called her glory hole – a small, old wooden box with a sliding lid. Stiff after years of non-use, I gently prised it open, pulling back the years.

Inside lay buried treasure – a worn leather pouch containing my grandfather's service papers from World War 1, his British War and Allied Victory medals, and a handwritten menu for a lunch of bully beef, oatmeal bread and a square of chocolate on Christmas Day in the trenches 1916. I recognised at once the immaculate copperplate from the handwritten labels he attached to all the photographs he'd take, years later, released from that hell along the Western Front, from trips to the Alps, Swiss lakes, Mediterranean cruises, the same care in spite of all the privations. I tried to picture him, huddled by a pile of sand bags, blowing on his fingers protruding from hand-knitted mittens sent by his mother, trying to force some last vestige of warmth into them, before taking out his fountain pen from the depths of his greatcoat pocket and writing out this menu for the amusement of his comrades.

He was that rare combination of tolerance and Methodism – teetotal, abstinent, moderate, yet forgiving, liberal and kind. If you met him now, you might take him for a Quaker, carefully measuring out his words, spooling out just enough for what was necessary, always saving more for later. And so I've often wondered what particular sense of duty it was that drove him to join up as soon as he was old enough in the spring of 1915: Manchester Regiment, Signal Corps.

He laid wire crawling on his belly across No Man's Land to carry the dots and dashes of encrypted Morse Code messages he'd later playfully teach me as a small boy delighting in the eloquent secrets carried in their elegant, binary, dancing script, like laying a trail of twigs you might follow on a child's treasure map, Indian tracks, animal paw prints, that only he could decipher, like some ancient shaman.

To me he was the source of all knowledge, his every utterance a fount of wisdom, endlessly patient. In the small room adjoining the kitchen, dubbed the morning room by his wife, and which also served as his study after he retired, the walls were lined with books, mostly atlases, ordnance survey maps, coastal charts, globes and manuals. He'd been a printer and in the drawer of his desk was a set of old wooden printing blocks, through which he taught me to recognise the shapes of letters and words by feel and touch. He was also something of an inventor, devising all manner of labour-saving devices for my grandmother in the kitchen, or the garden, and his desk was frequently strewn with meticulous pencil drawings.

Rooted in the traditions of his family and faith, a lay preacher, local councillor, he yet loved modern innovation, always seeking the most up-to-date technical refinements to the printing presses he kept rolling through the night in the works across the road from where he lived in the lee of the steel works, these same printing presses whose deep-throated rumble my mother would dance to as a child. In the 1920's he bought the second car to be seen in Cadishead (the first belonged to the local doctor); he flew aeroplanes at air shows; he befriended captains on cruise liners and discussed breakthroughs in communications, while he still remembered the language of the signal flags he'd used in the trenches.

He fought against the Ottomans in the Dardenelles, the Bulgars in Macedonia and the Germans in France, though it is impossible for me to imagine him raising a hand in anger. At Gallipoli, a piece of schrapnel lodged in his left buttock forcing him to make his way, alone, by mule to the nearest Field Hospital. He was lucky, he always said, for this meant that he missed the massacre that later took place there.

While he sat painfully astride the mule, he asked his C/O which road he should take. "Don't worry," he was told, "the mule knows the way." And indeed he did. For the rest of the day he rode through cypress groves in a narrow valley flanked by mountains, listening to the sounds of strange birds, insects and running water, the war a world away. Just as the sun was going down he caught sight of the hospital across a river, which the mule refused point blank to cross. Nothing my grandfather did could persuade it and the water was too deep for him to cross unaided. So he pulled out his flags from his haversack and signalled his predicament to the other side requesting further instructions. Once again he was told not to worry, that the mule would take him the long way round, a few miles downstream to a bridge where he could cross and be with them by the next morning.

But when he finally made his way there as the sun was coming up over the mountains, sleep-deprived and in pain from the added insult of a sharp wasp sting to the site of his injury, the field hospital was all but destroyed. A rogue shell had landed nearby in the night, leaving nothing but a huge crater. Mercifully there'd been no serious casualties but they were already packing up to find a new, safer base where they could set up, and my grandfather continued his weary exodus on foot, limping badly from his undressed wound, the mule now being used to carry supplies and equipment.

But he survived and rejoined his unit some weeks later, after the ignominious retreat from Gallipoli, in Salonika, where he contracted pneumonia, which was to recur throughout the rest of his life, flaring up every few years or so, and from which he finally died when he was just 68, but we're getting ahead of ourselves. He always felt he'd lived a full life, lucky to have survived when so many didn't. Following a period of recuperation back in Blighty, he returned once again to the war, this time to France, not far from the Belgian border, but not to the fighting. He stayed mostly behind the lines intercepting and interpreting further Morse Code messages, with occasional forays into No Man's Land to lay more wires.

The story of the mule is one of just two stories I know about his wartime experiences, and I didn't hear them from him. I pieced them together from snatches of conversation and occasional remarks from my mother and grandmother, and then from my own research. He himself would never speak of that time, certainly not to me. When, as a small boy, I caught sight of the schrapnel scar when he took me swimming one afternoon in the Irish Sea off the North Wales coast, he quickly changed the subject. "Just an old war wound," he'd said.

The other story concerns the handwritten menu I found in that old wooden box with the sliding lid when cleaning out the closet in my mother's flat. I can absolutely picture him writing that and reading it aloud to the other men as a gentle joke, and I can imagine them all smiling thinly. I remember my grandmother saying that he had once said there was always a mist along the front line, and as the pale sun tried to break through on that freezing, grey Christmas morning, they heard a voice calling to them, not a hundred yards away, across the mud and ice of No Man's Land.

"Hey, Tommy? Merry Christmas…" Then the faint, halting strains of *Silent Night* floating through the mist.

*"Stille nacht*
*Heilige nacht…"*

"The British Tommies," my grandmother said, "tried to join in, but a lump stuck in their throats." Instead, at the end, they offered a quiet, dignified round of applause till, emboldened, one of them started up with *Good King Wencelas*, which was followed by *God Rest, Ye Merry Gentlemen*, which gradually the rest of the men took up.

*"Glad tidings of comfort and joy, comfort and joy*
*Glad tidings of comfort and joy…"*

Through the mist my grandfather discerned a piece of white sheet being waved as a flag.

"Hey – Hubert, you're the signaller: what does it say?"

"I think we all know what a white flag means," he replied. "We come in peace."

And then, one by one, they climbed stiffly out of the trenches and proceeded to walk gingerly across the space between the two front lines, while, already emerging out of the mist, a small group of the Kaiser's men were walking towards them. There was a brief awkward silence when they finally reached each other, but then one of the Germans put his hand inside his greatcoat – the British soldiers all tensed – only to smile when the German pulled out a small flask of rum which he duly passed around.

"It was the only time I ever tasted alcohol," my grandfather ruefully recalled, "but it would have been impolite to have refused."

Then cigarettes were shared, photographs of families and sweethearts admired, and my grandfather showed them his menu and asked if they might care to join them for Christmas lunch. But the laughter was cut short by the sound of a shell exploding further down the line and both sides beat a hasty retreat back to their respective trenches wishing each other "Good Luck" and "Merry Christmas".

"If you'd have asked me then," my grandfather reportedly said, "what we were doing fighting men who were just the same as us, I couldn't for the life of me have told you. I still can't."

And that was it. Never another word did he speak about his time in the war, and now, as we commemorate the centenary of the outbreak of this so-called war to end all wars, I have that menu still in the same old leather pouch, while the box that contained it is now with my son in his home with his own family. The other day I asked him what he uses it for.

"Oh," he said, "I keep recipe cards in it that I cut out of newspapers, and memory sticks for my laptop."

My grandfather would have appreciated that.

## Remembrance

*Remember me when I am gone away,*
*Gone far away into the silent land…*

from *Remember* by Christina Rossetti: one of my grandfather's two favourite poems – see end

Inching his way forward in mud knee-deep
under a sniper's moon, edging past
the skittering horses, breath freezing in statues
settling on the shoulders of the men, grey ghosts
twitching beneath the humming barbed wire
starred with torn scraps of letters fluttering
in the wind, photographs of sweethearts,
snags of cloth from great coats, puttees,
calico and khaki prayer flags my grandfather
posts, a silent semaphore of hope
he squeezes under, flicking aside the rats
with glove-stiff fingers crawling clear
into the lunar landscape of no man's land
belaying the signal wire behind him…

Pausing to get his bearings he lets his eyes
accustom to the terrain, the ground hot
despite the winter chill, ice crystals forming
round his upper lip while smoke and ash
from the morning's battle still smoulders
smarting his eyes; he skirts the rims of craters
careful lest the wire catches, stuck fast,
caught in the random ruin of war –
piles of boots like some macabre rummage sale
(sometimes with feet attached, sometimes not)
form scattered cairns that mark his way
to the nearby camp, his second unit's HQ
where he's to join the wire to their transmitter,
a slender long umbilical that can't be cut…

My grandfather – preacher, printer, vegetable grower
who back home on his allotment plants
prize-winning dahlias between rows of beans and spinach –
looks around him as he crawls thinking

it will be a century at least before this land
bears fruit again despite the fertile bone meal
it's now fed with, the blood red poppies cling
to the craters' edge silver in the moonlight
leaching the land of all colour, monochrome mocking.
Three hours later he reaches the camp
and within minutes he's sending and receiving
the Morse code messages he reads like Braille
with his fingers in readiness for the next day's
carnage as clouds cover the moon…

The men on the night watch make room for him
by the fire, they are singing the soldier's anthem –
*and when they ask us, and they're certainly going to ask us*
*oh we'll never tell them, no we'll never tell them…*
My grandfather takes out a stub of pencil,
scratches on a scrap of paper a message in Morse
he knows he'll never send, blind dots and dashes
tossed on the dying embers of the flames,
smoke drifting high into the night sky
to float down the years in a petal shower
of dust and ash waiting for me, now,
to piece it all together, decipher and decode:
.-- .... .- - / -- . -. / --- .-. / --. --- -.. ... / .- .-. . / - .... . ... .
.-- .... .- - / -- .- -.. / .--. ..- .-. ... ..- .. - ...

Trans:
*… what men or gods are these…?*
*what mad pursuits…?*

from 'Ode to a Grecian Urn' by Keats,
my grandfather's other favourite poem

## Reparation

Why is it that my grandfather, who so loved people, elected to exclude them from all the photographs he took?

Living and working in the shadow of factory chimneys, cooling towers and spoil tips, the thickly polluted canal which one sticky summer's afternoon self-ignited and exploded at Bob's Ferry, every year on doctor's orders he'd take himself away on winter cruises or walking in the Swiss Alps, the clear sea or mountain air bringing welcome balm and reparation to war-damaged lungs.

On his return he'd bring souvenirs and stories, the ship's log he'd kept, noting the minutiae of ports and currents, wind direction and temperature, a ritual he repeated throughout the year, tapping the barometer in the hall first thing each morning, recording each month's rainfall, and then off to his home-made dark room to develop the photographs he'd taken, which he'd place into albums, meticulously annotated in immaculate copper plate, date, time, location. But never, if he could help it, any people.

There'd be the occasional exception – the ship's captain, the mountain guide, a distant goat herder.

I have some still today, but not many. Most were thrown out by my mother long ago. I can imagine her impatience with them, hear her child's voice asking that same question – why do you take such lonely pictures? – and then my grandmother's practised response: "Oh, you know Hubert and his views…"

I wonder if the answer isn't much simpler. Surrounded as he was the rest of the year by noise, the pounding furnaces of the steel works, the twenty-four hour rolling of the printing presses, the ceaseless choke of traffic along the Liverpool Road, I believe he fell into the solitude and silence of those empty seas and high mountains like a Lethean embrace.

He told me once, when he was a boy, Liverpool Road was little more than a country lane; children would play whip-

and-top along it undisturbed. It was 1910 and the newly crowned King George V was coming to cut the ribbon to open the just-completed Steel Works. My grandfather stood at the roadside to watch him arrive. He found himself a good spot where there weren't many crowds. A few minutes later a black Daimler pulled up and out stepped the King to stretch his legs. No one but my grandfather appeared to spot him. He took a silver cigarette case from his overcoat and then tapped in turn each of his pockets in vain for a lighter. My grandfather, then only twelve years old, did not smoke, but he had a box of matches with him. He stepped forward, struck one and offered it to the King, who nodded and drew deeply on his now lit cigarette.

"Thank you, my boy. And what would you like to do when you grow up?"

"I'd like to drive a car like yours, sir."

The King laughed and shook my grandfather's hand. "Here's a shilling for you." Then he climbed back into his car, which drove on down the Liverpool Road to the site of the steel works.

Five years later, larger crowds lined either side of it as my grandfather, having taken another King's shilling, marched with all the rest of the Manchester Regiment to overcrowded trains and trenches, to Europe and to war, bringing back with him a pair of broken lungs and a yearning for high mountain passes and wide, empty seas – solace and reparation.

# a day in the life

## Silence at Ramscliffe

In 2002 the dairy farmer at Ramscliffe, North Devon was ordered to have his entire herd of cattle slaughtered in a contiguous cull because of an outbreak of foot and mouth in a neighbouring farm. His own cows were at the time of the cull disease free. This was captured in a powerful photographic essay called *Silence at Ramscliffe* by Devon photographer Chris Chapman for Beaford Arts.

(a ballad and lament to be sung – make up your own tune)

Over the hills the smoke is rising
Forming a mist across your eyes
So you can't see what's really happening
So you don't hear our muffled cries

Nothing is left now but the ashes
Of more than a thousand funeral pyres
Only the silence here at Ramscliffe
As it hums along the wires

Telling of heroes and of villains
And of men all in white coats
Oh there is so much we could tell you
But it just sticks here in our throats

Now that the television cameras
And the bloodhounds from the news
Have left just the silence here at Ramscliffe
The time has come for you to choose

Between the city and the country
Between what's old and what is new
So when you come here for the weekend
We're not here to spoil your view

And you can build all your wicker statues
And erect all your concrete cows
Placing your art in the travelling landscape
With all the funds that the state allows

And you can push all your Tesco trolleys
To the check-out's constant bleep
Drowning the silence here at Ramscliffe
Lest it disturbs you from your sleep

But you can't shut us out completely
Or erase us from your mind
For if you tie up loose ends too neatly
There's always something left behind

Over the years we've fed and clothed you
Given you everything you need
Now you just trample over our bodies
As into the ground we bleed

But like a tide that's not for turning
We will return along this track
And like Canute along the shoreline
You will never turn us back

And the silence here at Ramscliffe
And in countless other farms
Will be broken by our singing
As we gather back into our barns

And our song is a song for freedom
And our song is the right to roam
Back to the bosom that is Ramscliffe
Back to the bosom that is home

Then the farmyards will fill with laughter
And the barns will fill with song
Over the hillsides and the valleys
This is the place where we belong

Over the hills the smoke's now clearing
Lifting the mist from off our eyes
Now you will see what's really happening
Now you will hear our heart-felt cries

Filling the silence here at Ramscliffe
Like a baby's cry new-born
Ringing with hope for all our futures
Ushering in a brand new dawn…

*

Over the hills the smoke is rising
Forming a mist across your eyes
So you can't see what's really happening
So you don't hear our muffled cries

Nothing is left now but the ashes
Of more than a thousand funeral pyres
Only the silence here at Ramscliffe…

## First Sighting

bird book in hand, pointing, eight years old
black smoke rising in a far field

this first day in their new home
look, she cries, the swallows have come

a high freewheeling swoop and dive
alighting on the cowshed roof

which overlooks the burning pyres
or strung out along telegraph wires

like notes on a musical stave
and she is their treble clef –

she folds her wings, muscles not yet flexed
heads back inside to try what's next

*

years later she sits at her laptop
designing logos – a swallow's curve and dip

## All the Ghosts Walk with Us

*In front of her a colony of ants had established a thoroughfare across the way, where they toiled – a never-ending and heavy-laden throng. To look down upon them was like observing a city street from the top of a tower. She remembered that this bustle of ants had been in progress for years at the same spot – doubtless those of the old times were the ancestors to those which walked there now.*

Thomas Hardy: Return of the Native

*walking, weaving, weaving, walking*
*where's time for wedding…?*

Alan Garner: The Stone Book

1

and you...

walking across an open field
threaded by footpaths made
by generations of women
who walked these same ways
more than two hundred years ago
to the flax mill in whose shadow
our cottage now sits in the wind's lee
which whips the hair across our faces
tosses sparrows like puffballs from hedges
as returning field fares flock before us
a lone buzzard's mewing cry
marking the years

...are bearing witness

you
cannot stop talking
are caught in a loop of memory
of speculation, all the unsung
unnamed lives who trod this path before us
two centuries of walking, walking
alone in silent contemplation –
the weary trek from work at week's end –
or in company like today's
as the field unfolds beside us
unwrapping its stories in
acorns crunching underfoot

you
steady yourself in the mud
from last week's rain
hold your hip
already troubling you despite your youth
your mother's and your grandmother's
history opening up before you
an inheritance that awaits you down the years
walks with you just a few steps ahead of us
on this muddy track sticky with leaf mould
and memory

you
at a gate crossing a stile
to an adjacent field where a carved wooden figure,
a woman mill worker, points the way
follow her gaze
a seagull behind a tractor
in search of scraps and leavings
all the ghosts walk with you
but no one special by your side

2

while I...

walking this same path
as I have done a thousand times before
seeing it fresh and reborn
rearing up new before you
a hare startled in the field's shorn stubble
eyes and ears alert straining

...can feel their breath on my neck
and turn my collar to the wind

I
am telling you stories
pointing out landmarks

the flax dam, the mill race,
the waving tree, shadows and voices
bubbling to the surface around us
from the muddied fields, the dark pond
where frog spawn swell in the spring
and water boatmen skim the surface
like ballerinas *en pointe*
(as you once were)
a kingfisher
dipping low spears the mirrored
sky pinprick shards of light
glinting blue electric
gone in a blink – memory burns
the retina's back at water's edge
clogged now with rank flags and weeds…
a dried old snail draws in its horns

I
am seeing my son
at seven, ten and twelve years old
running ahead of me along the track
seeking king cups, sloes and four-leaved clovers, he
roots out stoats or deer in the copses –
the trees are thinning now
the wind tears the leaves from the branches
reveals the teeming crowds of walkers
all the countless other lives
who've passed this way before us
these shades whose voices drown us out
now sharply etched
watching

3

so we...

back home in the warm
sipping sherry in the silence

of our newly renovated front room
the evening closing in around us
sitting by the window where the front door
used to be, the only door, in this
one-up/one-down cottage dug out of the earth
for the families who worked at the mill
along with all the women, all those walkers
who knitted the fields with their feet
fields which once were blue
with the shimmer of flax
fibres teased by the retting
to be carted north to Crewkerne
to be turned into linen or sail cloth
where Nelson's fleet for Trafalgar
was coaxed and kitted out
or south to Bridport for hemp
strung between back yard alleyways
looped along wide boulevard rope walks
where all the hangmen's nooses in England
were knotted and made
the poor man's friend

...hear a far off drop and swing

we
look at old photos, study their faces
peering out from their posed pasts
the workers at the mill gates
the picnic in Pond Field
the children playing outside
on the step of the front door
the window where now we sit, look out
see them dancing in the dusk
late season's midges swarming round a light
before the year's first frost

we
draw metaphoric curtains to keep out the dark
(for as yet we do not have any

our renovations continue)
warming our feet on the under floor heating
which now covers the blue lias flags
laid directly on the bare earth
we discovered when we started
excavating the layers and lives
of families here before us
hearing their talk hover
in the centuries-old fireplace
(where the bricks are so delicate
they crumble in our fingers)
voices creaking as we shift a chair

we
lift a shard of glass we found
from a walled-up window at the back
hold it to the light
frosted with patterns of moons and stars
all the ghosts walk with us
their dreams and hopes rise with them
their faces crowd the window
looking in, looking out
the room waits, holds its breath –
it wants a grandfather clock
to fill it with its slow tick tock

4

thus you...

the next day
walking once more across the fields
skirting around the skeletal trees
walking and talking, holding your hip

...are making your own path

you
carry all the voices, all the ghosts

behind you in your shadow
watching with a fearful hope…

*walking, weaving, weaving, walking*
*where's time for wedding?*

5

then he...

he…

standing with the ghosts
at the edge of the field
straining to catch a glimpse of you
walking with your head lowered

...separates himself from the crowd

he
takes one small step
then waits
his mouth half open
as if framing a question

you
walking, walking
sensing a new presence
rub your hip

he

you

look up

## Posting to Iraq

### Part 1: Last Post

Poppy's no longer wearing her ring;
she couldn't, she said, see it working out,
they spent too much time apart,
what with their jobs and everything.

Her girl friends offer consolation,
they moue and flick their hair and cluck.
"It all became one fleeting fuck
between each repatriation

and that's no basis for a marriage,"
says Poppy, "well not for me."
"And there are plenty more fish in the sea,"
her girlfriends wink and nudge.

They pick up their bags and totter,
arms linked, on their killer heels.
"Don't worry, love, we know how it feels.
Let's get legless, to the future!"

*

Next morning, nursing her hangover,
Poppy keeps the curtains closed,
she makes a coffee, picks up the post;
she knows the wife of a soldier

is something she's not cut out for,
all that waiting between the fighting,
but when she sees the handwriting
on the envelope in front of her

she pauses – the thing about the future
is that you can't foresee
exactly what it's going to be –
and holds the ring towards her finger.

Isn't that what 'for better
or worse' really means, she thinks?
She picks up her coffee, drinks,
looks back down at the sealed letter...

**Part 2: Send Off**

Poppy queueing up at the corner take-away
is distracted by the news on the TV
above the counter droning endlessly,
the rolling text announcing the latest state of play:

soccer scores, falling stocks, the ceaseless toll
of casualties in Kabul, Helmand,
this faraway war that no-one seems to understand,
the politicians least of all,

though crowds line the streets from Lyneham as the last
body bags are carted home, the huge cargo plane
disgorging its belly into the hard spring rain,
drenching the mourners as the coffins file past.

This time last year she was there too,
standing near his family, though respectfully apart,
(he'd already sacrificed his heart) –
it was, she felt, the least she could do.

She may no longer have worn his ring
but she propped his photo on the mantle
where she keeps it as a reminder still
of a road not travelled, a close run thing,

and now at the corner of the High Street it all comes back;
standing in some Middle Eastern grocery store,
she forgets what it is she's there for,
sees only his handwriting on the letter from Iraq,

the final one, the one she left unanswered,
(those months of coded silence
carrying their own especial eloquence
in all the words that neither of them said…)

Fumbling for her keys, she heads back to the car,
dropping her bag as her mobile rings,
bombarding her with bleeps and pings
texting where the latest bargains are.

She leans her head against the wheel
and tries to shut out all the noise,
specifically that insistent inner voice
that pokes and prods what is and isn't real.

*

Later that night back home in her flat
above the dry cleaner's, dinner cooked,
dishes washed and dried, she's looked
him up on Facebook, to check the site

for all who didn't make it home's still there,
and there he is as large as life –
she still can't play the army wife,
knows it simply wasn't fair,

for all his charm, the severe
buzz-cut, desert tan and boyish grin,
the unit's motto, 'play to win'
tattooed only she knew where

beneath the uniform that always made
him look so dashing. "Appearances
can be deceptive," he'd said, all defences
down in her creaking, narrow bed

that first time, back on leave between tours –
she hadn't told him then about the march
she'd been on, the way her heart would lurch –
instead she'd whispered, I'm all yours…

"… those recruitment ads," he'd said,
"the lure of adventure, like video games,
faraway places with exotic names…"
"… and roadside graves to mark the dead,"

she'd added, before she could censor.
"OK," he'd said, "there's no guarantee,"
and she'd looked away so he wouldn't see.
"What do you think you're signing up for…?"

Now he smiles back from the screen,
all doubts and fears erased.
Her finger hovers near the laptop's keys,
somewhere between delete and system shut-down…

### Part 3: On Parade/Inspection

Three years on and Poppy's moved house.
She lives on the edge of town
in a new estate where she's found
an unexpected happiness.

After supper she sits on the sofa
to nurse her new born son,
while Alma, his sister, smiling, looks on,
Poppy's inherited ten year old step daughter,

who asks if she might hold him –
he's tired and cranky and cross –
but in Alma's arms he ceases to fuss,
Alma, (Arabic for 'wise'), who'd suggested they called him

Faraj, meaning 'others have been called this',
"so that he won't feel too important,"
she adds, pausing a moment
before dropping a casual kiss

on his forehead. "He's asleep now –
here, he's getting heavy," and she passes
him back to Poppy, suddenly serious,
and Poppy wonders exactly how,

not for the first time, this miracle occurred.
"Tell me about *him*," says Alma and indicates
the photo on the wall. She waits
a nanosecond then whispers the b-word:

"Was he your *boyfriend*?" Poppy nods. Alma's
eyes widen in shock and awe.
"A long time ago." "Before the war?
Did he die too? Like Mamma?

Did the bomb that killed her kill him too?"
Poppy similarly experiences
these self-same fears and urgencies.
"Would you have married him? Would you?"

"I married your father." This uncloaked
quest for certainties,
the ifs, the buts, the maybes,
cannot, will not, be slaked,

but for now Alma seems satisfied enough
and takes a puff from her inhaler,
the simple act that will not fail her –
Poppy knows she's still to earn such love....

*

Later, in bed, she watches her husband's
breathing softly rise and fall in the dawn
light – Taymur, meaning 'brave', ("a lion,"
says Alma), and its truth can't be questioned.

Poppy still can't bring herself to believe
how, having survived the worst Saddam
could contrive to throw at him,
it was the peace and its aftermath

that would fling him to these strange shores,
and now, newly repatriated,
her friends, she knew, speculated
whether he'd become some kind of cause

for her, but that was way off the mark,
she'd never been interested in politics
*per se*, though at times certain specifics
would surface – all of them at work

had wondered if they should do a stint
at the nearby military hospital.
Poppy volunteered to be on call
but in the end she never went.

One slow afternoon Taymur
burst into triage carrying Alma
gasping in his arms: "She has asthma,"
he said, "she must see a doctor."

It was the strength struck Poppy most
of that unspoken love between them,
the way he held her as they worked to calm
her breathing, bound by what they'd lost

already, and so it was she fixed
things that she might be present
for Alma's follow-up appointment,
so that everything that happened next

seemed both pre-ordained and natural –
she'd never before believed in fate –
but now no warning voice said 'wait',
the time for being sensible

had passed: "You are like a drop of rain
in the desert", he would tell her,
"and who knows, we might heal, insh'allah,
a little of each other's pain,"

and her guilt, like the shedding of a skin,
had dropped away cell by cell,
and he retreated less into his own private hell,
until they felt emboldened to begin…

Now she watches his breathing rise and fall –
she no longer thinks that love's a spark
that's simply snuffed out in the dark –
she awaits her new-born's wake-up call….

**Part 4: Reveille**

The letter arrived a week ago –
Poppy had recognised the writing at once –
and it had lain on the sideboard ever since,
picked up, put down, unopened – just so…

Now, late one evening when Faraj was in bed
and Taymur and Alma were visiting an uncle's,
she picked it up on a sudden impulse,
peeled open the envelope, paused, then read,

on official MOD note-paper
bearing the regimental insignia,
*(we shall be worthy… merebimur)*
"… articles of a somewhat personal nature…

apologies for the delay et cetera…
items enclosed found in suitcase
tied up with army issue bootlace…
came to light when someone needed his locker…"

(the tone formal but not unkind),
then tucked inside, a card from his mother –
Poppy had several times wondered whether
she might – the usual one, with the signed

photo of Gary on his passing out parade
(the one which Alma had asked about),
the one his mother always sent out
now, in case, somehow she was afraid,

people might forget how once he'd been,
spruced up and polished like a new pin,
not a blemish on his flawless skin
(so different from the final one she'd seen –

a snapshot sent from his last R&R,
"a souvenir from old Baghdad",
pale beneath his tan, eyes dead
despite the smile, the seedy bar…)

"Thought you should have these", she'd written.
"*He'd* wanted to burn them…" (Col, her husband)
"… but I couldn't. What's happened's happened
and back then you were both so smitten…

We read about your wedding, saw the pictures
in the local gazette. Col thinks it's a double
betrayal, but I disagree, you must have trouble
enough without another of his lectures.

I think it's brave, what you're doing,
I really do, but I don't think we should
stay in touch, do you? Maybe something good,
something whole, will come from all this ruin…?"

Poppy lays the letters down, closes her eyes,
these concerns are no longer hers;
she hears Raji's soft snuffles from upstairs
and then his urgent, hungry cries…

## Bouncing

School Sports Day, Dorset 1989

Izzy is bouncing
like Tigger, she has
so much energy
it simply can't be
contained, it fizzes
from her with each bounce
but still the fizz won't
leave her, as if she's
struck oil which gushes
up from the field in
an unstoppable
flow this summer's eve

now she looks around,
her mother will be
there, sitting at the
side with her knitting,
smiling not speaking
unless spoken to,
and there is her friend
who lives down the hill
from the farm, who comes
to play hide and seek
in the old hay barn
jumping over rats
in the high piled bales

and there's her big slow
brother poking for fish
contentedly by
himself near the pond
with a stick that looks
like a tiny toy
in his huge ham fist
which breaks everything

it holds – the pen he
struggles with at school
tongue sliding from the
corner of his mouth
but not the gun he
pulls to shoot rooks and
pigeons for Sunday
lunches –

                engrossed he
doesn't notice her
still bouncing at the
finish line, she's won
three races already,
she's hardly started,
barely drunk a sip
of fizz, saving it
for when her father
comes (he's promised her)
right now she knows he'll
be cutting the grass
up in the top field
making the most of
the long, light night or
doing his final
check round the yard, dog
at his heels, calling
every cow by name

and then the gun fires
for the next race, she's
so busy looking
for him she forgets
to start but she can
give them twenty yards
and still fizz past them,
her bouncing run so
strong her father high
in the top field can

feel the ground vibrate –
that's my girl, he says,
spins her in his arms
like a weathercock
round again and round
till the fizz leaves her –
you'll outrun the wind...

*

... and later there are
times when she has to,
ladder placed against
the wall beside her
bedroom window for
those late night escapes,
those crept returns at
early morning when
it seems she has to
bear the whole world on
her teenage shoulders,
her mother's nerves, her
father's accident,
her brother's long, slow
retreat to silence,
the irrelevance
of school, it's hard to
keep bouncing then, but
somehow she does, from
cowshed to classroom,
homework to housework,
careering from one
set of demands to
another she bounces...

*

now she's two girls of
her own, a husband –
they're clutching tickets
for the Olympics,
high in the stands they
sit for the start of
the hundred metres,
where athletes gee them-
selves up, slapping thighs,
shaking out the stress,
bouncing – her girls glance
sideways at her, smile
(every year she wins
the mums' race, would win
the dads' race too if
they'd let her enter)
she winks, knowing what
they're thinking, the crowd
leans in, holds its breath,
runners take their marks
like Izzy on sports
day turning cartwheels,
bouncing, beginning...

## Property Ladder

*The Child is father to the Man…* Wordsworth

### 1. Tree House

Robert – Robbie – sometimes Rob
stands in the clearing catching his breath,
he's hacked his way through the undergrowth
undetected, he thinks, till a sudden grab

on his shoulder makes him whirl
around. "Caught you, she yells – you said
I wouldn't find you but there, see, I did."
Robbie grins – Jane isn't bad for a girl.

He turns away, surveying the terrain.
"This'll do," he says, puffing out his chest,
and Jane senses this is some kind of test.
He points to a tree. "You'll not tell Alan…"

This is not a question. She starts
to nod, then shake, her head.
"…as long as that's understood."
Her love for him's so fierce it hurts.

"I've been checking it out all summer," he says.
"I reckon from up there you can see the whole
village but still remain invisible."
He takes her arm and points. She tries

to picture it the way Robbie does.
"It can be our secret, with passwords and codes…"
"*My* secret," he corrects, and pulls her towards
the base of the tree. "Close your eyes…"

A minute later he lets her look,
then pricks some blood from both their thumbs
which he traces across their names
carved crudely with his sharpened stick.

From close by they hear Alan call out Jane's name.
Robbie puts his finger to her lips.
The leaves rustle in the tree tops.
"Sod you then," sulks Alan. "I'm going home."

Robbie and Jane smile. "Not a word.
Promise?" "Promise." They solemnly spit
on the palms of their hands, then silently part,
each knowing something momentous has occurred.

*

For weeks Robbie spends all his spare hours
building the tree house till it's just right.
Jane grows bored by the seemingly endless wait
but for Christmas gives him some old binoculars

she finds in her father's attic complete
with their leather case. Robbie is thrilled,
they shin up the top, then with ladder pulled
up behind them, he takes them out

reverently before surveying his kingdom.
He says nothing but his pleasure is deep.
Jane hangs back, watching. "I'll keep
them safe, " he says. "Here. Home."

"I know," she says, then looks around.
"You've made it nice." "Nice? It's fuckin'
brilliant." She laughs and something unspoken
passes between them. He reaches down

and pulls up a polished piece of wood.
"I got you this," he says, handing it across.
He sees the puzzled look upon her face.
"Write something on it. I'm no good

at stuff like that. We could put it where
only we would see it when we come in –
you know, like some kind of sign
that we can hang above the door."

He nods back towards a straggly curtain
of ivy that shuts out the world.
"But I don't know what to put." "It's old,"
she says. He beams. "I know. I found it hidden

in the top field. I think it was once part
of the old mill workers' cottages
that used to stand here ages
ago. They've ripped the heart

out of our village, my dad says." "Who have?"
"Incomers." "I'm an incomer too."
"No – you don't talk posh like the others do."
"What others?" "Like Alan does. Hey – you've

not told him …?" She shakes her head. "Let's
not talk about him. Not today. Why don't
you hand me that brush and that paint?"
He watches while the pale winter sun sets

behind her, bent in concentration,
studies her, still and patient,
as she labours slow and silent,
shielding with her body what she's written,

till finally she puts aside the paint:
*The Eyrie* – she sees the frown crease his brow.
"It's an eagle's nest," she says. "*I know*" -
lashing out more wildly than he meant –

"I'm not stupid." "I know you're not."
In the moonlight his face reddens.
"Eagles live in the high mountains,"
he says, "alone. I could handle that."

They stand facing each other a long time.
Jane is the first to break the silence.
"I've got to go," she says. "My parents…"
"I know," he says. "I'll walk you home."

"There's no need," she says. "I'll be OK."
Robbie grins. "I mean with these,"
and he picks up the binoculars.
"I can track you all the way."

He watches her cross the field, climb the gate,
run down the lane till she arrives
back at her house, where she turns and waves,
then steps inside. Robbie has never yet

been inside Jane's house and knows he never will
but he can imagine what it's like –
the lights and decorations – and waves back
then pans his gaze across towards the hill

where Alan is riding his new red bike
outside the big house where his family live
round and round till he falls off.
Robbie, rocking back, thinks, "What a dork…"

*

In the weeks and months that follow
Jane rarely gets to visit the house,
what with SAT's, tests, the eleven plus.
Robbie feels a gnawing in the hollow

of his stomach that life's about to change.
Jane and Alan go to the grammar school,
they move in a different social circle
now, and it feels awkward and strange

if Robbie ever bumps into Jane
by chance at the bus stop, he doesn't know
what to say, makes excuses to go,
wishes they could be the same,

but only makes things worse with each sullen
shrug and non-committal grunt.
Jane knows it's only a front
but now they have so little in common

that as more time passes he rarely
registers on her radar
until one day two years later –
they're both coming up to nearly

fifteen and Robbie's in the tree house,
he climbs up there almost every day,
bunking off school, keeping the world away –
when he sees her walking across

the field with Alan, they're holding hands,
she stops directly underneath
and Robbie stares in disbelief
as she points towards the hidden entrance.

Crows mock him with their raucous cries,
the sky above his head cartwheels.
He dares not show the pain he feels
and jams his fists against his eyes.

Jane and Alan start to kiss,
she leans her back against the bark,
her fingers trace the blood-smeared mark,
as Alan slides beside her on the grass…

Only when they've gone can Robbie breathe.
He howls his heartache to the stars,
snatches the binoculars,
a last, long look round, then takes his leave…

## 2. Tenant Farm

Robbie's mum died when he was eight,
since when he's lived with his dad on the farm
rattling around in the cold, comfortless home
that wasn't even theirs, merely let

to them by a distant land owner
who Robbie didn't know existed
till just before they were evicted
when he caught sight of the letter

unopened on the kitchen table
where his dad, mostly drunk these days,
piles everything. Robbie, fifteen now, is
hard-wired to try and stave off trouble

but this, he knows, is serious,
not something he can ignore,
confronts his dad while laying the fire –
"what's going to happen to us?"

"We'll be alright," he says, "the EU grant
will help pay off the overdraft,
then we'll sell whatever's left…"
"No, Dad" says Robbie, "we can't.

This…" brandishing the letter, "this
is a final notice to quit.
Even I can understand that.
'No option left but to foreclose',"

he reads – his dad throws it on the fire.
"It's finished, Dad, over, no use
trying to pretend otherwise…"
His stomach somersaults in fear.

For a long time silence holds them.
His dad reaches for another beer.

"I'll not let them put you in care."
Robbie knows it won't be up to him.

*

He gets up as usual the next day
before even the faintest crack
of light begins to pierce the dark,
he has his daily chores to do

he carries out routinely half asleep –
"Robbie the Robot," his mum would smile
tousling his hair when he was still small
struggling up the back step

uncomplainingly with each slopping pail –
he shrugs the memory of it away,
if he can just get through this next day…
The dog whimpers by the barn wall,

mechanically he strokes the collie's ears.
"Good morning, ladies," he says, about to enter
the still hush of the milking parlour
when some sixth sense makes him turn and pause.

The dog, still chained, is straining to reach
the barn door where Robbie detects
a chink of light catching the piled hay ricks.
He slowly lifts the heavy latch

and steps hesitantly inside,
its deep vaulted silence broken
by a low insistent creaking
whose source Robbie can't decode.

He feels his way forward, his hand
closing on a taut piece of rope
his eyes trace to a swinging shape
he knows at once, and sinks to the ground.

The dog won't stop barking even when
the police arrive, searching for a note,
Robbie still rooted to the spot,
before they finally cut his father down.

A kind lady from the Council
makes Robbie cups of tea,
asks questions concerning family,
notes the unwashed kitchen window sill.

*

By evening everything's arranged.
Bag packed, Robbie waits upstairs,
tightly clutching old binoculars
by his mother's dressing table, unchanged

since the day she died, like some exhibit
from a long ago forgotten age,
and searches for a keepsake which
he slips inside his threadbare jacket.

He trains the glasses through the window
to the gate, where he knows the car will come
to take him to some far-off Children's Home.
His footsteps make no sound, he casts no shadow

as he scans the far horizon
from his eagle's nest vantage point –
he's used to waiting, won't
move a muscle, shift position

till the moment that he has to…
When they ask him what he's holding in his hand
he says nothing, they wouldn't understand,
his keepsake, a tiny wind-up toy…

### 3. Student Living

Jane has won a place to study Law
at Cambridge, Alan's at Nottingham,
they're not now what she'd call an item,
they hardly even text any more,

both too busy settling in, Alan chose
Business, next stop the City,
then a career in property,
while Jane, although she knows

there's a core incompatibility
of different values, different goals
between them, nevertheless feels
a certain responsibility

towards their recent shared history,
going out together through sixth form,
each welcome visitors in the other's home –
closure requires ceremony

and nothing as yet's been actually said,
while into student life she plunges headlong –
clubs, classes, parties, the ceaseless throng,
till, waking up in someone else's bed

one morning, she knows she's letting go.
Strangely it's not towards Alan that her guilt
tends, but Robbie, to whom she's always felt
ambivalent, almost as though

a part of her still resides
back with him in the tree house
with her father's old binoculars
behind which, she suspects, Robbie still hides,

keeping himself separate, apart,
his faith in her almost feral
so that her subsequent betrayal
of him, with all its collateral hurt,

was, she feels, inevitable –
she thinks this now, not then,
(she saw him briefly again
around his father's funeral

and subsequently wrote to him
care of the Children's Home
several letters but no reply came
back, she wonders if he even got them) –

and so, this rainy Sunday morning,
in the arms of a guy she's barely met,
it's Robbie's face she can't forget,
and a faint future starts forming,

begins to surface in the grey light –
the essential difference between
herself and Alan, she now sees, is one
she can't allow to drift for one more night.

She catches the first available bus.
"We need to know exactly where
we stand," she says. "It's not fair
otherwise on either of us.

I really want us to stay friends
but you're on such a clear and chosen path
I'm not the one for you to travel with."
He nods and says he understands.

Next day she asks to volunteer
at the local Citizen's Advice.
"I want to give the disempowered a voice,"
she says. The future seems suddenly clear.

*

Alan takes Jane's announcement in his stride –
he'd long been expecting this rejection,
known all along that her affection
for him would in time have strayed.

He'd always felt a kind of stop gap,
now he can fully focus all his mind,
really put his nose to the grind,
to forge his way to the top,

which he feels is his predestined right –
Agamemnon freed from Clytemnestra,
*per ardua ad astra* –
a creed he daily will recite,

a mantra on each morning's jog,
rain or shine, hail or snow,
he knows which way he has to go
to stave off ending up a cog.

*

Jane, too, cruises through uni –
she sails through the next three years
with serene and peerless grace
envied by few, admired by many.

After a year in Halls of Residence
she shares a house with three friends
she makes at Greenpeace, really finds
out who she is and her confidence

blossoms, she sings in community choirs,
joins Drama Soc, learns to play
the accordion, writes her first plea,
speaks in a debate, marches against wars.

She falls in love passionately
with a host of radical causes,
(romantically with hopeless cases),
throws open her door indiscriminately

to every digger, leveller,
argues with her tutors,
some of them would-be suitors,
shares a bed-sit with a fellow traveller,

sends postcards to Robbie's last address
signed "a humanitarian",
becomes a vegetarian,
donates old clothes to charities for peace,

so that when she graduates she wants,
beyond the double first, the praise
heaped on her, *the summa cum laudes*,
to go out there and make a difference.

### 4. Training Camp

It's a big year for acronyms –
Jane vacillates between the PSC,
GDL, LPC, CPE,
and contemplates the LLM's,

while Alan enrols with the AAT,
speedily joins the CIMA,
fast-tracks a distance MBA –
Robbie applies for the AFC…

PSC = Professional Skills Course; GDL = Graduate Diploma in Law; LPC = Legal Practice Course; CPE = Common Professional Examination; LLM = Master of Laws; AAT = Association of Accounting Technicians; CIMA = Chartered Institute of Management Accountants; MBA = Masters in Business Administration; AFC = Army Foundation College

*

At 17 years 5 months Robbie joins
the Army, the earliest that he can,
he makes the long trek up north by train
to Harrogate the day he leaves the Children's

Home with not a single backward glance,
the start of a new chapter, year zero,
sights set on becoming a hero,
he's not thought of it since.

He'd made no attempt at all to fit
in there, regarded it as doing time –
just show me where I have to sign,
he'd said when the Army came to recruit –

and after training less than a week
he already feels himself at home,
his confidence visibly grown,
as he settles down to graft and work,

excelling at every single task –
no one's uniform is slicker
or re-assembles rifles quicker –
he's the one the other newbies ask

on how to pass their BFT's,
the proper protocols in the Mess,
which Ruperts it's best not to cross,
the meaning of the seven P's.

When they go on TAB's he's always
first to reach the planned objective,
carries out each new directive
to the letter with such ease

BFT = Basic Fitness Test; Rupert = Officer; 7 x P's = Prior Planning & Preparation Prevents Pretty Poor Performance; TAB = Tactical Advance to Battle

he's already, he can tell,
being singled out, lined up
as potential leadership,
maybe officer material,

but Robbie's not interested, prefers
instead to be one of the lads,
always on hand to give a heads
up when the red mist clears

after one of the SCC's tirades
or crack a joke at his own expense
to boost another's confidence
if he's just emptied his insides

after falling from the assault course
which Robbie loves, nor is he ever
spooked, even on some night manoeuvre,
they all remind him of the tree house,

before Jane, before Alan, just him,
high up in his eyrie, captain
of all he surveys, this bleak terrain
he can truly call home.

He makes bivouacs from broken
twigs, locates a long-forgotten field well.
fashions cunning invisible
scratchers from scraps of bracken.

Back at base he can take apart
and repair quite ingeniously
the most complicated machinery –
he can give anyone a head start

SCC = Section Commander Corporal; scratcher = a place to sleep in an open field

and still be through before them.
He's a natural, the sarge avers,
but Robbie merely shrugs, demurs,
that's what growing up on a farm

does for you, it forces you to fix
stuff, never throw a thing away,
you'll find a use for it one day,
you can't teach an old dog new tricks

but Robbie's still a young pup
hungry for every bone they throw,
for every pace they put him through
feeding off each meagre scrap

till he receives, training over,
orders for his next assignment,
to join 33 Regiment
Royal Engineers, Carver

where his reputation precedes him –
as he's laying out his kit to dry
someone spots the wind-up toy
and it at once becomes his nickname –

Robbie the Robot, sapper, friend,
joining the ranks of Cob and Chaz,
Bandit, Zorro, Peanut, Jaz,
brothers in arms, on whom he must depend,

so even he can't keep much secret
as he places in his locker
postcards from Cambridge, a pair
of old binoculars, a toy robot…

*

For Jane's and Alan's graduations
each respective family preens with pride
but at Robbie's passing out parade
no one's there to hear his lone citation

save the other squaddies, wedges,
who shampoo his shaven head with beer,
a fully fledged Royal Engineer,
the world's his oyster, rags to riches.

He wouldn't want it any other way;
he's with the one family
who understand him properly –
there's nothing else to say.

That night, legless, all the walled
up anger tearing him in half
for years releases on the barracks roof:
"Look at me, Ma, I'm King of the World!"

The roaring boys tear up the town.
"All for one and one for all," he cries.
"Listen, mate, what you've got to realise
is he who pays the piper calls the tune,"

says Cob, the calm one. "Nothing comes for free –
you, me, Jaz and Bandit,
we're for the Bomb Disposal Unit,
dismantling our first UXB

tomorrow." Robbie grins. He can't wait.
For him the prospect holds no fears –
a bomb's been ticking deep inside for years.
Bring it on, he thinks. Time to detonate.

UXB = Unexploded Bomb; Carver = army base in Essex; wedges = new recruits

### 5. Starter Home

Alan completes his first major deal
in less than six months – a modest bank loan
unlocked by a simple business plan
is all he needs to set the wheel

in motion and pretty soon
he's bought the vacant lot
with building scheduled to start
the moment planning permission

is granted, which proves an absolute breeze –
councils are falling over themselves
to build affordable, straight-off-the-shelves
homes for young professionals. Soon he's

purchased three more sites – brown field,
in-fill, green belt – he's invited
to join the Rotary; he finds it
helpful to oil any troublesome wheel.

It's through them he meets Amina,
who proves the perfect partner, colleague, lover.
They see themselves reflected in each other,
design a ten year plan over dinner.

What's wrong with making a profit,
they argue, it's simple market forces,
and everyone needs houses,
so everyone can benefit.

Amina, like Alan, has succeeded
on merit, her rise meteoric,
her goals equally specific,
she's exactly what he knows he's needed –

within a year they've opened offices
in London, Leeds and Cardiff,
their client list's impressive,
plus major online consultancies.

Their wedding's featured in the FT
under "ones to watch next year",
they jointly win the "Young Entrepreneur
Prize" awarded by the City,

live within easy reach of Marylebone
out in GX, a stress-free commute,
flat white to go, sharply tailored suit,
checking their stocks and bonds on smart phone.

*

Jane spends the next year pursuing
only human rights cases. While
this undoubtedly raises her profile
it threatens potential ruin

to her career prospects longer term.
She reluctantly agrees to compromise
(as damage limitation exercise)
so she can join a more respected firm.

She moves from trendy Hackney Wick
where she's been renting a studio
above a slightly dodgy video
rental store claiming to unlock

mobile phones, wire money transfers,
next door to an Asian beauty
salon scrawled with edgy graffiti,
close by other bargain basement offers –

GX = Gerrard's Cross; LSE = London School of Economics

she loves its multi-cultural mix,
is on familiar first name terms
with shopkeepers, kids and single mums,
makes daily use of blue Boris bikes –

to a more desirable postcode
in Islington from where each dawn and dusk
she runs the four miles to and from her desk,
the saving from her gym members card

donated to a range of causes
close to her heart, she volunteers
at various refuge crisis centres
for victims of political abuses –

it's at one of these she meets Khaleel
recently arrived from Syria,
temporary visa carrier
seeking asylum – she knows she'll

in a heartbeat take his case
swept away by his dignity,
charisma, not seeking pity,
not love even, but justice.

It takes two years of constant battle
to navigate the torturous,
lengthy, labyrinthine processes
to secure his right to settle

in the UK permanently.
A month later they marry,
friends close to her worry
though say nothing of expediency

but such fears prove unfounded:
he lectures at the LSE
on Middle Eastern policy,
his views tempered, firmly grounded

in first hand experience,
and less than one year later
Jane gives birth to Sri, a daughter,
Khaleel the most solicitous of parents.

Jane returns to work part time –
a few *pro bono* cases –
Khaleel takes on extra courses,
financially they manage between them.

Running into Alan one day by chance,
"I wonder that you've never thought
he's only with you for his passport…"
Appalled the gulf's grown so immense

between them, she asks idly about
Amina. He stiffens. "You can't compare,"
he says. "She was born and raised here."
Politely furious, they part.

Then, one night after Sri's asleep,
she turns the TV on to watch the news
and there before her is a face she knows
but hasn't seen since when she failed to keep

a solemn childhood promise.
The pictures show the latest raw recruits
loading APC's in steel crates
bound for NATO forces

from the Royal Chatham Dockyards, Kent –
she picks up the remote and presses pause,
his image flickers on the screen in freeze-
frame-hold, his body bent

APC = Armoured Personnel Carrier
NATO = North Atlantic Treaty Organisation

beneath the weight of ordnance:
Robbie – there's no mistake,
and she feels a deep, remorseful ache,
recognises the artless innocence

behind the forced camera smile.
Her husband sits beside her, draws her near.
"Poor bugger, he's simply no idea
what he's walking into," says Khaleel,

but when the cameras fade, Robbie's grin
doesn't, he walks into the belly of the plane
with only one thought in his brain:
his life can truly now begin.

### 6. Gated Community

1

"Robert Hann, you have been found guilty
on one count of illegal possession
of a firearm with intent to threaten
plus one count of aggravated burglary…"

The judge waits, looking Robbie directly
in the eye. "Before I pass sentence
is there anything by way of circumstance
extenuating you wish to say to me?"

Robbie stares back, remaining mute,
as he has done throughout the trial.
The judge sighs and shakes his head. "Very well.
You give me no alternative but

to commit you for a term of five years
at Her Majesty's pleasure
where you may repent at leisure
upon this judgement by your peers."

Robbie looks up sharply at that word.
"They're not, and never will be, my peers…"
he says. "So you do speak," the judge avers.
"… not after all I've seen, or heard."

The judge raps his gavel sharply.
"Then hear this. You have squandered
every opportunity afforded
you by the Armed Forces, wilfully,

I would say, and, I might add,
betrayed the faith entrusted you
by your Commanding Officer who
nevertheless took time to provide

this glowing detailed reference
by way of mitigation
with its full account and explanation
of those most distressing incidents

which led to your medical discharge,
an act of extraordinary lenience
in my view, requesting a second chance,
and it is within this context I urge

you not to forfeit further
any right to clemency this court
might choose to exercise if it so thought
it might improve your coarse demeanour.

He brings his gavel down one last time hard.
"Take him down." The attending officer
gently guides him down the corridor
towards the holding cell. "Keep your head

down, son, that's my advice. With good
behaviour you could be out in less
than three, no matter what the Beak says.
Stay focussed, sharp, and always on your guard."

Robbie pauses. These are the first words
to have made sense in nearly a year.
"How…?" "Paras." Robbie nods. "Engineer."
An exchanged look, then he steers Robbie towards

the armoured police van which waits
to transport him to his new billet.
"Time passes quicker if you fill it,"
he says, "with *future* thoughts."

But Robbie can't help dwelling on the past
rewinding it, reliving it,
trying to retrieve the moment that
it all began unravelling first…

2

The plane arrives at dead of night.
Shivering, sleep-deprived, they step
out into this strange lunar landscape
shrouded in ethereal, ghostly light.

The first thing he encounters
surprisingly is the cold –
nobody has ever told
them about Afghani winters,

it's always been the desert
(which comes soon enough) they warn you of –
but when he, Jaz, Cob and Bandit first arrive
a snow blind blizzard's at it its height,

the wind whipping through the high mountain
passes that they have to drive along,
GPS down, they make several wrong
turnings before reaching Camp Bastion

exhausted, scared and travel sore,
but the next day dawns clear and bright,
he experiences the shock of Afghan light,
sharp as a needle, that will sear

his memory ever after.
The temperature grows daily higher
and soon the camp's a cauldron fire
in which everyone must suffer.

Their CO's waiting with a welcome:
"A city as large as Reading at least,
airport the size of Gatwick almost –
think of it as your home from home."

The one thing everyone notices
is its size – he can't get his head
around the sheer scale of it, spread
across miles of desert – it encompasses

local Afghan troops too, assigned
to follow Robbie and his team
defusing different types of bomb
buried in the shifting sand;

but what he can't escape's security –
the gates and fences, codes and checks
to ward off terrorist attacks.
"Our very own gated community,"

CO = Commanding Officer; GPS = Global Positioning System

jokes the CO when they're on parade.
The brutal sun beats down without remission,
they shut their eyes to the rendition
they all know takes place inside

the windowless huts on the outer
limits of the camp, the nightly
trucks of hooded prisoners driven out of sight
beyond the far perimeter.

"If I might read from *Ozymandias*,"
the CO adds: "…this 'colossal wreck, boundless and bare –
Look on my works, ye mighty, and despair'."
"Poofter, obviously," mouths Cob to Jaz.

Robbie tries to take in the statistics,
the 40km long boundary fence,
the cheek-by-jowl surreal existence
of Pizza Huts by Ballistics,

the more than ten thousand metal
containers that will all revert to sand
blown in by the desert wind
after they leave, after the last battle.

*

Robbie gets his bearings week by week.
He and Cob and Jaz and Bandit
head off each day before the main unit,
their job a simple one, to seek

and destroy each home made UXB
that line the road like poppies,
their DNA the carbon copies
of a blueprint that might set them free.

UXB = Unexploded Bomb

They soon acquire a reputation
for their bravery and expertise,
with fewer casualties
than any time in Operation

Helmand's chequered history;
they're dubbed the Dream Team,
acquire the status of a good luck charm,
Robbie and Cob especially,

whom they nickname "RoboCob",
so it hardly makes a ripple
when he's fast-tracked up to Corporal
and then given the crucial job

of supervising training
for the Afghans' own disposal squad,
becoming like his own Jihad,
with hours of endless rote-explaining,

but each time Robbie bends down low to listen,
the movement he detects beneath the sand
sounds like voices carried on the wind
whose meaning he begins to think he's missing.

His once-clear sense of direction
falters. He knows the enemy is wrong
but he cannot find his own song
to match their pure conviction.

His respect for the Taliban deepens,
the fact they have a clear cause,
no matter it's misguided, makes him pause.
A long-buried ache opens

up inside him, as vast
as the high, wide desert skies
whose moods he starts to recognise,
a freedom and a joy he thought he'd lost.

Army issue field glasses,
complete with GPS, night vision,
helmet-mounted, high precision,
have long ago replaced his

old binoculars from the tree house,
but he finds himself more and more
thinking back to that time before
what he now sees as a fall from grace.

He tries to get to know his charges,
their hopes, the reasons they enlisted,
what kind of life existed
for them back home in the villages

before the Taliban came.
They can't remember that far back,
but, insha'allah, plus a little luck,
they might all one day go home.

*

As Robbie grows familiar
with the new rules and routines
he gradually gleans
he has a shadow, a follower,

a young Pashto boy who haunts his footsteps
each time he tours the Afghan market-place
patrolled by joint US/UK police,
the Union Jacks, the Stars & Stripes,

a replica for orientation
so they'll learn to recognise
the tell-tale signs of IED's
when they're out on active operation.

IED = Improvised Explosive Device

But soon the boy's becoming bolder.
He waits for Robbie outside *Heroes* bar,
runs behind his armoured car,
salutes and marches like a soldier.

"Don't encourage him," warns Bandit.
"You'll open Christ-knows-what new can of worms.
There's hundreds like him, none of them with homes,
they blame us, can't you understand it?

We can't make friends, we don't know who to trust –
simply follow orders, do our tour,
then get the hell right out of here.
It's not for us to count the cost

of what we're doing. Let others worry
over that. He'd blow you up
as soon as look at you. Our job's to stop
him, nothing else." "You sound like Prince Harry,"

says Robbie, smiling. "That's fine with me,"
says Bandit. "Take a life…"
"… to save a life – I know. But what if
it's already been taken?" asks Robbie.

"You've lost me there, mate," Bandit grins.
"You'll make your head ache with all that thinking.
Best do that instead by drinking."
Robbie laughs, looks back, and so it begins…

*

His name is Bashir.
He crawls inside a concrete pipe
each night to snatch some sleep.
It seems that he has always lived here

in Bastion, for as long as he can
remember, which isn't that long.
Although he's small, he's strong,
he says, just watch him run,

which Robbie does – he sees him
racing other boys around
the rim of the Parade Ground,
while working out inside the gym.

Soon he's running errands, not just
for Robbie, but all of them, on a beat-up bike;
he knows which cigarettes they like,
whose soccer team has won or lost,

and that gives Robbie an idea –
to organise a one-off special
football match to boost morale:
Lashkar Gah versus Royal Engineers.

The CO's all for it. "I firmly believe
this kind of PR exercise
can only serve to emphasise
the brighter future when we leave.

Good show, Hann. Put me down for referee."
The game draws a huge crowd.
The atmosphere is colourful and loud.
With seconds to go a doubtful penalty's

awarded to Lashkar Gah with the score
at 2-1 to the Engineers.
Inevitably it's Bashir
who steps up to take it. The roar

Lashkar Gah = nearest Afghan town to Camp Bastion

dies down to a held, expectant hush,
then the noise that greets his equalising goal
must be heard as far away as Kabul,
the mountains of the Hindu Kush.

Bashir is carried shoulder high
in adulation from the field as far
as right down next to *Heroes* bar –
the CO catches Robbie's eye.

"I think a fair result, don't you?
The best that we can hope for
here's an honourable draw –
to the victor the spoils, what, riven in two…?"

*

After the match Robbie's taken to one side.
"I'd like you to meet Akhtar.
He's to be your interpreter,"
says the CO, "chief liaison and guide."

It seems there's to be a big push on
deep into a once controlled
former Taliban stronghold.
"To make the right impression

take Akhtar with you. He's Afghan police,
he knows the terrain,
will help you better explain
we're here as allies, friends, in peace."

Robbie's happy to comply,
so are Bandit, Jaz and Cob –
if they're to make a decent stab
of carrying this out properly

they're going to need all the help they can get,
and it's not long before Akhtar seems
he's always been a part of their team –
they each acknowledge with a mute

respect it takes a special courage
to do just what he's doing,
foot in two camps, risking ruin
when he speaks to elders in each village

that they come to on their mission,
who listen darkly, who with good
reason have come to regard
soldiers from all sides with suspicion

equally. Akhtar takes great care
reliably to act
with the caution and respect
each new negotiation might require:

he knows the land without recourse to maps,
has a sixth sense when it comes
to finding water, resolving rival claims
to irrigation, avoiding mishaps,

misunderstandings based on cultural
difference, scenting dangers,
potential ambushes by strangers,
an arrangement that brings mutual

benefit; for Robbie, Bandit, Cob and Jaz
guarantee him safety
in return, status born of loyalty,
attainment of a common cause.

*

Akhtar invites them all to meet
his family. The landscape gently unfolds,
a day's drive through endless poppy fields,
mirage in the shimmering heat.

They lounge on cushions inside a tent,
a simple dish of lentils, rice and lamb,
followed by songs as old as time,
shooting stars in the firmament.

They talk deep into the night
taking turns to keep watch,
it's ingrained in them, they judge
it's better safe than sorry, and they're right –

Robbie thinks he sees a shadow
creeping but he can't be sure
and then he thinks he hears Bashir
whispering to Akhtar in Pashto,

but that makes no sense, he's
a hundred miles at least away.
They start their journey back at break of day,
Robbie's anxieties

fade, he must have been mistaken.
By the time they reach Camp Bastion
such fears have been forgotten,
all thoughts focussed now on their operation.

*

They make good progress. Soon a whole
swathe of desert's been swept clean.
Overlooking the entire plain
they set up camp upon the highest hill.

They share a smoke, content but weary,
then radio back to base.
Robbie smiles, remembering, says,
"Let's call it The Eyrie."

(They have orders to report their position
on this as yet unnamed hill
with the merest hint of detail
so as not to jeopardise the mission).

Akhtar nods. "A good name. Look..."
An eagle, patrolling the escarpment
from above, carves escapement
for its young high up on the rock,

before swooping in a ruthless dive
like a guided missile on its unseen prey.
Robbie knows he will remember this day,
this moment, for the rest of his life.

*

The year turns. The onset of winter,
the end of their six months tour close.
The high Shamal wind blows hard and fierce
from the Kazakh steppes. The days grow shorter.

They wait. They wait two days and two nights.
Early on the third day a fighter jet
tears across the sky, ripping the heart
out of the silence, its tail lights

blazing red in the bleached dawn sky.
It can only mean the main unit's
near. Akhtar, Cob, Jaz and Bandit
make their way down to the road, close by

a three-arched stone bridge
that spans a wadhi, a dried river bed.
While they go on ahead,
Robbie stays up on the ridge

scanning the plain for signs of dust
whose rising spirals signal
the imminent arrival
of the ATF heading out of the east,

the sun rising behind them.
When the leading vehicle
is less than half a mile
away, Robbie's gaze is pulled below him.

Something's not quite right.
He magnifies the focus
on the Steiner Optics lenses
of his field glasses, trying to make out

just exactly what is going on.
Incredibly it's Bashir
warning them not to come near.
He's pointing at what looks like a loose stone

towards the middle of the three bridge spans
shouting frantically
he's spotted an IED.
Robbie shakes his head. This makes no sense.

They only swept that spot last night; it's clear.
He watches Akhtar hang back at the rear,
then trains the glasses back towards Bashir
still gesticulating wildly with fear.

ATF = Advanced Task Force; IED = Improvised Explosive Device

The convoy's less than two hundred yards
away now. Akhtar begins to run.
Bashir, intoning the Koran,
with Cob inching his way towards

the bridge, pulls open his shirt to reveal
a bomb strapped to his body.
The convoy starts to cross the wadhi
when Cob thinks he hears Robbie yell

as down the mountainside he races.
Jaz and Bandit hit the ground behind a rock.
Robbie clocks Cob's face, the sudden shock
as he sees Bashir and realises

what's about to happen just too late.
Time stretches. Robbie's dimly aware
of an eagle's wing trembling in the air,
then Bashir flicks the switch to detonate.

The blast blows Robbie from his feet,
hurls him through the air, hitting his head.
He just has time to shoot Akhtar dead
before he finally blacks out.

*

When he comes to, the world is silent,
muffled by the first flurries of sleet
and snow that have begun to fall, the light
drains from the sky moment by moment,

mixed with debris from the bomb,
particles of bone and metal
floating in a dream-like petal
shower of smoke and ash, a ghostly plume

drifting down the mountain. Dazed,
Robbie stumbles through the carnage,
searching madly in the wreckage
for something he might recognise

till finally he comes to it –
lying in a roadside ditch
beneath the rubble from the bridge,
Cob's lifeless body, still, inert,

at peace, eyes surprised and open,
face unspoiled, as if death
has simply sucked the breath
from deep within him and then moved on.

Robbie cradles Cob to him close,
the ringing in his ears
rising deafeningly, roars
up through him till his own voice

returns, howling to the moon
as the world crashes in around him,
when Jaz and Bandit find him
and try to hold him down,

but his grief-fuelled strength's too great –
he wrenches himself free,
stares about him wildly,
runs off into the freezing desert night.

3

They find him thirty-six hours later
jabbering half way up a tree.
Escorted back to base by the MP,
suffering from acute hypothermia,

he's placed in an isolation ward
(technically he's been on AWOL)
and not interrogated until
the doctors declare he's recovered

sufficiently. He refuses
to speak to anyone, not to Jaz,
not to Bandit, or his CO, appears
indifferent to his diagnosis

confirmed as post-traumatic stress
disorder, though there's talk for a while
of disciplinary measures, possible
court action even, nevertheless –

killing Akhtar outright without
clear, verifiable, hard
evidence can't be ignored,
it casts a serious doubt

over his previously unblemished
record, which his CO steps in to correct
and with immediate effect
Robbie is medically discharged.

MP = Military Police; AWOL = Absent Without Leave

*

He leaves the Army with nothing –
no job, no money, no place
to live, just the address
of a charity, offering

temporary shelter,
but this reminds him
too much of the Children's Home
and so he steers clear.

He keeps taking his meds, which induce
a numbness that helps him not to think
and when they run out he finds drink
and then drugs fulfil the same purpose.

He's losing his edge but he doesn't care.
He wanders the streets, sleeps where he can –
days, weeks, merge into one
indistinguishable blur

until one day he wakes up in a police
cell, not knowing how he got there,
and without someone to vouch for
who he is he can't be released.

He stares blankly at the walls,
sectioned in a bleak secure unit.
He has a visitor – Bandit –
who grabs him tightly by the balls,

whispers fiercely in his ear,
"This is not what Cob would want, mate, get a grip,
pull yourself together, time to snap
out of this self-pity, get out there."

The words jolt Robbie back awake,
eyes locked tight together, face to face.
"I've brought you this," says Bandit, starts to place
Cob's regimental tie round Robbie's neck.

"An Engineer wears his badge with pride.
Once a sapper, always one..."
With these last words Bandit's gone.
Robbie's ready now to go back on Parade.

*

*If you've got no address*
*you can't get a job*
*and if you can't get a job*
*you can't get a house –*

that's the mantra they all share
each night in the white caravan,
Robbie, Lev, Mirek and Jan,
over a game of cards and a beer.

"It is like," says Lev, "Catch 21."
"22," says Robbie. "Yes. 22.
Damned if you don't, damned if you do."
Robbie nods. He's not read it. But he's seen

the film – when he first joined up
there were always DVD's to watch.
Now they all seem to merge
into each other and he can't press stop…

They've been here nearly twenty weeks,
labourers on a building site,
constructing an exclusive estate
that will close its doors on the likes

of them when the work's all done –
a gated community,
electronic security,
each home costing a cool million.

Lev's an electrician, Mirek's
a plasterer, Jan
a plumber, while Robbie can turn
his hand to anything, he can fix

Jan is pronounced 'Yan'

whatever they throw at him –
he's the Army to thank for that,
above all else the one thing they taught
him was how to solve a problem.

The whole set up reminds him of when
he first enlisted, sharing quarters
in cramped spaces with complete strangers,
instead of the barracks, this caravan

where they crash each night bone weary
after working a double shift –
for the first time since he left
he feels no need to say sorry.

It's simple here – work, sleep, eat –
cash in hand, no questions asked,
maximum effort, minimum risk,
cheap accommodation, right on site.

No-one asks him why he's there
(though Mirek, Lev and Jan assume
that what to them seems like a fortune
is next to nothing when compared

to what someone like Robbie might expect
to earn in normal circumstances,
but another man's experiences
they treat unjudging with respect).

Each of them has beneath his bunk
a box, their sole inviolable
space, where things too preciously personal
are kept, brought out over a late night drink

to be cried quietly over,
letters, photographs, a keepsake,
longingly traced blindly in the dark,
while Lev plays his harmonica…

Robbie never looks at his save
for when he needs to check the heft
of that other thing that Bandit left
carefully wrapped in its small black cloth,

familiarly snug, a reassuring weight
amid the lightness of his current
state of being, impermanent,
tethered only by a sense that fate

is holding one more surprise
and he needs to be ready –
his hand remains rock steady
as his fingers slowly close

around its pure, uncompromising shape.
Some nights the others will sing – songs
that strangely make Robbie feel he belongs,
lost and wandering on some far-off slope

on an Afghan mountainside, their cracked
voices evoking a deep sense of pain
and loss that, through singing, is found again,
a purpose naked and uncloaked –

but mostly time is taken up with work,
Robbie can sometimes go a whole week
without opening his mouth to speak.
"Man of mystery," jokes Mirek.

*

As completion date draws nearer
the four are pushed to the limit.
There's talk of a large bonus if it
comes in on time and under

budget. It's all hands to the pump
now with each of them having to work
quite literally around the clock,
there's something of a siege camp

mentality, corners are cut,
safety measures ignored –
it's squeaky bum time, mistakes are made –
but somehow they get through it

more or less unscathed, until it's time
to get paid. Suddenly the gang
master's nowhere about. They hang
around the site waiting for him

to show – he'll have to at some point –
but Lev and Jan and Mirek
have another contract
lined up already, they can't

wait indefinitely, there are dark
mutterings, a deep, brooding sense
of betrayal, humiliation descends.
Robbie retreats from further talk,

heads towards the white caravan
as wet, grey snow begins to fall,
he's running down that Afghan hill
towards the three-spanned bridge again,

when the gang master enters the yard –
all the talk and promises
of extra pay and bonuses
are coldly, flatly, denied.

He hasn't, it seems, even got
the money to pay them for the work
they pulled out all the stops for this week,
voices are raised, then silenced by gunshot.

They all turn as one. Robbie alights
from caravan steps, the gun
pointing skywards. He lowers it down
slowly, deliberately, training the sights

towards the gang master's head.
Lev spreads out his left palm.
"Robbie," he says, "please. Let's stay calm."
Robbie motions the gun towards a shed

in a corner of the yard, silent,
ignoring the others' frightened looks.
The gang master nods, nervously unlocks
its reinforced steel door, each moment

elongates like taut, coiled wire
stretched so tight it might just snap
in a heartbeat, a child's spinning top
humming in the heavy, snow-filled air.

Robbie points towards the safe,
the gang master punches in the code,
each blue symbol digitally displayed,
then slowly pulls the heavy, stiff

door open, the automatic light
inside revealing neatly piled stacks
of twenties that Robbie counts, checks
and evenly metes out

between Mirek, Lev and Jan
just as the site alarm shrieks.
Robbie stays calm, coolly speaks
for the first time. "Quickly – run,"

and when they object, "it's fine.
Just go. It's best if I stay here."
Lev presses his harmonica
into Robbie's hand, and then they are gone.

*

After the police convoy's arrived,
tyres squealing, Robbie's flung head
first down in the snow, arms stretched wide,
a cruciform, silent, smiling, saved.

4

The ex-Para attending officer
who escorted Robbie from court
when the trial was over's proved right.
Two years and ten months after

starting his sentence he's surprised to hear
in a brief, terse letter
signed by the prison governor
that owing to his good behaviour

he's to receive parole.
He's summoned to an office
where he's obliged to sign various
papers. He hardly reacts at all.

Throughout his time there he's kept
his head down, spent days working
in the machine room making
donkey jackets, has hardly slept

a single night, instead he's watched
the night sky's orange glow through the bars
of the cell subtly shifting down the years
rediscovering his edge.

He makes no friends, but no enemies
either. The other inmates steer
a wide path around him, taking care
to avoid close contact with his hooded eyes.

He doesn't notice them. They mean
less than nothing to him,
each hour he clocks up in the gym
brings him one step closer to the plan

he's formulated those long, dark nights –
he's done the crime,
he'll do his time –
and silently, patiently, he waits.

*

Back in civvies, by the outer gate,
the screws shake his hand, wish him luck,
he hoists his kit bag on his back,
clock ticking, takes his first step out –

a deep exhilaration
fills him, he quickens his pace,
each new stride takes him close,
close, closer, to his dreamt-of destination.

### 7. Loft Conversion

Alan and Amina move three times
in five years, each location a further
step up the property ladder.
They also acquire holiday homes

in Sardinia, Miami and Crete,
which they mostly use to impress
new clients, make deals, showcase
their next big idea, complete

with finance packages, tax free
benefits all designed to induce
an 'A' list clientele - a rich recluse,
a rising celebrity

or two, to endorse the latest scheme
of AA Associates
with champagne parties on chartered yachts –
the rise of the double 'A' Team

seems irresistible, their London
residence Clink Wharf, all shabby chic
exposed girders, distressed brick,
reinvented smart Victorian

former jute warehouse loft,
its trendy Borough Market site
with views across the river to the Tate
regularly photographed

for *Time Out, Square Mile, Vogue*,
frequently they're interviewed
on day time TV, *Loose Women* regard
them as distinctly *nouvelle vague*,

claims Amina will dismiss
with studied style. "We're glorified
estate agents, nothing more. We pride
ourselves in never settling for less

than what our clients expect.
My grandma back in India
was the local village matchmaker
assisting families to select

a husband for their daughter.
I like to think I do the same,
helping people choose a home…" –
cut to studio applause, cue laughter –

"… wish lists, mood boards, style charts,
replacing astrological
with pragmatic aspirational,
our heads must rule our hearts

when market forces are in play,
but not forsake entirely childhood dreams –
if I'd lost sight of my own personal schemes
I wouldn't be where I am today."

The front cover of *London Magazine*
highlights their ingenuity;
they each receive an MBE
personally from the Queen.

While Amina is their public face
Alan's busy buying brown field sites,
developing different types of estates,
their bread and butter, not so glamorous

but profitable. On a rare
visit to his family, they walk around
the still overgrown waste ground
and hatch a scheme to build some houses there.

Amina thinks it makes a great news
story: "Local boy strikes gold,
returns to roots to build
hash-tag *#homes for heroes.*"

*

Jane, too, begins to climb
the property and social ladders.
She joins a set of top-ranked Chambers,
takes the silk, has breakfast with the Home

Secretary, appears on *Newsnight*,
speaks before Commons Select Committees,
sues for political amnesties,
on which she's a much sought expert,

challenges rulings in the High Court
supported by her senior partners
who act as guides, advisors, mentors,
aware her photogenic light

can work to their advantage too,
especially in those cases that attract
significant attention from the media pack
which she seems to relish. *Who's Who*

lists her in their top one hundred
"young professionals on the cusp",
an opportunity she knows to grasp –
it's *her* time and mustn't be squandered.

Khaleel is also on the rise –
he's published a book, writes
for the more discerning broadsheets,
still walks the hallways of LSE's

more elevated echelons,
occasional guest appearances
on *Question Time*, his smart responses
capturing the headlines.

He's being groomed by New Labour
for a north London marginal
that's eminently winnable,
currently courting favour

among local party constituents,
his likely opponent a token
Tory glamour girl who's widely spoken
of and regularly trends

across the blog-and-twitter-sphere.
Media darlings both, each at home
with the new rules of an old game,
Khaleel and Jane are firm and clear

to keep the personal and professional
separate. Jane's had a second baby
(Sri now has a sister, Ruby)
creating need for additional

space – rather than moving house
they opt for upward expansion,
design their own loft conversion,
hire a live-in nanny from Manaus,

who drives Sri to school each day,
the local state primary,
whose Head invites Jane to be
Chair of the Governing Body,

where she makes an instant impact
by resisting calls from the PCC
to become a Gove Academy –
local radio dubs it "The Jane Effect".

She goes to see her parents for a break.
On a whim, just as she's almost there,
she makes a detour past the waste ground where
she sees a sign that stops her in her tracks.

PCC = Parochial Church Council

*

Robbie's feeling giddily light-headed.
He's been walking for ten weeks straight,
his destination now almost in sight,
this time alone's been what he's needed.

He's tramped through cities, towns and villages,
crossed fields, strode along dual carriageways,
seen England's landscape open down the days
unfolding as his courage has.

He's slept in ditches, bus shelters, graveyards,
walked with miners trudging weary in the dark,
waved to children texting in the park,
followed farmers heading homewards,

cut along towpaths beside canals,
been chased by dogs on sink estates,
sat on sofas dumped on roundabouts,
passed boarded up shops and closing down sales,

seen seagulls scrapping over land-fills,
nose-to-tail car lights snaking through the nights,
twenty-four hour service stations, factory gates
shutting, the winking bleeps of check-out tills

balancing the haves and have-nots in their scales,
he's marched through army firing ranges
dodging bullets as the season changes
and kicked his way through sodden piles

of fallen leaves, as the year turns.
He sees his breath form ghostly statues,
grey wisps dissolving as they rise.
An urgent sense of mission grows and burns

inside his belly as he nears
his final destination –
soon he'll place his long-planned operation
onto high alert, he's ready, no fears,

this is what he's trained for down the years.
The last day he passes row after row
of houses, looks in each lighted window
at lives he's never known, at doors

that haven't opened for him, never will,
cobbled terraced streets, high rise, back-to-backs,
garden semis, crescent *cul de sacs*,
right up to those mansions on the hill.

The ferris wheel stops turning round,
dodgems sputter one last spark,
ghost trains banging in the dark,
no one rides the helter skelter down –

he hears their final shout.
In a muddied field on the edge of town
The Last Fair in England's being taken down,
one by one the twinkling lights go out.

*

He turns down a newly surfaced lane,
towards the rundown tenant farm
where he was born, now a holiday home,
all past associations gone,

the barn his father hung himself in
torn down, replaced by modern stables,
the farmhouse has freshly painted gables,
an oak front door, over which a sign

proclaims "The Elms", though Robbie can't recall
actually seeing one, at least not alive.
He doesn't recognise it, can't believe
he ever lived there. He needs to pull

himself back on track. He retreats
to the main road, pauses, looks around,

then makes a bee-line for the waste ground,
which is where he's always set his sights.

*

The first thing he notices is the fence –
grey steel mesh, electrified, twelve feet
high, topped with barbed wire, double thick, floodlit,
a rash of garish warning signs:

*Trespassers Will Be Prosecuted,*
*Guard Dogs Patrol This Site,*
*Danger – Keep Out – Private*
*Property of A.A. Associated;*

an advertising billboard
nostalgically depicting, complete
with artist's impression, the small estate
surrounded by a bluebell wood

the developers plan to build there.
"*Imagine waking up to all of this,*"
it asks. "*Set within the timeless*
*tranquillity of English nature,*

*but with all the modern amenities*
*contemporary living requires we need,*
*within easy reach of rail and road*
*links to nearby towns and cities,*

*this luxury but discreet hideaway*
*offers two-, three-, four-bedroom homes fit*
*for heroes, because we think you're worth it –*
*we can all be heroes just for one day.*

*Completion date expected early*
*next spring, mortgages available,*
*dreams have never been more attainable:*
*An Englishman's Home is his Eyrie.*

*We hope you have a pleasant flight."*
Logo of an eagle's head, bright eye fixed
on happy families posing next
to shiny new front doors, a kite

dancing in the sky above
the artist's airbrushed painted scene
of houses round a village green.
*"Let's all celebrate the Good Life."*

Robbie, seething in the fading light,
scales the steel fence – time for Plan B –
cuts the wire, drops noiselessly
down, a lone wolf swallowed by the night...

*

His feet lead him unerringly
to the tree – blindly through the dark
his fingers trace initials in the bark –
he looks up. The moon casts a pale glow

through skeletal branches to the base
of the platform – he climbs swiftly up,
parts the tangled ivy, takes his first step
across the threshold, back in the tree house.

Owl droppings lie scattered on the cold floor,
spiders scuttle in far corners,
a trail of threaded whispers
hang gossamer light in the night air.

He listens for those lost, familiar noises –
a fox barks emerging from its earth,
badger snuffles through the undergrowth,
the ancient murmur of ancestral voices...

*

He wakes to a faint mewing cry,
a buzzard, hanging on the high thermals,
making slow, lazy circles,
tries to climb the sky,

its flight is intercepted,
mobbed by two persistent, nagging crows,
forcing its retreat, Robbie's gaze
is shifted, redirected

back to stake his claim on the ground,
marking out his territory,
an absolute necessity,
with everything meticulously planned.

The tree becomes a fortress for a siege,
the wood a palisade with sharpened sticks,
he smears dirt across his brow and cheeks,
wears combat camouflage

fatigues, digs in for the duration,
sets booby traps beneath rope nets,
trip wires that will trigger warning shots
at the first sign of enemy intrusion.

At dawn early, heart rate slow and steady,
he scans the land's perimeter,
his battered old binoculars
back where they belong. He's ready.

*

Jane calls Alan the next day.
By now it's known what Robbie's done.
Already news hounds have begun
to sniff around, scenting prey.

"You did grow up here after all,"
she argues. "You might show some degree,
some small pretence, at least, of empathy."
"The times we live in are more mobile,"

he counters, "we have to let the market
set the value, Jane, you know that's true;
if we engineer the prices of a few,
falsely, surely you can see it,

we run the risk we jeopardise
the investment potential of the rest.
Trust me, Jane, the real test
is what these homes might realise

in ten years time." "But *homes for heroes*,
Alan? That's so deliberate,
the way that you manipulate
an already loaded phrase

and hijack it for your own ends,
it's dishonest, it betrays a total lack
of feeling to the soldiers coming back –
like Robbie…" "You two were friends,"

says Alan, "though I never could see why,
so you can't remain impartial."
"But that's my point," says Jane. "It *is* personal.
I want to look him in the eye

when this is all over and say
I'm on your side, you've made a start."
"Spare me please the bleeding heart,
you and I both pursue the middle way.

It's a property *ladder*, Jane."
"But how do you get your foot on that first rung,
Alan?" "Go for cheaper if you're young –
you can always come back here again

when you're older, when you can afford it."
"You're trampling on our history."
"No, Jane. It's what we've done for centuries,
and as for Robbie's rights, they're forfeit."

Jane's voice lowers to a whisper.
"Let me talk to him. Let me try. Please."
A brief pause. "I'll give you twenty four hours –
then I send in the bulldozers."

*

*Robert – Robbie – sometimes Rob*
*stands in the clearing catching his breath,*
*he's hacked his way through the undergrowth*
*undetected, he thinks, till a sudden grab*

*on his shoulder makes him whirl*
*around. "Caught you, she yells – you said*
*I wouldn't find you but there, see, I did."*
*Robbie grins – Jane isn't bad for a girl.*

*He turns away, surveying the terrain.*
*"This'll do," he says, puffing out his chest,*
*and Jane senses this is some kind of test.*
*He points to a tree. "You'll not tell Alan…"*

*This is not a question. She starts*
*to nod, then shake, her head.*
*"…as long as that's understood."*
*Her love for him's so fierce it hurts.*

*

"Hey," she says. "Found you." He nods.
"Hey." She twists her wedding ring. A long pause.
How to start again after twenty years?
"I see you're married," he says. "Kids?"

"Yes," she says, "two. Look."
She brings up photos on her phone.
"Nice." "Are you going to come down?"
He shakes his head. "Can I come up?" "If you like."

He lowers the ladder, she slowly climbs.
"It feels higher than I remember it."
"Were you scared back then?" "No. Not
with you. They were good times."

Robbie narrows his eyes. "I know,"
she says, "I spoiled it. Sorry."
His face softens. "Not to worry –
all a long time ago now."

She looks around. "You've made quite a home,"
she says. The floor's been swept clean,
he points towards the re-hung sign.
Her eyes widen. "Is that the same…?"

"Of course," he says. "It's been here ever since.
When you first painted it, I didn't know
what the word meant. I do now."
She looks away. She scarcely understands

one tenth of what he's been through.
She's only just beginning
to register the camouflage he's wearing.
"What are you going to do?"

she asks, suddenly fearful.
"Homes for Heroes – that's what he's written.
I'm here to remind him in case he's forgotten
what a hero looks like." Jane becomes tearful.

"I don't mean me," he adds, "I fucked up before.
But my mates – what can they expect? This?
Not on a private's pay. He's taking the piss.
Like he always has. Well – not any more."

He's trembling. His eyes roll back inside his head,
she takes a step towards him, he recoils
so violently it fills
her with a sudden dread.

"You mustn't touch me," he explains,
"do you understand?" He carefully adjusts
his combat jacket sleeves beyond his wrists.
She nods, retreating from him as he turns

his face away from her. "You can't win,"
she says, barely audible.
"It simply isn't credible,
you know that. You'll have to come down.

In the end you'll have no other choice."
"Oh, I think I shall," he says.
"I've survived the desert for days
in circumstances far worse

than this. I'm in control up here.
I set the agenda. *He*
is going to listen to *me*."
"No he isn't, Robbie. He doesn't care.

But I can change the rules if you'll let me.
Right now he won't allow the newspapers,
radio or TV cameras
anywhere near. But put me

outside the fence with a microphone
and I'll make sure your voice is heard,
all you have to do is say the word,
and then you'll see: you're not alone.

You're a symbol, Robbie, a cause
who people will relate to, rally round…"
"No," he says, "you don't understand.
I don't want to be a symbol, or a cause.

I just wanted to come back home,
to this place, this ground, this tree.
There's nowhere else I can truly be,
and now, even its name's

been taken from me."
Jane takes all this in quietly.
"OK," she says, "but listen, Robbie,
you've got one day, then he'll call in the Army."

Robbie smiles. He feels no regret
at what's about to happen.
"Eagles live in the high mountains,"
he says, "alone. I can handle that."

*They stand facing each other a long time.*
*Jane is the first to break the silence.*
*"I've got to go," she says. "My parents..."*
*"I know," he says. "I'll walk you home."*

*"There's no need," she says. "I'll be OK."*
*Robbie grins. "I mean with these,"*
*and he picks up the binoculars.*
*"I can track you all the way."*

*He watches her cross the field, climb the gate,*
*run down the lane till she arrives*
*back at her house, where she turns and waves.*
Robbie breathes. Time to detonate.

*

The roar drags Jane from the pit of sleep.
Her first thought's to pick up Ruby, go
to the window where a red glow
illuminates a fire-bombed landscape.

In the aftermath of the explosion
parachutes of tiny flames
shower down on waking homes
lighted hopes of liberation.

### 8. Homes for Heroes

Another year passes.
A small crowd gathers in the village square
to listen to the local Mayor
deliver a short speech. He expresses

his gratitude to AA Associates
for their act of generosity,
this gift of land in perpetuity,
before the two ornate, wrought iron gates

which mark the garden's entrance.
Alan and Amina acknowledge
the polite ripples of applause which
drift across the freshly cut lawns

in the warm early spring sun.
Jane's there too, holding Ruby's hand
while Sri perfects her latest handstand,
her father looking proudly on.

Jaz and Bandit in full dress
uniform stand to attention throughout,
their presence lends a sober note
that's picked up later by the Press.

The Mayor now hands the microphone
to some minor TV celebrity
who's here to cut the ribbon, she
went to school nearby, is locally known,

who, though she's not been back in years,
is still regarded favourably,
cheered enthusiastically –
"she doesn't put on airs", "one of us",

Jane hears the people round her say
and wonders if that's how they think of her,
with a husband who's a foreigner,
then quickly shuts such thoughts away.

The soap star moves towards the ribbon,
takes the scissors from the Mayor,
poses for the photo, then: "I now declare
this Peace Garden open,"

she says, cuts it, and the gates swing wide,
white balloons rise high above the green,
the brass band plays *God Save The Queen*
and everybody pours inside

to view the former waste ground's rebirth,
the flowers in their regimented rows,
the newly planted trees which rise
like bayonets from the scorched earth.

Games and picnics have been planned,
children make a bee-line for the swings,
in the distance a church bell rings
over England's green and pleasant land.

*

The day draws to a close, the sky grows dark.
Jane leads the girls towards a spot
that's stayed neglected, kept apart
from the rest of the carefully tended park.

By the stump of a charred tree
set into a square of flattened grass
she points towards a simple brass
plaque plainly inscribed: "*In memory*

*of Corporal Robert "Robbie" Hann*
*who never showed a trace of fear,*
*who built his home for heroes here,*
*the child is father to the man.*"

"Did you know him, Mummy?" asks Sri.
"Not well enough," says Jane, "not since
I was your age, when we were, briefly, friends…
Come on, let's go back to Grandma's for our tea."

As they walk away for the last time
they pass by Jaz and Bandit keeping still
their lone silent, night-long vigil
and the promise they made to bring back home

and lay to rest upon the grass
a harmonica, a regimental tie,
postcards from Cambridge, a wind-up toy,
a pair of old binoculars.

## Gaudete

Gaudete - an anonymous plainsong from the early 15th century collection Priori Cantones made famous by Steeleye Span in the 1970's.
(See end for translations)

Heard in Blackpool 1975, remembered now – for Gareth: 1953 – 2013

the day passes in a blur
a loop of light around your head
kicking a football on a beach
crystals of sand in your hair
a Frisbee frozen in mid
flight which when I try to catch

it down the years, to grasp
it, hold it close, eludes
me, flutters down, a dip and curve
back to each memory's cusp
flickering with your eyelid's
pulse, the seagulls' wild dive

swooping as we race the waves
and though you cannot swim
you smile as we go under –
all the sounds of muffled lives
crashing like an unheard drum
rise up through the half glimpsed future

jolting me awake, that same song's
call to arms now turned to lament
*carmina laetitiae*
*devote redamus* flings
a faint rebuke defiant
undiminished since the day

we first heard it soar above
the crowd and out across the town
back towards the water's edge

your footprints in the sand leave
no trace along the shore line
as from the haze you re-emerge

striding with that Ghost Train grin
fearless through each fairground
ride, haunted swing, hall of mirrors
where each phantom broken
image carries no cruel hand
print yet of what mockeries

lie in wait, the Golden Mile
kiss-me-quick/squeeze-me-slow
souvenirs, like candy floss,
which innocently beguile…
*tempus ad est gratiae*
*hoc quod optabamus*

I try to fix that summer blur
now, capture in a single frame
that one-time shot to take me back
to that always golden hour
your whoop of joy urging home
the Frisbee's final hanging arc

Translations from the Latin:

*Gaudete*
Rejoice

*Carmina laetitiae devote redamus*
We offer these songs of joy with love afflicted

*Tempus ad est gratiae hoc quod optabamus*
Let us give thanks for this time of grace - we long for its return

# the long and winding road

## What Survives

But if you place each rescued moment of high alert
beneath the latest high-spec microscope
to probe beyond the loss and the regret
and salvage what survives of each first spark of hope

what will I do if, when you load the slide
with this or that culture on the tray,
adjust the focus, magnify the lens,
you tell me what survives has drained away;

how am I then to see what happens
washed up with the rubbish on the tide:
do I sieve the filtered water pure
or drink untreated sewage raw?

No – rather I'll explore fresher, less primeval slime;
hold my breath, dive deeper to a half-remembered home...

## Delivering Memories

If ever I'm asked what has been my favourite job, I answer immediately: driving a delivery van for a local florist's, for the simple reason that everyone was always so pleased to see me. Except for once. I arrived on the doorstep of a thirties semi early one morning bearing a beautiful, wrapped bouquet of mixed blooms, to be greeted by a young woman still in her dressing gown. She took one look at the flowers and was instantly horrified: "You can't deliver those," she said. "My husband is here!" She was just about to shut the door when she added *sotto voce*, with a nervous glance over her shoulder, "Come back in half an hour. He'll be gone by then."

Otherwise people were delighted. Even when it was a funeral, they were quietly relieved to see that everything was being done properly. Weddings and funerals were our biggest and most regular orders. Each morning Mr Monks, the owner of the shop, would drive to Smithfield Market in the centre of Manchester before dawn to make sure he had the pick of the freshest flowers as they arrived from the growers. You never quite knew what you were going to get – in February and March it would be daffodils and narcissi from the Isles of Scilly – but he would frequently surprise the rest of us working for him with an unexpected glut of anemones, or dahlias, or freesias. As well as Mr Monks, there was Linda, the shop girl, straight from school, who served the customers; Rosie, the actual florist – "what else could I do with a name like mine?" – who designed and arranged all the displays and who'd been to college; Old Fred, who'd previously driven the van, but who now swept out the cellar, brought more stock up when it was needed, and helped out in a whole range of ways; and then there was me – just graduated from university, part of a small touring theatre company with friends, working for a drinking buddy of my dad's as the delivery boy.

It suited me perfectly. I'd begin work each morning around 7am, deliver flowers till midday, then rehearse all afternoon and evening. As well as the weddings and funerals, we had our weekly round of regular customers: board rooms, hotel foyers, the Mayor's Parlour, council offices, and every Monday morning to Kellogg's in Trafford Park, where there were displays in the two works canteens. (I used to enjoy these weekly Kellogg's drop-offs, partly because of the excellent bacon barm cakes they used to serve, but mostly because the previous summer I had worked for a month there, and if delivering flowers was the best job I ever had, working at Kellogg's was up there with the worst. I was what was called a "Quality Assurance Operative", a ridiculous hyperbole for what in fact involved me wearing a white lab coat and standing next to a conveyor belt for hours at a time while thousands upon thousands of Corn Flakes flowed past me: if I saw a burnt black one, my job was to lean over and pick it out).

But mostly the work was delivering bouquets to individual houses – wedding anniversaries, birthdays, get well wishes, apologies. Each morning I'd wash the van, clear out all the bits of leaves from the previous day, then load her up with the first set of orders. We delivered to an approximate ten mile radius of the shop, and during my first week, Old Fred would hand me the A to Z and test me on all the roads and pretty soon I got to know every one, including all the short cuts, cul de sacs and one way systems. Saturdays were always the busiest days because of the weddings, and I would pick up lots of tips then, too. I would usually be tipped at funerals as well, but more quietly, almost secretively, as a thank you for being discreet and on time. I usually gave these back to whatever charity was being collected for at the service.

This carried on for about six months, by which time I felt like an old hand. More and more Mr Monks would take me with him to Smithfield Market to help him buy from the growers, and once or twice he'd let me go by myself. This meant getting there for 4am, but it was worth it for the overtime, and also for the atmosphere of the market as the sun was coming up. Traders began to recognise me and the smells and the colours were intoxicating. I settled into the routines of early mornings, the jokes and banter, the scalding cups of tea, the feeling of being valued, the sense of belonging.

I remember trying to articulate some of this to my father one evening over a beer. "But is this really what you went to university for, son?" was his only comment.

The next week the theatre company got its first significant tour – three months on the Isle of Man, followed by three more in the Trough of Bowland. I spoke to Mr Monks and tried to explain my predicament. I'd love to come back one day, perhaps he could hold the job open for me when I returned? He raised a rueful eyebrow. "This isn't a hobby, Chris. This isn't something you can just put down and pick up again like some kind of toy. This is my life. I've built this business up from nothing, it's taken me years to get it to where it is now. I need people I can rely on, not some fly-by-night here-today-gone tomorrow. Someone I can trust. You've got to make a choice, lad…"

Well, there was no choice really. I handed him back the keys to the van and went off on tour the following week. Inevitably, within a year, the theatre company folded as we all went our separate ways, and I drifted back to Urmston and dropped into the shop one morning to say hello. Rosie had moved on – "seduced by *Interflora*," said Fred, who was still there – while Linda was now arranging the displays. Someone else was driving the delivery van of course, Derek Lightfoot, who'd been in my class at school, but who'd left after 'O' levels. He looked a bit like Phil from The Everly Brothers, and at school he'd played the guitar.

"Are you still singing then?" I asked him when he came back from his first round.

He looked at me like I'd stepped off the moon. "No."

"Why's that then?"

"I grew up."

Just then Mr Monks came into the shop. "That's right. I might retire next year and I'm thinking of asking Derek to become manager."

Over the next couple of years, I'd sometimes see the van driving towards me down the old familiar streets, its twin taglines *You Bring the Thought, We Bring the Flowers* and *Delivering Memories* painted on each side. It would go one way, I the other.

## Passing By

*My life is like a music-hall...* Arthur Symons

"... and chiefly yourselves!" The Music Hall Chairman, resplendent with handlebar moustache, in top hat and tails, brings down his gavel with a flourish; the band strikes up *The Old Bull & Bush*, and a packed, swaying auditorium begins raucously to sing.

"And now, for your further delectation and delight, *The Victorians* are proud to present that Prince of Prestidigitational Prowess – that's a magician to you, madam – Professor Paul Prosser!" And down comes the gavel once more.

With similar sleight of hand, my father, too, disappeared before my eyes as if he had walked inside one of those magic cabinets. The conjuror closes the door on him, reopens it and he's vanished; then he spins it around, opens the door once again, and out steps my father as if he's never been away. When he returned, he had reinvented himself – from export clerk to impresario. He set himself up as an agent, specialising in Old Time Music Hall, which he promoted as *The Victorians* to pubs and clubs across the north-west.

There were singers, dancers, comedians, as well as conjurors and other so-called "novelty acts", including *The Harmonica Seven*, a family of three generations who each played a different sized mouth organ, from the tiniest, which could fit easily into the palm of your hand, to the largest, which was as long as your arm, performing the *William Tell Overture* or *Flight of the Bumble Bee*, followed by a silver-haired, lugubrious man who played the musical saw. Introduced by the Chairman in cod German as a celebrated, virtuosic maestro, he would enter the stage carrying a music stand and a violin case. He would then speak in slow, sonorous tones, his accent vaguely Central European, about the need for absolute silence and concentration from the audience (a request usually greeted with amused *oohs* and *aahs*); he would adjust the height of his stool several times, take out his sheet music which he would place with a flourish on the stand, announce that we were about to witness the premiere of a long lost sonata by Brahms, or Beethoven, or Schubert, trusting that we fully realised the import of the occasion, and then proceed to take from the case his musical saw, which he would polish reverently with a cloth before producing in high glissando a very recognisable version of a well known classical tune.

These acts were interspersed by a Chorus singing well known music hall songs, which the audience joined in with lustily; there was also a melodrama, *The Lighthouse Keeper's Daughter*, complete with Drunken Father, Blushing Daughter, Dastardly Villain and Dashing Hero, together with much audience participation, and the whole evening was knitted together by the Chairman, who stood to one side of the stage, introducing each of the acts with a series of increasingly outrageous alliterations.

At the heart of these performances was my mother, who bore a striking resemblance to Marie Lloyd, and who would offer rousing renditions of *My Old Man, Don't Have Any More Mrs Moore, One of the Ruins that Cromwell Knocked About a Bit, Oh Mr Porter* and, my own favourite, *The Boy I Love is Up in the Gallery*. Sometimes she'd throw in some of Marie Lloyd's original patter, with the Chairman standing in for the judges and magistrates who would try to censor her…

*

Chair: And now, ladies and gentlemen, that Most Mellifluous Melodienne, the Queen of Covent Garden, the Duchess of the Double-Entendre, who though she may have dillied and dallied, lost her way and can't find her way home, has in all respect and favour, won our hearts and made her home for ever in them, I give you Miss Stella Fogg, bringing you the undiluted delights of Miss Marie Lloyd!

*(The gavel comes down and the orchestra strikes up).*

Marie (*singing*): "She sits among the cabbages
and peas…"

Chair *(banging his gavel)*: No, no, no, Miss Lloyd. We cannot have such lewd licentiousness here.

*(The Audience registers its disapproval at his interruption).*

Chair *(continuing)*: This is a decent establishment.
Audience: Ooh! Speak for yourself etc
Marie: *(approaching the Chair)* Very well, sir. What would you have me sing instead?
Chair *(flustered, blushing)*: Couldn't you substitute a different vegetable?
Marie *(winking)*: I'll see what I can do for you, sir.

*(The orchestra takes up the song once again).*

Marie *(singing)*: "She sits among the cabbages and leeks…"

*

As well as *The Victorians*, my father handled all the individual acts which comprised the show and was always arranging separate bookings for them in working men's clubs, miners' welfares, golf clubs, night clubs, cinemas and theatres. Occasionally he would be so stretched to meet demand that I would be drafted into the Chorus and would quickly have to learn the routines to all the various sing-along numbers. And sometimes he could even be persuaded to perform himself. He was no longer singing Puccini arias by then, but he was always a great hit with the ladies singing well known Irish tenor favourites, formerly made famous by Joseph Locke or John McCormack, songs such as *Danny Boy, Roses of Picardy, Macushla*.

I would listen to him then and wonder if, as he sang, his thoughts turned to all the different parts he had played, not just on stage *(The Merry Widow, Carousel, The King and I, Kismet)*, but in life – footballer, soldier, steeplejack, clerk…

The last time I heard him sing in public was just a few months before he died, at the height of *The Victorians'* success, when he was just 52. It was a Victorian parlour song, Thomas Ford's rendition of an anonymous Elizabethan love poem:

*There is a lady sweet and kind...*
*... I did but see her passing by...*

The following year I was invited to direct a full length Music Hall at a theatre where my father had staged many such events. I was delighted to be able to do so. I decided to see if I could construct a single narrative that could weave its way through all the traditional music hall elements. It told the story of young Billy Button, who enlisted for World War 1, and who afterwards came back, for a while settling into a rather humdrum life, before unexpectedly being discovered, going on to strike it rich as a singer on the stage. The Chairman was a thinly disguised Arthur Symonds, the celebrated music hall poet, and for one section we wanted to contrast the brightness and gaiety of the world inside the theatre with the grimmer reality of life on the streets outside, as two small children danced to a tune on a barrel organ begging for change from the rich folk passing by. I asked the sound technician if he could find a recording of a barrel organ that we might use.

"How about this?" he said.

The theatre was dark and empty apart from the two of us. The haunting, lilting cadence of the barrel organ floated up through the dimly lit auditorium. I recognised the tune at once. Thomas Ford's *Passing By*. I could feel my father's presence watching over us as we put the finishing touches to the show in his honour.

We are all of us just passing by, and it was as if my father was trying to tell me to make the most of every moment, not waste so many of them, as he had been forced to do whilst enduring a successions of jobs he hated, only following his heart when it was almost too late.

*

*Lonely, save for a few faint stars, the sky*
*Dreams; and lonely, below, the little street*
*Into its gloom retires, gloomy and shy.*
*Scarcely the dumb roar enters this soft retreat;*
*And all is dark, save where come flooding rays*
*From a tavern window: there, to the brisk measure*
*Of an organ that down in an alley merrily plays,*
*Two children, all alone and no one by,*
*Holding their tattered frocks, through an airy maze*
*Of motion, lightly threaded with nimble feet,*
*Dance sedately: face to face they gaze,*
*Their eyes shining, grave with a perfect pleasure.*

*The Little Dancers:* Laurence Binyon

*

I picture my mother as a small child, in outsized, grown-ups' red shoes, dancing to the rhythm of the deep-throated rumble of my grandfather's printing presses rolling through the night, waiting for her dancing partner, a barefoot boy, to step down from his brick tower, and ask her to join in with a new beat, to jive and jitterbug, clearing the floor, before he sings to her one more time:

*There is a lady sweet and kind*
*I did but see her passing by…*

## Timelines

for Martell Linsdell

Scrambling to the summit of grassed-over slag heaps, we try to fix a toe-hold in the sliding scree of coal still poking through the surface this cold March morning, cobwebs of mist clinging to our clothes and hair. She points back down to the pithead where trucks tip spoil into mud-churned hollows.

"Think of it as drawing," she says, "making marks on the land, with the earth as a canvas."

A crow, feathers tugged by the wind, hunkers down on an outcrop of hard stone jutting from the slick shale like a bleached bone.

"For all this," she continues, her arm sweeping across the rain-swept wreckage of demolition down below, the headstocks, the steel tracks, the winding gear, "despite being so recent, feels almost prehistoric. That digger looks like a dinosaur, about to dredge up fossils – ammonites, trilobites – from when it was all under the sea…"

As does she: the spoke of a wheel from a broken wagon, the blade of a shovel like a ploughshare, part of an old pick-handle, and other more domestic finds – a willow pattern tea cup, a lace doily stiffened with frost and years, brittle as a bird's wing. The crow caws a half-hearted, ragged protest, lifting into the wind. Across the empty ground two hares buck and box through the driving March rain.

For the next two years she walks across the coalfields collecting stories and memories, random found objects she mounts in cases like a museum, or arranges carefully in small metal tins like secrets waiting to be discovered. She likes to tease us with context: she places a series of drill bits she has found in framed boxes around the walls; they are identical, but beneath each box she has placed a different label – gallery exhibit, industrial artefact, archaeological find; mechanical tool, disposable waste, art work – make your choice…

She coaxes pitmen twice her size to hand over their brass tallies, name tags with numbers embossed in the plate, each containing a unique fingerprint, a distinct identifiable individual. Every miner has two: at the start of each shift he hands one over to the site foreman as he steps into the lift that will carry him down the shaft to the coal face, keeping the other safely on his person; when he returns to the surface he reunites this one with its twin, so that the foreman knows who has ascended safely and who is still underground. If ever there was an accident, these tallies were vital in determining whether you were alive or dead; they were as important to the men as their wedding rings.

She places all of the tallies the retired miners surrender to her onto a silicon slab, each one delicately positioned after careful, sometimes contentious deliberation, to reflect special relationships, particular places, status and roles. Then she casts them into bronze sculptures to be placed as an installation in the landscape, recording their continuing presence, a sign saying even though the pits are closing we can still leave our marks on the land, timelines, a trail of tears…

As the millennium turns, like the slow creak of the winding gear on the last surviving headstock at the only working pit, she knows she is ready. She will attempt a giant drawing, she tells me, making her own marks, to capture all these stories, all these memories, in one unbroken line drawn at a single sitting. In the concert hall of an old Miners' Welfare building, she gaffer-tapes huge sheets of paper to the floor in a vertical line, as if delving underground. She takes a deep breath, holds up a piece of charcoal, closes her eyes, then begins. For a silent eight hour shift she continues to climb across the floor, her feet and fingers never leaving the paper, her body descending as if on a rope down to the coal face.

When it is finally done, she fastens it to a series of old railway sleepers found at the surface of the most recent pit to close; these she attaches with chains, which are then lowered deep into the mine…

The press has a field day.

"Public art the public can't see!" they gleefully proclaim.

"But we know it's there," she counters. "We can feel it in our bones, muscle memory, lines on the skin, marks on the land..."

In memoriam.

The day the exhibition is hung is just another Tuesday, we think. Tuesday 11th September, 2001.

When the first plane flies into the North Tower, she is under the earth, putting the last sleeper in place. When the second plane hits the South Tower, she is just reaching the surface, her face and body completely covered in black coal dust. There are safety workers with her, with hard hats and breathing apparatus. Behind them the wrecking ball swings into the twin headstocks, the tallest in Europe, imploding, collapsing in on themselves, leaving only a rusted skeleton. She stands for a long moment…

*

In the late summer of 2014 I visit *1 World Trade* in New York. It is coincidentally 9.11, and as a silent tribute, two vertical pillars of light are beamed into the night sky, occupying the space once filled by the twin towers. The names of the dead are etched in black granite, recording their continuing presence, the water plunging to infinity in the empty space below.

artefact landmark

monument identity

memorial timeline

## Crossing the Water

Each morning to get to school I caught the steam train that still ran from Flixton to Irlam, crossing the Ship Canal via one of many iron bridges. The canal incorporates sections of the rivers Mersey and Irwell alternately, linked by newer waterways constructed to provide an unbroken link between Liverpool and Manchester. When it opened in 1897, at just under forty miles in length, it was the longest continuous river navigation for ocean-going vessels anywhere in the country, and it led to Manchester, despite being so far inland, becoming the third largest port in England. But it also cut off Irlam from Flixton irrevocably. What were once adjoining villages now became entirely separate communities, with different occupations and different ambitions. Whereas Irlam was all heavy industry – steel, tar, chemicals – Flixton became suburban, aspirational, a dormitory town for workers in nearby Trafford Park or Manchester. Crossing the canal became a symbol of stepping up in the world, so if you crossed the water at all, it was preferable to do it from Irlam to Flixton and not look back.

And so it was something of an anomaly that saw me crossing the other way back over into Irlam, followed by the short walk along the thundering Liverpool Road to Cadishead, where I went to school. I was accompanied by my mother, who was a teacher at the same school, and who had grown up as a child there herself, so for her this was more like a homecoming, passing on our way the house where she was born, the printers where my grandfather still worked, the old Rialto Cinema (next to the canal, but there the similarity with Venice ended), the Wesleyan Chapel on the corner, the bomb site on the Bama, the library on the edge of the Moss, where families lived in makeshift shanty homes built on stilts, where fierce dogs and feral children roamed, and where there was a gypsy encampment.

It was on the Moss, my mum would tell me, that as a girl she went to the annual travelling fair that pitched there each

Midsummer's Eve. She loved its tawdry glamour, the freak shows and hoopla stalls, the rifle ranges and dancing girls. "She wears red feathers and a hoochy-coochy skirt," she'd sing as we walked to school. (This was when she wasn't telling me the story of *Treasure Island*, complete with different voices for all the characters. How I'd been thrilled and terrified by Blind Pew tap-tap-tapping his way towards The Admiral Benbow Inn to serve Billy Bones with the black spot). The Cadishead Moss Fair also had a boxing booth, where a bare-knuckled champion challenged all-comers. "Five guineas for the man who can go three rounds with me!" My mother's cousin Jack, a red-faced farmer from the adjoining Rixton Moss, who'd once tied my mother as a girl to a tree in the orchard and then left her there all day, challenged him but was, as he quite cheerfully recounted to anyone who'd listen, "knocked into the middle of next week".

But while there was some currency to be had in having crossed the water, it also quite literally cut me off from all of the other kids, who looked on me as posh, not one of them, even though my family went back generations there.

A more pressing currency was to be found in the squares of hard pink bubble gum, which we traded fiercely in the playground, for each wrapper contained two postcards depicting various flags of the world, and I was desperate to collect the whole set of eighty flags. Frequently you'd open the wrapper breathless with anticipation, only to discover that the flags were ones you already had, and so exchanges were bartered and traded. It soon became apparent which countries were worth more than others. Union Jacks were ten a penny, as were French Tricouleurs, or American Stars and Stripes. Much more difficult to find, and therefore much more collectible, were Iraq and Afghanistan, Syria and Saudi, but rarest and most sought after of all was Albania. It was not uncommon, therefore, to witness the sight of small boys and girls tearing across the playground like flocks of starlings swooping and converging, dividing and separating, finally reforming around clusters where trading was most active, with as many as ten Stars and Stripes changing hands for a single Saudi scimitar.

I personally disliked bubble gum and never mastered the highly admired art of forcing large, round pink bubbles to blow up and then burst across my cheeks, and so I hoarded dozens of the thin square slabs to use as additional trading currency. Gradually my collection grew until it reached 79. Only Albania remained to be found. Nobody had ever seen it – the only reason we knew about it at all was because a full list of all the flags was printed on the inside of the bubble gum wrappers; we began to suspect that it didn't actually exist, either as a flag or as a country. Who knew anything about it back then? I asked my mum on one of our walks along Liverpool Road, and all she could come up with was King Zog, who sounded more like a character from a fairy tale than an actual real person.

Then one day, when the train was late and my mum and I didn't arrive till nearly the morning playtime, I slipped into Pook's Sweet Shop on the corner of John Street where the school was situated, paid over my penny for the bubble gum, and there it was, tucked inside beneath the hammer and sickle of the USSR. Albania. A black double-headed eagle in triumphant flight on a red background beneath the outline of a gold star. Each card, as well as a flag, showed characters in traditional costumes and a famous landmark – Albania has a young shepherd boy wearing a green waistcoat over brown shirt and trousers and a *qeleshe*, a strange, conical woollen hat, behind him a lake and snow-capped mountain – while the reverse side of each card gave snippets of information about that particular country (capital: Tirana; monetary unit: lek; miles from London: 1200), plus phonetically spelled handy phrases, should you ever find yourself there. *Loom-too-me-ray, Mik!* (Farewell, friend!)

When playtime came I duly showed off my complete set, only to learn that the bubble had, quite literally, burst, and now everyone was into trading something entirely different. My collection had become, overnight, worthless. I have the flags still, on a shelf in the room where I write; they have outlasted several of the countries they depict which have, for various reasons, ceased to exist, while another of their legacies is that I still know every single capital city, from the hours spent poring over these bubble gum flags of the world. I've noticed, though, that such knowledge has questionable value and carries little currency – girls were far less impressed by my ability to tell them the capital of Tristan da Cunha (The Settlement of Edinburgh) or Pitcairn Island (Adamstown) than they were by other boys' more successful efforts at blowing large round bubbles with shiny pink gum...

Journeying home back across the water my mum would continue the latest episode of *Treasure Island*, where flags also featured strongly – Long John Silver and Israel Hands hoisting the Jolly Roger on the mast of the *Hispaniola*, Jim Hawkins and Captain Smollett raising the Red Ensign over the stockade on the island.

I loved the idea of treasure islands, imaginary places with strange tribes speaking unknown languages, just waiting to be discovered. I drew endless maps with detailed landmarks – Smugglers' Cove, Skull Mountain, Devil's Hollow – and designed exotic flags for them all. So when, together with Pete from next door, Michael and Charlie the twins from a few doors down, and Barbara from across the street, along with her pet Sealyham terrier Candy, we decided to form The Cross Swords Club, it was only natural that I would design our flag – lifted almost in its entirety from the crossed swords on the flag of Saudi Arabia, but replacing its elegant Arabic script with the more prosaic initials CSC. Very much in thrall to Enid Blyton, we referred to ourselves as The Super Six, and we met in our garage. Although we didn't have a car (and wouldn't until I was 13) we had a garage, where there was a coal bunker and a magnificent mangle with lethal rollers, plus an enormous metal wash tub, which were dragged into the yard every wash day. Barbara, who was very bossy, drew up lists of rules we had to abide by, and there were complex knocks and codes and passwords with which we would let one another in to hold our secret meetings and plan our next daring adventure.

I remember my grandmother, quite baffled, asking me one day. "But what do you actually do?"

Wasn't it obvious? I rolled my eyes theatrically. We solved mysteries of course. We would lay trails – chalked arrows along the pavements – hide behind lamp posts as we followed unsuspecting passers-by and concocted all manner of fantastical plots to explain the most trivial of happenings: washing hanging on a line would be a message we had to decipher; sweet wrappers dropped as litter on the street would contain clues to the whereabouts of stolen jewels.

I also discovered through the Cross Swords Club the difference between boys and girls, as Barbara and I would pee quite companionably next to one another in the overgrown tangle of weeds at the bottom of our garden, taking care to avoid the nettles. (It was around this time too that my father, embarrassingly trying to explain to me the facts of life, got me so confused that I felt certain that, by handing Barbara a dock leaf to wipe herself dry, I must have got her pregnant).

Having a girl friend of course gained you more currency than anything else – even though you never actually went anywhere, or even spent any time at all together. It was the unaltered ritual of it all that counted.

"Will you go out with me?"

(Pause. Look away. Coil bubble gum around finger. Shrug).

"Alright."

Then off you would whoop like a cowboy riding your imaginary horse to join the other boys at the far end of the playground, running up and down the sliding piles of coke before Mr Nuttall the caretaker could catch you, while the girls hung about by the school wall playing complicated games catching balls and spinning while chanting unfathomable rhymes. My own special sweetheart was Margaret Ness, whose dad had emphysema and no longer worked in the steel mill, but was a park keeper, and who in 1961 put a shilling each way on the rank outsider Psidium to win the Derby because it was named after a flower. In a huge upset – so big that you can watch it still on Pathé News clips on you tube – it won, coming in at 66/1, which meant that Mr Ness won more than four guineas. The next day Margaret, who had shy dimples in her cheeks when she smiled, came to school with a new ribbon in her hair, white for a psidium.

St Mary's school was surrounded on three sides by the

Steel Works with Liverpool Road less than twenty yards away down John Street, a narrow cobbled alley between Pook's Sweet Shop and Martin's Bank, beneath a tall, blackened stone bridge, which carried trains from the steel furnaces to the Tar, Soap and Margarine Works further down the track and out along the Moss. There would always be clouds of smoke from the trains and factories hanging like a pall over the school playground, and some days this would turn a sickly sulphurous yellow, and then there was a chance we might all be sent home early. (Unfortunately this did not happen enough). All the kids except me lived within walking distance, either from the Bama (a bomb site) close by, or from the Moss, from where many would turn up barefoot, or in shoes they'd long outgrown, so that their toes poked through the ends, wrapped up in newspaper in winter.

One day, shortly after Psidium won the Derby, we had a school outing to visit the Steel Works. I must still have been just eight, almost nine, but I remember it as if it were yesterday. We walked in pairs, crocodile-fashion, along the Liverpool Road, holding hands. Or, if you were put next to a girl, you each pulled the sleeve of your jumper down over your hand, so that you didn't have to make any real physical contact. I was paired with Margaret Ness, and she permitted me to hold her actual hand with my own all the way till we reached the gates where we waited to be met by the foreman who was to show us around. But it was not the thrill of holding Margaret Ness's hand alone which made this day so memorable, but what followed.

After standing around for a few minutes in awe, dwarfed by the huge cooling towers, we were ushered across the main yard and into one of the cavernous rolling mills. Inside the scene was almost biblical. I was reminded of Daniel and the fiery furnace: Meshach, Shadrach and Abednego. Years later, as a student reading *Dante's Inferno*, I recognised immediately that this was what I had witnessed that day. Great plumes of fire fountained into the air above us; white-hot molten lava poured beside us from enormous vats into cascading open pipes which transported it to giant bare-chested blacksmiths in the cathedral-sized dome of the forge. Their faces and arms bathed in an eerie red glow, they lifted these ingots of white liquefied steel with large tongs from the rivers of fire flowing endlessly past them and dipped them into dark troughs of water where they hissed, cooled and solidified.

We were allowed to wander through this scene from Milton's Hell more or less unsupervised, with many of those from the Moss still barefoot. After a while I closed my eyes and pictured all those Flags of the World from my bubble gum collection and tried to imagine myself in some of those countries, as far away from Irlam Steel Works as possible.

When we got back to school afterwards, many of the children were incredibly excited. Some had seen their fathers there, while everyone knew that their futures, in some respect or other, would be played out there, as steel workers or steel workers' wives. I was determined that that would not be my fate. I had found the whole experience a nightmare and knew that the only route out of such a fate lay in education. If I could pass my 11+, that would mean another trip across the water, to Urmston (the suburb adjoining Flixton) and the Grammar School. I was determined there and then to do everything I could to ensure that this might happen.

"There's no way I'm ever setting foot back in there," I announced to the teacher in class afterwards.

As you might imagine, this did nothing to endear me to my classmates. Later that day, during playtime, I got into a scrap with one of them, George Hodson, one of the barefoot boys from the Moss. "You think you're somebody, don't you?" he said. "You think just because your mum's a teacher, and you live in a posh house, and you talk proper, you're better than us. But you're not. You're just stuck up, that's all."

And with that he launched into me, pushing me into the coke pile, where we wrestled and fought till Mr Nuttall came running across and we both scarpered. In the afternoon, when we were lining up for home time, Margaret Ness brought us both together, telling us not to be such silly boys and made us shake hands.

George and I became quite good friends afterwards, and we would work next to each other in the small school garden once a week, a blighted patch of scrubby land that Mr Nuttall somehow coaxed to produce a few potatoes each year, as well as some scraggy dahlias for the Headmaster's classroom. Mr Coleman. He taught the top juniors, where George, Margaret and I had now reached, and prepared us for the 11+ exam. It was a small room, facing the Bama. Unlike the rest of the school it didn't have the benefit of the huge, cast-iron, pot-bellied stoves, which looked like monsters from a fairy tale and which heated the school hall, itself partitioned by sliding blue doors to form two classrooms. (Once, some years before, Margaret Ness's best friend, Penny Williams, who lived behind Prospect Library at the edge of the Moss, pulled my hair because I'd beaten her in a test, and our chairs fell backwards as we crashed through these partition doors. Here I learned another of life's important lessons. Even though it was she who'd pulled my hair, because I was a boy, I was caned by Mr Coleman, while Penny was simply given a telling-off). But Mr Coleman's room did have an open fire, which George would come in early to light. He was still only ten years old and was always getting into mischief. Frequently he would shin up a drainpipe and climb up to the top of the school roof, where he would sit astride the weather cock. Yet he was immensely practical and could turn his hand to almost anything (except for holding a pen) and so it seemed perfectly normal to us that, despite being just ten, he would be entrusted with this daily task of lighting the headmaster's fire each morning.

But for most, preparing for the 11+ was not really a priority. Their lives were mapped out for them . When the results were announced, I was the only boy to pass, while from the girls, only Margaret and Penny secured a place at the Grammar School. But we would still be going our separate ways, for the boys' and girls' schools were on opposite sides of the town.

I went to North Wales as usual to spend the whole summer with my grandparents, and it was while I was there I stumbled across an article in the newspaper they had delivered each morning. *"Boy, 11, dies in Swimming Pool Tragedy..."*

George Hodson, the boy I'd fought with over our

futures on the coke pile, the boy whose hand Margaret Ness had forced me to shake, the boy next to whom I stood each week raking the weeds in the school vegetable plot, was dead. He had just taught himself to swim in one of the shallow inlets of the Ship Canal and one day he had taken himself off on an adventure, a train ride across the water to the swimming baths in Urmston, and there he had got into difficulties in the deep end. But it was so crowded that nobody had noticed, and he simply sank to the bottom, where he had drowned…

*

Two years later, I was still being troubled by dreams of George. You sort of knew that older people died, or pets (like Candy the Sealyham terrier who had died the same summer as George, leading to our disbanding of the Cross Swords Club, though in truth we had long since stopped meeting in our garage) but you didn't somehow think that someone your own age might. This first intimation of mortality shook me deeply. I had not seen anyone from St Mary's since. I was a Grammar Bug through and through. But one morning during a half term week I woke up particularly heavy of heart after another dream about George gasping for air unheard at the bottom of the pool, and I decided I had to try and lay his ghost to rest.

I skipped breakfast and walked alone the mile and a half to Flixton Station to catch the early train. Over the iron bridge, I crossed the water back again to Irlam. As I walked down Liverpool Road, past my grandfather's printers, past the Rialto Cinema, the Wesleyan Chapel, Prospect Library, the bomb site at the Bama; past Pook's Sweet Shop and Martin's Bank, past St Mary's School and under the blackened granite railway bridge, towards the gates to the entrance of the Steel Works, I paused. I fancied I caught sight of my former classmates heading home from an all night shift (as in a couple of years they would be) or pushing prams to the park. I turned down Fir Street, where Margaret Ness lived (though there was not a fir tree anywhere in sight). I had not seen her since we had each left St Mary's and I didn't know what I was going to say to her when I did. All I felt was that, if I spoke to her about George, she might understand.

As I reached her front door, I paused. A dog started barking across the street. From next door a woman with her hair in curlers underneath a head scarf, wearing a pinny and slippers, came round from the ginnel between the two houses. There was a cigarette hanging from her bottom lip. I started to move away. "Oi! What do you want?"

"Oh," I stammered. "I was looking for Margaret Ness."

"They moved," she said.

"Where to?"

"Mind your own business," she said, then walked back down the ginnel.

There were a few kids now playing on the street with bikes and scooters – I'd forgotten it was half term – and a couple of small girls were sitting on the kerb by the edge of the road unwrapping cards of pop stars from packs of bubble gum.

"Who do you like best?" said one of them. "The Dave Clark Five or The Swinging Blue Jeans? I've got these already."

"So have I," said the other. "I'm waiting for Herman and the Hermits. He lives in Flixton, you know. Our Gloria went across the canal to see him at the youth club."

"Was he any good?"

"He was rubbish," our Gloria said. "Still, he gets to go all over, doesn't he? He's on *Top of the Pops* next week."

I walked slowly back towards the station and crossed over the water for the last time. I never saw Margaret again.

## Penny Bridge

*The greawnd it sturr'd beneath my feet...* Samuel Bamford: Tim Bobbin's Grave

I'm back in the town I was a teenager in. Shaw Town. Though it's not called that now. Nor was it then. That belongs to an older time, two and a half centuries ago, when it was merely a collection of outlying farms spread along the water meadows on the flood plains between the Mersey and the Irwell.

John Collier lived there, a lace maker (like my great grandmother), who took from his trade the name he is better known by: Tim Bobbin, the father of Lancashire dialect writing. His most enduring work, *Human Passions Delineated*, or *The Tale of Tummus & Mary*, tells a simple love story between a dairyman and a milkmaid.

Hard to credit when I was approaching 18 with the steel works across the canal, the heavy visible industry of Trafford Park just three miles away (where my father worked in an asbestos factory), and the huge petro-chemical works at Partington closer still. A permanent eerie glow hung above them every night as the sky burned red like Mordor.

But there were still traces of the old Shaw Town to be found if you knew where to look, where Tummus might have wooed his Mary: the Cinder Track that ran from Acre Gate to Abbotsfield over Penny Bridge by way of the railway line and the Thunder Tunnel, a low arch directly under the track where, as small children, we'd crouch waiting for a train to thunder over us shrieking at the tops of our voices, or later a trysting place for courting couples; then up through The Grove to the Jubilee Tree and the Village Green.

Such anomalies, these names – Acre Gate an old people's home built on the site of a demolished farm; Abbotsfield an overgrown waste ground where wild dogs roamed; The Grove a rat-infested slum, and the Village Green only an old road sign by a pub car park. Hardly known then; resurrected now by property developers as misleading names for new estates.

The Cinder Track remains however, still unadopted, still unsurfaced, and Penny Bridge still crosses the railway. You can follow this path on old maps threading its way across fields, between farms, all the way to Barton Dock, linking the Irwell to the Mersey over several miles, and as I was nearing my 18th birthday I walked its entire length, trying to reclaim a sense of continuity, a timeline, weaving between more recent marks on the land, which I tried to capture in a song I wrote back then:

*From Brooklyn Grange to De Brook Court Farm*
*The road runs ever on*
*Copper beech tree, sycamore*
*Lean towards the sun*
*And grow…*

I suppose I fancied myself as Tummus, always looking for my Mary – not that I'd have admitted this to anyone. I'd have got pretty short shrift if I had.

Now, four and more decades later, I retrace my steps. I lean on the granite stone wall of Penny Bridge looking out across the water meadows, those few patches of green still not built on, down towards the thirties estate I lived on back then, close to Stott's Orchard, gone now. It's early. A mist rises from the river, creeping towards me along the track. I see my younger self emerging from it, striding confidently towards me, his arm around a pretty girl with raven black hair. They are both talking animatedly as they head down towards the Thunder Tunnel, a few yards below me. They disappear from view but snatches of what they are saying drift up to me. They are arguing about the future.

"I'm thinking of staying," I hear myself say. "I've got a place at Manchester. I can go there."

"And live at home?"

"No. I'll get a bed-sit."

"Where?"

"Moss Side. I've already looked. It's just across the road from the Student Union."

"But you'll not get a grant. You'll have to go back home."

"I'll manage."

"The whole point of university is to get away, find out who you really are."

"But I feel I belong here." I'm struggling now. "This place, this track, these fields. I feel connected." I'm looking straight at her.

"Oh no," she says. "That's way too much responsibility. You can't stay here because of me. This time next year it'll be my turn to make this choice, and I'm telling you right now, there's no way I'm staying here. I'm leaving and I'm not coming back. You won't see me for dust."

And I see her now in my mind's eye storming out across the fields back towards the main road. A train roars across the Thunder Tunnel drowning out my shouts of pain and anguish, but after it's gone, they just become mixed with the raucous racket of rooks, the low rumble of distant traffic, a constant buzzing tinnitus that never quite goes away.

Years later I finally left this Mersey flood plain, crossed the city to an old cotton town a few miles to the north. I only discovered when we got there that this is the path Tim Bobbin had also taken. In a Rochdale churchyard an unremarkable head stone marks his grave, on which is inscribed the epitaph he himself wrote, just twenty minutes before he died:

*Jack of all trades – left to lie i'th dark...*

Time to let in the light.

## Choose Your Own Adventure

before there were apps
or sony play stations
before the collapse of analog
before xbox
instagram, facebook
sparred for our attention
replacing dialogue
with postings, tweets and likes

before tablets or netflicks
i-pads or e-books
or the latest must-read blog
an early interaction
placed the reader at the centre
to *choose your own adventure*

where you the hero
fought off devils
ascended levels
up to ten from zero
took the right fork
or the left
made the pieces fit
the puzzle with deft

manoeuvrings of pages
enabling you to navigate
while hounds of Hades bark
or lightning tempest rages –
you chose each new adventure
to safeguard every future

## The Stranger at the Cross Roads

This is a Choose Your Own Adventure story, which means you decide on the order in which you read it. You may choose to read it through continuously as it is set out below in the form of a single narrative, ignoring the italicised instructions at the end of each section; or you may follow their suggestions. Alternatively, you may make your own route and navigate your way through the various choices on offer in as many different ways as you wish. Bon Voyage!

### 1. The Riderless Horses:

You are standing at a cross roads marked with four ash trees on the edge of a forest at the bottom of a steep valley. You have never been beyond the borders of the valley, and you are curious to know what might lie beyond, but you don't know which way to go. After you have been standing there undecided for three days, two Riderless Horses appear, one from the east and one from the west. They reach the cross roads at exactly the same moment and stop momentarily to paw the ground. They have identical dark green saddles on their backs, and golden bridles in their mouths. One appears to want to head north, the other south. They are waiting for you to climb up onto their backs.

Which one do you choose?

*If you choose to go north, go to: 2. The Running Girl*
*If you choose to go south, go to: 8. The Foreign Princess*

*

### 2. The Running Girl:

You choose to head north. The instant you climb up onto the horse's back, he gallops away up the steep-sided valley towards the distant mountains. As you near the foothills, you see a young woman running across the fields. She appears as fast as a gazelle and even lighter on her feet, and soon she is outpacing the horse. But suddenly she loses her footing quite unexpectedly, tumbles and cries out in pain. You bring the horse to a halt beside her and ask if you can be of assistance.

You climb down to where she is lying and realise that she has sprained her ankle. You tear your shirt into bandages, which you bind tightly around the swelling. You then lift her onto the horse, which carries the two of you gingerly across the uneven terrain.

"You look like a frightened deer," you say. "What are you running away from?"

She looks at you, surprised. "Not away from," she says. "Towards."

"Where?" you ask.

"Wherever the road takes me."

"In that case, I think we should travel only as far as the first town we reach, for you are hurt and need to rest."

The horse then pauses, for he has reached a fork, where the road divides. He turns round to look at you, as if to ask which way he should take. In the distance you can just make out a tall stone lighthouse, shining far out to sea.

"Whichever way the wind is blowing," she says.

You lick your forefinger and raise it into the air to test it.

Which way is it blowing?

*If east, go to: 3. The Five Bridges*
*If west, go to: 7. The Handsome Giant*

*

**3. The Five Bridges:**

You head east. By nightfall the horse arrives at a great northern city along the eastern sea board. There are tall ships with high masts docking in the harbour, which lies in the estuary of a great metropolis crossed by Five Bridges. You stay with the Running Girl while her ankle heals. Day by day she grows stronger until soon she is ready to begin running again. She runs down to the harbour where she hears songs and stories from all over the world. When she returns each morning, she sings and tells these to you. She runs a little bit further as each week passes. Most days, you accompany her, try to run alongside her, but soon you can no longer keep up with the pace she is setting. She runs faster and faster, further and further, until one day she runs right out of the city, out of your sight, but not out of your mind. As she disappears beyond the Five Bridges, you call after her. "What are you running towards?"

"Not towards," she answers, her voice mocking as it echoes. "Away. Away… away… away…"

And she doesn't come back. She is nowhere to be found. You make enquiries of all who know her, but they either can't, or won't, tell you where she might be.

Just when you think all hope of ever finding her again is lost, an old friend, whom you have not seen since childhood, turns up on your doorstep.

"Running Girl runs fast, Kemo Sabe," he says. "Running Girl runs hard. Put your ear to the ground. Feel the vibration of her feet running. Like drum beating. Listen, Kemo Sabe. Look with your ears."

You close your eyes. You listen. You shut out all other sounds until all you can hear is the sound of her feet running, like the pulse in your blood, and when you open your eyes, there she is – running across each of the Five Bridges and then down to the shoreline. You follow her all the way to a Lighthouse standing far out to sea on a narrow spit of land. She runs round and round its spiral staircase until she reaches the top, where she stands and spins like a weather cock.

When finally you catch up with her, aching and gasping for air, you have breath enough for just one question: "Will you run back to me?"

What does she answer?

*If she answers yes, go to: 4. The Denial*
*If she answers no, go to: 5. The Red Feather*

*

**4. The Denial:**
She doesn't say yes.

*Go to: 8. The Foreign Princess*

**5. The Red Feather:**

She simply runs right past you all the way down to the bottom of the Lighthouse and appears to skim across the water and out of sight. Even the Lighthouse's most powerful beam cannot pick her out.

You live alone on the Lighthouse for a long time. Sometimes you think you hear her voice singing one of those far away songs she heard from the sailors on the quayside in the City of the Five Bridges. You shine your light towards the rocks where you think she might be hiding, but she is never there, and the ships pass through safely.

Late one night, your friend suddenly reappears at your side. "I have story for you, Kemo Sabe. Let me tell it to you, and then after I have finished you must decide what you must do."

And this is the story he tells you:

*We were riding through frozen fields in a wagon at dawn*
*A red wing rose in the darkness.*

*And suddenly a hare ran across the road.*
*One of us pointed to it with his hand.*

*That was long ago. Today, neither of them is alive,*
*Not the hare, nor the man who made the gesture.*

*Oh my friend, where are they, where are they going:*
*The flash of the hand, streak of movement, rustle of pebbles?*

*I ask not out of sorrow but in wonder.*

You look at his face for a long time after he has spoken. Even when he has gone, you continue to stare after him, so that you can still see his reflection imprinted on the glass at the top of the Lighthouse. It resembles a red feather. You realise that you must leave the Lighthouse and live your life not out of sorrow, but in wonder. At the same time, it is so long since you have moved that you are nervous to try.

What do you do?

*If you leave, go to: 7. The Handsome Giant*
*If you stay, go to: 6. The Darkness*

*

**6. The Darkness:**
You will your legs to move but they refuse. You remain in the Lighthouse until they turn off the light. You continue to linger in the darkness, listening for the Running Girl's song. Your story ends.

*Go to: 8. The Foreign Princess*

*

**7. The Handsome Giant:**
(You slowly stand up. Your legs feel weak and your balance is unsteady. You nervously descend the spiral staircase until you reach the door at the bottom. You turn the heavy handle, push open the door and step out once more into the light. You walk west. The sun rises behind you as you walk, leaving the Lighthouse further and further behind.)

You remember that today is your birthday. Just then a car pulls up beside you. A handsome Giant is driving; a Fairy sits beside him. They have a cake with sparklers fizzing brightly.

"Make a wish," they say. "Close your eyes."

And suddenly you are on a beach. The three of you are laughing and running into the sea, jumping over the waves. The Giant throws a bright orange Frisbee, which spins towards you, arc-ing just beyond your reach. You stretch your fingers as far as you can and just manage to catch it. The Fairy claps her hands. There are donkeys, and fairground rides, and ice cream, and a Punch & Judy show along the Promenade. "That's the way to do it!" shrieks Mr Punch. "Gaudete! Rejoice!" And there you are, leaping fences, chasing rainbows, running free.

The Giant and the Fairy place a folded piece of paper into the palm of your hand, then fly away, soaring above the clouds in an aeroplane, bound for new adventures, leaving behind a vapour trail, which spells out the words: "There's No Place Like Home..."

As you wave them goodbye, the piece of paper falls from your hand. You pick it up, unfold it and read the message written there:

"Listen to the Small Voice in your Ear."

You hear it singing:

*"Unde lux est orta*
*Salus invenitur..."*

Where there is light, let there be hope.

*Go to: 27. The Dancer*

*

**8. The Foreign Princess:**
You choose to head south. The instant you climb up onto the horse's back, she gallops away up the steep-sided valley towards the distant sea. Sailing towards you out of the sunrise from over the sea is a beautiful Princess. When she reaches the shore, she tells you she is an exile from a far away country, where she longs to return. You love the strange sound of the words on her tongue when she asks you to marry her, but first you must help her return to her Castle, which has been taken from her by a Cruel Priest, who plans to keep her locked up in a high tower where only he will be able to see her. She wishes to return to the Castle, for she was happy there before the Priest came, and she feels sure that you will love it too. But first you will have to help her banish the Priest for ever.

What do you do?

*If you climb aboard the ship and sail back with her, go to: 10. The Doldrums*
*If you decide to stay on shore and let her sail back alone, go to: 9. The Far Horizon*

**9. The Far Horizon:**
You decide to stay on shore. You watch the ship sail away with the beautiful Foreign Princess standing at the helm until they disappear into the sunset. You never see her again. Your story ends here with you staring for ever at the horizon, wondering: what if…?

*Go to: 2. The Running Girl*

*

**10. The Doldrums:**
You climb aboard and at once the Foreign Princess turns the ship into the wind and sets sail for the far horizon. You sail for forty days and forty nights. Sometimes the sea is smooth, sometimes it is stormy. Suddenly you become becalmed. You drift for what seems like an eternity in the flat, dry doldrums, waiting for a wind to stir the sails. The Princess seems quite content to wait for as long as it takes. Sometimes she declares she would be happy to stay there for ever, so long as you are by her side. But you grow restless. You long to see the Castle she has been describing to you for so many weeks, to walk in its enchanted gardens, to bathe in its crystal fountains. Suddenly, the mist which has been surrounding the ship clears, and through a telescope, standing from the high crow's nest, you spy a distant land and the Dark Tower atop a magnificent Castle. But still there is no wind to take you there. You become more impatient than ever to set foot on dry land once more. Hanging alongside the ship from a yard arm is a small rowing boat. "We could row ourselves there," you say. But the Princess will not hear of such a thing. "You may row if you choose," she says, "but I shall wait for the wind."

What do you do?

*If you stay on board, go to: 11. The Wind*
*If you row to the distant shore, go to: 12. The Castle*

*

**11. The Wind:**
You stay on board. A wind never materialises and you drift for ever in the listless doldrums.

*Go to: 13. The Bottom of the Sea*

*

**12. The Castle:**
You row ashore and discover that the Castle, which looked so golden and magical from afar, is in fact cold and draughty, with damp stone staircases and iron grilles on all the windows. The Priest is nowhere to be seen and you wonder if perhaps he left too once the Princess had escaped. There was nothing there for him any more, and nor is there anything for you. You are disappointed for you wanted the chance to show off your bravery and daring, and prove yourself a worthy hero. After a week has passed you decide you will leave the far-off land and the Castle and try to return to the Cross Roads in the valley and take a different route. But as you are rowing away from the island, a wind suddenly starts to pick up, the ship is sailing towards you, and less than a mile off shore the two vessels collide. You are thrown out of your boat but you manage to stay afloat by clinging to an oar. The Princess is swept ashore, where she takes the veil and lives out the rest of her days, not as a bride, but as a nun. She grows fruit and flowers in the shadow of the Castle Wall; she makes medicines from herbs. The Priest returns, but he is old and ill. The Princess prepares special ointments and infusions for him, nursing him back to health, looking after him for many years.

You drift with the currents, clinging fast to the oar, for many days, until you grow so weary that you feel barely able to hold on. You are tempted to let go, but a Small Voice in your Ear urges you to keep going.

What do you do?

*If you let go of the oar, go to: 13. The Bottom of the Sea*
*If you keep holding on, go to: 14. The Galley Ship*

**13. The Bottom of the Sea:**

You let go and immediately you begin to sink towards the bottom of the sea. At first this is a lovely, warm, luxurious feeling as you gently drift down, passing shoals of fish towards banks of anemones on the ocean floor. The fish seem completely unaware of you, busy with their own pursuits.

"Take me with you," you plead.

"Not this time," they sing, bubbles escaping from their mouths.

But the anemones, once you reach them, latch on to you and will not let you go. You see something disturb the waters above you at the surface, a great commotion of people from many lands and a concerted hauling of nets. You wave your arms to try and attract their attention, but they do not see you, and the spines of the anemones wrap themselves around you ever more tightly till you drown.

*Go to: 16. The Net*

*

**14. The Galley Ship:**

You make one last desperate effort to keep hold of the oar. Your every muscle burns with exhaustion but just then a large ship appears at your side and rescues you. The Captain of the Ship promises he will take you to the nearest port, but that is many leagues away, and in the meantime, you must work your passage. You are so grateful to have been rescued that you agree at once. It is only then you notice that this is a Galley Ship, as you are led below deck to join the other slaves chained to their oars. The Captain commands one of the crew to begin beating a large drum, and you are ordered to row in time to the rhythm, which grows faster and faster. You have to work harder and harder just to keep up. The Captain, just before he leaves to go up on deck, whispers in your ear. "Loyalty will be rewarded."

But that does not seem to be the case. Years pass, during which you row the ship, remaining in the darkness of the world below deck. You have no clear idea of where you are heading, but every time you put into port, the Captain says that he cannot spare you just yet. Although you change positions in the galley, gradually moving nearer and nearer to the front, now with a view through a port hole to the far horizon, you remain chained to your oar, and there seems little prospect of escape.

As time passes, you grow thinner and thinner, until one day you notice that you can slip your wrists in and out of the chains. You do nothing with this discovery, however, and another year passes.

Eventually you hear once more that tiny Voice in your Ear. "Leap," it says, "and a net will appear."

The next day the Captain asks you to climb to the top of the crow's nest and to call below as soon as you sight land. "Does this mean my loyalty has been rewarded?" you ask.

"Possibly," he says.

"And will you release me when we reach port?"

"We'll see."

The Voice in your Ear tells you not to believe him. "Trust your own instincts," it says.

And at once, as soon as you begin to look up, you see land looming out of the mist.

"Leap and a net will appear."

You can see the harbour quite plainly. The jetty is busy with people from all over the world exchanging skills and crafts, speaking in many languages. You could escape here, you think. You could lose yourself in the crowds.

"Or find yourself," says the Voice.

What do you do?

*Should you shout out "Land ahoy"? If so, go to: 15. The Promotion*
*Or should you remain silent and dive from the top of the mast? If so, go to: 16. The Net*

*

**15. The Promotion:**
You look down at the drop from the top of the mast to the roiling sea below and your courage fails you. It is too far; you might drown. There will be other chances like this. So you call out, "Land ahoy!" You climb back down from the crow's nest. When you reach the deck, the Captain is there to greet you.

"I have done all that you have asked of me, sir," you begin. "Will you now reward my loyalty and let me go ashore?"

"I will indeed reward your loyalty," he says. "I shall make you my Chief Drummer. You will beat the time below to which your former colleagues can row. Your many years of service have taught you how to do this better than anyone else."

You stare open-mouthed at such bare-faced betrayal. "I fear I must decline your offer, sir," you say. "As you say, those who row below are indeed all my former colleagues and friends. I could not subject them to more misery."

"Then do not ask me again if one day I might put you ashore. You have shown yourself to be disloyal and ungrateful. You shall live out the rest of your days chained to your oar."

And this is what happens. You are taken below deck and, as the Galley Master shackles you once more to your place, you notice that the chains are tighter and that you cannot now slip your wrist through, while you no longer have a port hole next to you, through which you might gaze longingly upon the distant horizon. Your story ends.

*Go back to: 11. The Wind*

*

**16. The Net:**
(You look down at the drop from the top of the mast to the broiling sea below. You listen hard for that tiny Voice in your Ear. "Now?" you whisper.

"Yes," she answers. "Now."

"Leap and a net will appear," you both call out together.)

You dive headlong into a whirlpool that spins you round and round, sucking you deeper and deeper towards the ocean floor, where the anemones are waving their coloured arms joyfully towards you. But just when you think your lungs will surely burst, a net does indeed appear. It sweeps you up in its fine roped mesh and carries you back towards the surface. As your eyes grow accustomed to the thrashing waters all around you, you see a shoal of fishes who look oddly familiar.

"We told you we would see you again," they bubble. "What an adventure."

"But where are we going?" you ask.

"Do not worry," gurgle their watery mouths. "Just enjoy the ride."

And before you have time to reply, you are whisked into the air, and you can feel the strength of many hands hauling you ashore, just as you'd known somehow would happen.

"This is indeed a strange catch," says someone. He wears a brightly coloured shirt and gathers the others around him. "Look at the chains on his wrists. He must have escaped from the Galley Ship. We don't often meet survivors. Let us welcome him amongst us."

Everywhere you look there are people pressing around you, eager to shake your hand, invite you to their homes. They speak in strange accents using unfamiliar words, but you soon grow accustomed to their ways and begin to feel one of them. The Man in the Brightly Coloured Shirt is like a King, but one who listens to the people and bestows his largesse upon them. You begin to learn new skills and soon you are able to go down to the jetty to greet the new arrivals and help them find places to live and work.

At the back of the port lies a forest where nobody seems to go. You ask the King about it and he tells you that once upon a time there used to be a deep mine there. The mine went far underground, and people came from miles around to dig deeper and deeper until eventually it stretched right out under the sea. He tells you that they brought out black gold from the deepest seams of the mine, but that when they brought it to the surface, thieves snatched it from them and built grand palaces near and far with their ill-gotten riches. In the end, the people refused to go down the mines any more unless the thieves gave them back what they had stolen, but the thieves refused; nor would they go down themselves to mine the gold, and so they sealed them all up, so that no one else might try and take it for themselves. The people who had worked there decided to stay, however, for they had nowhere else to go, but they had not yet discovered what else they might do instead.

"Couldn't you have prevented this?" you ask him.

"I did not arrive here until afterwards," he tells you, "and this is where you come in. Perhaps you might help them to find something different to fill their lives."

"But how can I do this?" you ask. "I have not lived as they have lived. This is their land, not mine, and though they have welcomed me and treated me with kindness, I do not belong here, for I did not grow up here. I have not breathed the same air. I will always be a stranger."

" Be not forgetful to entertain strangers," he says, " for thereby some have entertained angels. And besides, you are not so very different, I am thinking."

"I need to walk into the forest," you say, "and see the mines and the people for myself."

"What is it that you are hoping to find?" he asks.

"I think it might be home."

"The shortest way is the way to home. But the longest way is to reach the first bend."

"Then I'd better set off at once."

"There's no hurry. The winter is approaching. The days grow colder and the nights longer. Stay till the spring comes, and then, if you still feel the same desire, go with the thaw…"

What do you do?

*If you wait until spring, go to: 17. The Thaw*
*If you leave at once, go to: 18. The Mine*

*

**17. The Thaw:**
But when the thaw does come, late, you no longer feel much like leaving. You have become dug in during the long, hard winter. You have made new friends, you have begun to learn new songs to sing, you have acquired new tastes. You begin to feel that perhaps this is where you belong now, not some dark, forbidding mine deep in the mountains beyond the forest. You have heard there may be wolves there, roaming in search of unsuspecting travellers.

"As you wish," says the King. "There is plenty of work still to be done here, for there are always new people arriving, new stories to hear."

And so you stay and begin to put down roots. For most of the time, the forest lies in shadow, and for weeks at a time, you hardly give it a thought. But every so often, when the wind changes and the skies clear, a light falls on the mountain and you see traces of the ancient mine workings, and you wonder: what if…?

*Go to: 21. The Barefoot Boy*

*

**18. The Mine:**
You leave at once. The forest is dark and foreboding but the track is wide, for it was made long ago by machines, even though parts of it are overgrown and sometimes you have to climb over fallen trees. Just as night is falling you reach the old mine workings. There are no trees here any more, only bare rock and mud. There is a dark hole like a scar in the side of the mountain, which you are drawn towards, for you can hear the distant sounds of chains clanking, gears winding and voices calling to one another. An old man greets you at the entrance.

"Come," he says. "You are just in time for the Night Train. We have been waiting for you."

"How did you know I was coming?" you ask.

"We have been watching you."

"Who are you?"

"You have never met me, but you have always known me. I am your great-grandfather, and I worked here in the mine, along with my father, right back to my own great-grandfather."

"But surely, you must have died many years ago?"

"There are many memories still alive deep in the mine. Come."

You take the miner's hand as he helps you to step across a narrow crack that runs deep into the mountain and into a wire cage. No sooner have you done so than he slides a mesh gate across in front of you, and you plunge down into the darkness of the mine shaft. Tiny rivulets of water trickle down the bare rock, which is jet black with iridescent crystals sparkling within it. With a jolt you reach the bottom and there waiting for you is a small tank engine. A fireman is shovelling coal into its boiler, where a fire glows red. The miner walks you past the engine, through the clouds of steam billowing around it, towards a series of coal wagons attached behind.

"Climb aboard," he says. "Welcome to the Night Train."

"Where are we going?" you ask.

"Patience," he says. "You will see soon enough."

Something holds you back. You wonder if it might be a trap.

"Quickly," he says. "We must run to time. We cannot wait a moment longer."

What do you do?

*If you climb aboard, go to: 20. The Night Train*
*If you step back from the train, go to: 19. The Explosion*

*

**19. The Explosion:**

You hesitate. The train's whistle sounds loud and shrill in the tunnel. There is an enormous hiss of steam and you are enveloped in a thick, dirty cloud.

When it clears the train has gone and you are left alone

at the edge of the track. It is unnervingly quiet and your eyes take a long while to accustom themselves to the utter blackness that surrounds you. You think you can hear slight tappings in the distance, and what might be footsteps approaching, but you cannot be certain. After what seems an age you begin to make out strange troglodyte figures clambering up the rock walls towards you, stooping, skeletal. When they reach you, they pluck at your arms and legs pulling them with you, pointing to a labyrinth of steep stone steps cut into the rock face, beckoning you to climb down. They hand you a tiny cage. Inside is a small yellow bird, which sings a tune you can dimly recollect. As you descend the stone stairs, the air grows hotter, thicker. The bird's song falters. When you reach the bottom, it ceases altogether. You look around you. All the other figures have disappeared. You are in what seems like a labyrinth of deep trenches.

You are utterly alone.

A pungent smell of gas fills your nostrils, the high distant whine of a far-off explosion. The darkness takes you.

*Go to: 27. The Dancer*

*

**20. The Night Train:**

You hesitate. The train's whistle sounds loud and shrill in the tunnel. There is an enormous hiss of steam and you are enveloped in a thick, dirty cloud.

At the last moment you leap aboard just as the Night Train pulls away. You soon pick up speed and you appear to be descending deeper and deeper into the mountain. You pass through wide subterranean caverns, the track weaving between a forest of stalagmites and stalactites. Suddenly you plunge into a narrow tunnel with another whoosh and hiss of steam. For a while there is absolute nothingness until, without warning, you emerge into a completely different landscape.

Tall, blackened chimneys are belching dirty, grey smoke high into the air, as are huge cooling towers, dwarfing the town, which is criss-crossed with different railway tracks shunting ores and goods between the various factories. The train pulls into a small station with plasticine porters with looking-glass ties.

The Old Miner is once more at your side, but he now resembles more closely your grandfather. "We need to take on water," he says. "Stretch your legs and look around. We leave in an hour."

You climb down and begin to walk through the bombed out streets, picking your way carefully between broken glass and mounds of rubble. Feral children are playing in the hulks of roofless, windowless houses. They seem to know you and call you over. As you join them, you feel yourself shedding the years. You are a child once more, like these others. Girls are playing with whips and tops, swinging round lamp posts on lengths of wire, or chanting rhymes jumping over an enormous skipping rope, which a few minutes earlier had served as a washing line strung across the whole of what remains of the street. Tired housewives are standing outside more bombed out houses, leaning on door frames, or donkey-stoning front steps, as the girls keep on singing.

*"The big ship sails down the alley-alley-o*
*The big ship sails down the alley-alley-o*
*The big ship sails down the alley-alley-o*
*On the last day of September…"*

Meanwhile boys are trundling by on home-made soap-box racers, bowling old car tyres across the cobbled waste ground, chalking stumps on a brick wall, shaping an old plank for a bat, while a posse of cowboys gallop by on their broom-handle horses pursued by whooping Indians wielding shrapnel tomahawks. Across the way, by a warehouse from where you can hear the thundering roar of printing presses rumbling under your feet, you see a small girl dancing alone to the rhythm in a pair of outsized red shoes.

Just then you hear the whistle of the Night Train summoning you. You turn and see the Old Miner urgently beckoning you to hurry.

"Quickly," he says. "We must run to time. We cannot

wait a moment longer."

You start to run, but your legs feel as though they are wading through thick sludge.

Will you make it?

*If yes, go to: 22. High Noon*
*If not, go to: 21. The Barefoot Boy*

*

**21. The Barefoot Boy:**

You get to the station just as the Night Train pulls away. You have missed it. You look around you as the steam clears. The soap-box racer rattles towards you.

"Hop in," says the driver. He has just come from the Wild Moss at the edge of the Town, he says. His feet are bare and his pockets are stuffed with coal. "I'm on my way to light the Headmaster's fire at the school," he says. "You can come too. We get a bottle of milk each and a straw, though sometimes, when it freezes, the milk pops up through the bottle top like an icicle."

You look around at the bomb-scarred, scorched town. "And what do you do when you leave school?" you ask.

"That's easy," says the Boy. "Look."

At that moment a loud siren fills the air. It is so loud that you cover your ears. Rats scurry into cellars, starlings rise up from the ashes of smouldering bonfires to fly south. With the sound a pair of giant metal gates creak open and out pour hundreds of men and boys all heading home from their shift. Their faces are streaked with grime and sweat. Behind them you can see huge plumes of fire shooting up high into the night sky from the blazing furnaces of steel, stoked by giant, heaving bellows. More and more men and boys are spewed out. A grit of something hard and metallic gets caught in your eye. You rub it hard to try and remove it. When you open it again, you find that you too are streaming out of the Furnace Gates. The Barefoot Boy, who is now a young man, but who still wears no shoes, claps you on the back.

"Same time tomorrow," he says.

You walk away from the Steel Plant knowing your story has ended.

Just then the Barefoot Boy lights a cigarette. He asks you if you would like one too. Why not, you think. He cups his hands round yours to shield the match from the wind as he lights it, then tosses the match over the low wall that separates the factory from the canal, which no longer flows beside you, for its surface is a thick crust of polluted sludge. As the still-lighted match alights it explodes and you are thrown off your feet with the force of it. The Old Miner turns your face away so that the last you see of the Boy are his arms and then his hands as he is sucked down into the canal's murky depths.

*Go to: 24. The Magic Bus, part 2*

*

**22. High Noon:**
You get to the station just as the Night Train pulls away. But just as it does so, an arm reaches down and hauls you aboard.

"That's cutting it fine," says the Old Miner, and suddenly you are speeding along once more.

The factory town gives way to fields. An iron bridge carries you across a canal. Far below you see many people walking beside it like tiny columns of ants. But even from this great height, you think you can make out someone you recognise lighting a cigarette, but you cannot be sure. He looks around, as if expecting someone to be walking beside him, and then blows out the match, putting the stub back into his pocket, when he realises no one is there.

You have crossed the water and left the factory far behind. The Night Train is now running through a low, flat water meadow in the early morning. The sun is burning through the mist rising from the grass. Through the mist you see the Running Girl, her sprained ankle fully healed, racing along in the opposite direction. She waves, smiling, as she speeds past you.

The track makes a wide, long curve between the high banks of a river's bend. As it makes its way across the flood plain it passes over a low stone bridge. A courting couple are walking beneath it – a young man, little more than a schoolboy, and a Girl with Raven Hair. As the train thunders over the bridge, you hear shouting from beneath you. The Girl with Raven Hair storms out from the arch and, without looking back, walks swiftly away across the fields. A few minutes later the young man emerges too; except that now he is no longer young. This older man looks towards the Girl with Raven Hair, an apparition disappearing before his eyes.

The train continues its journey. By high noon it has reached a seaside town. Seagulls wheel overhead screeching, together with the crowds of people who are now riding the train with you, as the track buckles and dips like a roller coaster. You scream through every fairground ride the train can carry you on, until you are flung out of its carriages as it dives into the sea, rolling over and over, until you find yourself lying on the soft, golden sand. A song soars over the town. It is a song you can remember, the singer a yellow bird released from its cage. You pick yourself up and walk towards the waves, your feet leaving no prints. Out of the haze you see a Giant striding out towards you. You lift your arm in recognition but he, too, fades from sight, an orange Frisbee hovering towards you before it falls just beyond your reach.

The train pulls up behind you, its sudden sharp whistle startling you from your dream. You turn around just as the Old Miner is stepping down.

"This is where I get off," he says, looking less like your grandfather now and more like your father.

"Can I come with you?"

"Not yet."

"Why not?"

"You have promises to keep," he says, "and miles to go before you sleep… I expect you'll hear from me again". You watch him walk towards a tall tower at the end of the beach, which he begins to climb like a steeplejack.

You walk back to the train, which hisses impatiently on the promenade.

"Quickly," it says. "We must run to time. We cannot wait a moment longer."

The Fireman, leaning on his shovel, winks at you as you pass, halting you in your tracks. It is the Barefoot Boy.

"You?"

"The very same. I've always enjoyed lighting a good fire. Climb aboard. Want to drive? Come on – doesn't every boy want to be an Engine Driver when he grows up? I shan't ask you twice."

You are uncertain. Of course you would like to drive the Engine. But what if you lose control and crash it with all these people on board?

What do you do?

*If you decide to drive the train, go to: 23. The Magic Bus, part 1*
*If you decline, go to: 27. The Dancer*

*

**23. The Magic Bus, part 1:**

You climb up beside the Barefoot Boy, who is once again busy shovelling coal. "We're building up a big head of steam now and no mistake."

You sound the train's whistle and call out at the top of your voice, "All aboard!"

Slowly the train pulls out of the station and begins to pull away along the Promenade, where crowds of people are lining the streets, waving flags and cheering you on your way. The sun is shining down fiercely, bouncing off the gleaming, polished engine, which, you notice, now appears bright red, more like a bus than a train. As it reaches the pier head it lurches off the tracks and makes its way towards a Passenger Ferry bound for France. You nervously drive up the ramp leading to the back of the ship, though it's a close-run thing, for a number of the deck hands leap over the retaining ropes into the shallow waters of the Channel below to avoid being mown down, until finally you manage to steer into the narrow space they have reserved for you.

The Barefoot Boy wipes the sweat from your brow. "You'll get used to it," he says.

"I think I'll go and check on the passengers," you say. "Make sure they're OK."

"You do that, sir," he says. "It'll be hours before we need to take her off again on the other side."

The carriage is a double-decker and all the passengers seem blissfully unaware of the near miss they have just experienced. They are smoking and drinking cheap wine. They are, you realise, all young officers in hard hats and high spirits, a band of travelling players en route to perform the Scottish play in theatres across France – Paris, Nice, Narbonne. It is an adventure and they welcome you in their midst with open arms. You are to be one of them, it seems.

Among them you see a Girl with Raven Hair, who is smiling at you mischievously. "Who are you meant to be?" she asks. "The Porter? The Ghost?"

"The Engine Driver," you reply somewhat sheepishly.

"You look too much like a schoolboy to me. I can see we are going to have to make some changes." She begins to rearrange your clothes, alter your hair.

You disentangle yourself from her just long enough to say, "Here. Why don't you drive the engine?" And you hand her your cap. "You look much better in uniform than I do."

She gives you a kiss, winks, then waltzes off towards the others, whom she also busily starts to undress. Later you learn she does take a turn at driving the engine, wearing her grandmother's wedding dress.

The Ferry pulls out and on board the double-decker train the party continues. Lines are practised, scenes rehearsed, but people seem more interested in smoking, in drinking, in each other, By the time you are half-way across the windows are all steamed up. You wipe one of the panes and try to look out, to see if you can see any sign of land.

Instead you see a Tall Sailing Ship, making slow, idle circles, seemingly going nowhere. On the prow you see a Beautiful Princess. She is waving to you pleadingly. Your mouth tastes swollen and dry, as if you have been sucking a large round pebble.

What do you do?

*If you abandon the double-decker train to try and recue her, go to: 10. The Doldrums*
*If you turn over and go back to sleep, till the party starts up again on board the next morning, go to: 24. The Magic Bus, part 2*

*

**24. The Magic Bus, part 2:**
The red double-decker bus drives down the twisting, narrow country lanes, criss-crossing France. In Paris the theatre has burned down. In Nice you cannot find it. You spend a drunken night on the shores of the sea, dancing naked round a camp-fire. Far out to sea, calling to you across the waves, you hear a mermaid singing, and you think you might try to swim out to reach her.

What do you do?

*If you decide to swim out, go to: 25. The Rock*
*If you decide to stay by the camp-fire, go to: 26. The Magic Bus, part 3*

*

**25. The Rock:**
She is sitting on a rock combing her long, straight hair.

What does she say?

*If she says yes, go to: 4. The Denial*
*If she says no, go to: 6. The Darkness*
*If she says nothing, read on…*

*

**26. The Magic Bus, part 3:**
The next morning you head off at dawn. The other students are either asleep or hung over. You stare out at the unfolding landscape as the sun rises. You see a wide, flat expanse of marshland. Herons and flamingos lift from the water, the sun gilding their wings. You see a herd of wild horses stampeding across the Camargue. Among them you think you see, just for an instant, two which appear to have dark green saddles and golden bridles.

The journey continues.

Rising from the mist above the marshes, as the sun climbs higher, you see a Fairy Tale Castle, its tower reaching to the clouds.

The bus stops to take on more water, and you step outside to see if you might get a closer look. You are torn. You feel a strong force pulling you towards the Castle, while a Small Voice in your Ear whispers caution, whispers loyalty.

What do you do?

*If you are drawn towards the tower, go to: 12. The Castle*
*If you feel you should stay, go to: 27. The Dancer*

*

**27. The Dancer:**
You are back on the Promenade. The vapour trail, which spells out "There's No Place Like Home", is fading in the sky, leaving only a wisp of memory.

You look around you, wondering which is your next way.

Just then the Small Voice in your Ear murmurs, "Look at the Moon."

You turn to see a sickle moon rising in the late afternoon sky, just at the point where the final wisps of vapour trail disappeared. You walk further along the Promenade towards it. As you move between the rows of houses that line the way, it appears to follow you.

You stop. It stops.

You move. It moves.

You look more closely. Where the shadow of the waxing crescent lies, you begin to detect a Swan, in a perfectly balanced *attitude en l'air,* her left leg in arabesque behind her. She is dancing.

You run. She runs.

You leap. She leaps.

*Un grande jeté,* which carries her right across the night sky, sees her skimming over the moonlit sea on *demi-pointe*, until she arrives before you with a dazzling series of *fouettés*, no longer a swan, but human, placing her hands on your shoulders, leaning in to plant a chaste kiss on your left cheek.

"Will you be my dancing partner?" she asks you.

"I don't know how to dance," you say.

"I'll teach you," she says. "First you have to learn how your body moves. Isolate every muscle – hip, abdomen, rib-cage. Find your core, your centre, your balance."

You watch her every movement, you mark her every gesture. The line, the grace, the suppleness.

"We shall choreograph our own private dance," she says.

"And where will we perform it?" you ask.

"Home," she says.

"But where is home?"

"We are making our first tentative steps towards it."

"And how will we know when we have got there?"

"Why, this is home, nor are we ever out of it, so long as we are together."

"And when we are apart?"

"You will still be able to hear that Small Voice in your Ear."

You walk together along the road, and your walking is itself a dance.

You dance along more and more streets full of houses. The Moon no longer stalks you from between them. She walks by your side, and the glow that she radiates lights up all the windows that you pass, so that you can both look inside. You see tables laid for Christmas dinner. You see trees and decorations and lights. You see love and laughter shining on people's faces.

Sometimes you see people alone. A young woman reading her book, or listening to the radio, pauses to look up as you pass by. An old woman putting out a saucer of milk on her doorstep for a stray cat nods towards you. A man standing in front of a mirror above a fire in the hearth places a music score on a stand, preparing to conduct the imaginary orchestra he hears in his head, catches sight of your reflection and raises his baton, as if to signal your entrance.

The twilight deepens. You hear the sound of children playing in the street. It is that golden hour, when they know they would usually be indoors, getting ready for bed, but for some reason they are being allowed to play outside just that little bit longer. You turn a corner. A small boy is kicking a football against a wall with his father. An older boy arrives on a bicycle. The small boy passes him the ball and the older boy juggles it expertly from foot to foot, on and on, never allowing the ball to touch the ground, flicking it to his knee, his thigh, his chest, finally up on to his forehead, where he sways from side to side maintaining a perfect balance.

They do not see you as you pass them by, but as you do so, your shared light falls upon the ball, creating a silver orb, so that the small boy will no longer be frightened each time he looks up and sees the Moon.

In the window of a house across the street, a small girl sits on her window sill, the curtains closed behind her, looking down on you all, waving as you smile up at her.

You walk all through the night and into the next day.

You pass the Girl with Raven Hair dressing a Scarecrow in a field. A circle of admirers has gathered around her. You pause momentarily, but the Small Voice in your Ear chuckles.

"You are no longer a schoolboy."

The Running Girl flies past in a blur so fast you barely have time to register her, the echo of her song hanging on the breeze, ("towards… towards… towards…"), while the words spoken by the Foreign Princess drop like stones which, when you stoop to pick them up, you do not recognise, feeling rough and strange.

The Dancer loops her arm through yours and together you walk towards the Cross Roads.

*Go to: 28. The Cross Roads of the Four Ashes*

**28. The Cross Roads of the Four Ashes:**
You walk slowly but purposefully towards the Cross Roads. It has been many years since you were last here, but at the same time it feels like only yesterday. The Dancer signals the way before you with a graceful *port de bras.* As you reach the Four Ash trees that stand on each corner of the Cross Roads, she raises her arms in a sun salutation. At precisely the same moment, the two Riderless Horses with dark green saddles and golden bridles gallop towards each other from out of the Forest.

They appear to be on a collision course, but at the last second they swerve and veer off in separate directions. This time they do not stop. When they have gone, they leave behind a huge cloud of dust covering the sun. Out of the haze you become aware of a teeming crowd of walkers heading towards the Cross Roads, women threading the fields, carrying cloth bundles on their backs. They acknowledge one another as they pass before you, converging, then separating again, before disappearing back into the cloud of dust, which, as it lifts, reveals a Stranger standing at the centre of the Four Ashes, where the different roads meet.

"I have been waiting for you," he says.

"Who are you?" you ask.

"Oh, I think you know. After all, it was you who named me."

The Small Voice in your Ear begins to sing softly:

*"Oh Camille,*
*Tell me why are you in this place....?*
*When you tell me your story, are you making amends...?"*

"But you weren't here before," you say.

"I was travelling back from the War. I had been away a long time and you had forgotten about me."

"I too have been on a journey, only to return from where I began."

"But it is different now. Even you must see that, surely?

"I don't understand."

"You set off alone, but you come back..." he gestures

towards The Dancer, "…accompanied."

Out of the trees another voice begins to sing, a high, light tenor, rustling the leaves.

*"There is a lady sweet and kind,*
*Was never face so pleas'd my mind;*
*I did but see her passing by,*
*And yet I love her till I die…"*

The Stranger steps towards you. From the haversack on his shoulder he takes a small packet, which he offers towards you. You take it and slowly begin to unwrap it. Inside is a thin square of hard pink bubble gum, and beneath it is a postcard of a flag.

"To add to your collection," he says.

It is a blank white square. You look back at him, puzzled.

"You can fill in your own design," he says. "Or you may find it quite sufficient as it is. For white contains every colour, does it not?"

You thank him and hand him the gum. He smiles as he takes it from you. "I must be going," he says.

"Where?" you ask.

He does not immediately answer. The Small Voice in your Ear whispers softly:

"The woods are lovely, dark and deep
But I have promises to keep…"

"And miles to go before I sleep," says The Stranger.

"And miles to go before I sleep," you echo.

He pops the square of gum into his mouth, then proceeds to blow a large round pink bubble, a perfect sphere, which grows and grows and grows, like a waxing moon. It becomes so large that it swallows up the entire horizon, as far as you can see. It stretches until it encircles the sky, when an aeroplane bursts through it, a vapour trail hanging behind it. But the words they create fade before you can read them. The bubble explodes like the shattering of a glass paperweight globe into a thousand pieces. The Four Ash Trees drop their keys in a cascade of dancing leaves.

Eventually there is stillness and silence. The Stranger has gone. Where he stood is now a small house at the centre of the Cross Roads. You walk towards the low front door, but it is locked. You turn around. The Dancer picks up one of the ash keys and places it in the lock. The door opens. From inside the high tenor voice is singing:

*"Her gesture, motion, and her smiles,*
*Her wit, her voice, my heart beguiles,*
*Beguiles my heart, I know not why,*
*And yet I love her till I die..."*

Together you step across the threshold. The house is full of light.

## Infinity

just turned sixty
pension, bus pass beckoning
steps from his car
after the six hour drive
back north, older
back aching, legs stiff
not necessarily wiser

*

cars crawl bumper to bumper
roads reach beyond sight

*

dialling 999
the first time
forgets his lines
mother… confused… stroke

*

space between seconds
stretches
each tic(k) a life

*

ambulance arrives
paramedic's huge hand
enfolds her brittle bird bones

*

do you know where you are
- here with you
do you know who I am
(holding a syringe)
- the man with the golden gun

*

closes her eyes

*

red, she says, red
it has to be red
red shoes, red dress
yes

*

last words
yes

*

final hours
her face grows younger
breathing slows
mouth slackens
relaxed, cares
lifting from her

*

eyes open
seeking his
full of moon
urgently squeezing
his hand, smiling

*

making sure
he understands

*

this long held moment
time stops

*

parallel lines
meeting
infinity of red

*

transfiguration

## Alma Mater

*Easy to open, push hard:* sign on a door

Back on the campus
of my old *alma mater*,
seeking the familiar
among the sleek glass

towers sprung up since,
I spot the old German
church still hunkered down
beside the picket fence

where I studied Drama…
Forty years have passed since then
that set the wheels in motion
to all that's led to this summer's

pilgrimage to return here
hoping to find… what exactly?
The truth of it eludes me –
when just as I reach the door

("easy to open, push hard")
a flock of Asian girls
surges past me, high-pitched squeals
like the song of some exotic bird

uncaged, set free to scatter
as confetti on the wind;
they flutter to the ground
followed a few moments later

by an older student, hair
framing her face, head down
mumbling sorry, *aisumesen*,
mind completely elsewhere,

drawing a cigarette
half way to her mouth, she wears
what might be an old U.S.
Marine combat jacket

looking for all the world
through the rimless tinted lenses
of my John Lennon glasses
like Yoko Ono, she holds

the door open for me –
echoes of student protest
roar up from the past
and briefly it is 1970

once more, till she takes out
her cell, flips it open, checks
for updates, missed calls, texts
and the door slams shut.

The mirage fades and here am I,
an old guy in his 60's,
hair unfashionably long, whose
parade has passed him by.

I check my own phone –
a message tells me I've been
tagged, sender's name withheld, I turn
and there I am at 21:

this younger version of me
seems to sense my shadow
falling briefly in the glow
of that endless hazy

campus afternoon,
he sits up shielding his eyes
which seem to recognise
me, masked by the sun,

and beckons me across.
I shake my head – that was then –
he smiles, lies back down again
as if to say, could be worse,

stretched out easy on the grass
carefree, golden, finals over,
his eyes scan a future
whose promises seem endless…

The Japanese girl appears
invisible at his side –
see, he says, life's not so bad –
a tear catches me unawares…

Rain suddenly rips
the sky, we run helter skelter
seeking refuge, shelter
beneath bending tree tops

where the Asian girls alight,
shiver like dancing leaves,
the frisson of old loves
shimmering out of sight,

leaving a faint trace,
a pale palimpsest
of lingered lives lost
unflattening the grass.

I head back toward
the door of the German church,
I lift its creaking latch –
easy to open, push hard…

## Privet

it takes us more than half an hour
to climb the short hill back home
we have to stop while our son
pauses to examine every single
privet leaf of hedge next door
in the sharp early morning

ten months old he scrutinises
each one minutely
sniffing, stroking, licking
testing their uniqueness
we have lost that essence
he senses so completely

our instinct's to hurry on
get back inside in the warm
but he's absorbed, oblivious
to our breath freezing
in statues so we wait till
he's nothing more to show us

## Afterword

Imagine you are faced with two choices and you don't know which one to take. So you toss a coin. Heads for one choice, tails for the other. You call out heads. While it spins through the air, before it lands and finally comes to rest, there is a 50% chance that it will fall on either heads or tails. It lands, it teeters this way, then that, till eventually it tumbles and stops. Heads. You take the appropriate action. Only after you have done so, do you begin to wonder: what if? What if it had landed on tails? Would that have been better? But you've made your call and you carry on. There is now no choice to be made.

Imagine the coin is still spinning in the air. While it has not yet landed, there is still a chance that it may land on tails after all. That possibility still exists. An alternative universe in which you follow a different path from the one you have just taken, running parallel to it.

In the world of quantum physics, the world of sub-atomic particles, instead of a single coin with just two possible choices, there are now billions of these leptons, quarks and baryons, all colliding and interacting, simultaneously offering an infinity of outcomes, a multi-verse. The differences between each of these outcomes may be immense, or they may so infinitesimally small as to appear identical. Like the different leaves on a privet hedge. From a distance they may seem identical, but if we examine each one closely, minutely, we might discern who-knows-how-many distinct varieties.

These poems and stories have attempted to describe what happens once the coin has landed and the call has been made; a subsequent collection might explore a different set of choices altogether.

**Acknowledgements**

I would like once again to thank my late parents and grandparents for providing me with so many stories and memories that I have been able to draw on here (and Amanda for reminding me about those endless childhood Sunday afternoons); Mudlark Press for their commitment to this project and for their unfailing support for my work; Sally Chapman-Walker for her design expertise; Chris Waters for his constant friendship and advice at every step of the way, and for his continuing companionship along the Long & Winding Road; Mark Vivian and Luci Gosling for arranging permission for us to use Shirley Baker's wonderful photographs; the ChagWord Literary Festival, Appledore Book Festival, Netherhay Chapel, Dorset, and Kate Gowar and Steven Brett of the wonderful Nightingale Theatre, Brighton for providing opportunities to test the work out in front of audiences; Andrew, Chris and Julie (and everyone else from Qualtagh) whose "first-foot" footfalls still resound today; Theresa, Mark, Lucy, Ben W, Theo, Quentin, Suba, Ben D, Sharon, Rosie, Charlotte, Gavin, Kate and Beth in the UK, and the Crossing Paths Writers Group in The Berkshires, Massachusetts for reading various versions of individual pieces and for so generously offering their comments and suggest-ions; the artist Martell Linsdell, who first introduced me to timelines and showed me the marks we make on the land; Gavin Stride, who more or less saved me, who continues to make me believe that anything is possible, and who never stops encouraging me; Kay, Mari & Rhiannon, whose remarkable courage has taught me how to celebrate as well as grieve – gaudete – and Mari for providing the image of a playground raining children; Theresa Beattie, for her constant kindness, hospitality and friendship; Eva Martinez and Hetain Patel for their loyalty and support; Rowena Price, who despite being a life-long Chelsea fan, nevertheless supported United for May 1968, who chased a hard day's night (even if, in the end, we could not catch it) and who walked purposefully with all the ghosts; Ben Wright for opening up a whole spectrum of infinite colour; Laila Diallo and Phil King for agreeing to go on an exploratory creative journey with me, and all the dance artists I currently collaborate with, who keep on artistically feeding me; and, last but by no means least, the poet Irene Willis & her husband Daves Rossell in Great Barrington MA for their unending inspiration, friendship, warmth and welcome. There is nobody I know who is more passionate about poetry than Irene, and it is she who, as well as offering so much wise advice, has been such an invaluable guide and mentor to me and who continues to urge me to keep on telling stories. Without her this book would not have been possible.

Chris grew up in Manchester and currently lives in West Dorset, after brief sojourns to Nottinghamshire, Devon and Brighton. Over the years he has managed to reinvent himself several times – from florist's delivery van driver to Punch & Judy man, drama teacher, theatre director, community arts coordinator, creative producer, to his current role as writer and dramaturg for choreographers and dance companies. Chris is married to Amanda Fogg, a dance practitioner working primarily with people with Parkinson's.